IN THE
HOUSES
OF THEIR
DEAD

OTHER BOOKS BY TERRY ALFORD

Fortune's Fool: The Life of John Wilkes Booth

Prince Among Slaves

Abraham Lincoln with medium Nettie Colburn (seated, center).

IN THE
HOUSES
OF THEIR
DEAD

൭

THE LINCOLNS, THE BOOTHS, AND THE SPIRITS

Terry Alford

Liveright Publishing Corporation

A Division of W. W. Norton & Company
Celebrating a Century of Independent Publishing

For information about permission to reproduce selections from this book,
write to Permissions, Liveright Publishing Corporation, a division of
W. W. Norton & Company, Inc., 500 Fifth Avenue, New York, NY 10110

For information about special discounts for bulk purchases, please contact
W. W. Norton Special Sales at specialsales@wwnorton.com or 800-233-4830

Manufacturing by Lakeside Book Company
Book design by Chris Welch
Production manager: Lauren Abbate

Library of Congress Cataloging-in-Publication Data

Names: Alford, Terry, author.
Title: In the houses of their dead : the Lincolns, the Booths, and the spirits / Terry Alford.
Other titles: Lincolns, the Booths, and the spirits
Description: New York : Liveright Publishing Corporation, A Division of W. W. Norton & Company,
[2022] | Includes bibliographical references.
Identifiers: LCCN 2022005165 | ISBN 9781631495601 (cloth) | ISBN 9781631495618 (epub)
Subjects: LCSH: Lincoln, Abraham, 1809–1865—Religion. | Lincoln, Mary Todd, 1818–1882—Religion. |
Spiritualism—United States—History—19th century. | Parapsychology—United States—History—19th
century. | Presidents—United States—Biography. | Lincoln family. | Booth family. | Booth, Junius Brutus,
1796–1852—Family. | Lincoln, Abraham, 1809–1865—Assassination.
Classification: LCC E457.2 .A267 2022 | DDC 973.7092/2—dc23/eng/20220207
LC record available at https://lccn.loc.gov/2022005165

ISBN 978-1-324-09358-9 pbk.

Liveright Publishing Corporation, 500 Fifth Avenue, New York, N.Y. 10110
www.wwnorton.com

W. W. Norton & Company Ltd., 15 Carlisle Street, London W1D 3BS

1 2 3 4 5 6 7 8 9 0

TO

L. L., BESS, JOHN, AND NATHAN ALFORD

AND TO

JOYCE AND MORTON STEWART

LOVING IN LIFE. IN DEATH, NOT DIVIDED.

CONTENTS

INTRODUCTION

I n the 1820s two families, unknown to each other, worked on farms in the American wilderness. The Lincolns had a homestead in the backwoods of Indiana. The Booths lived in a forest clearing in Maryland. The former farmed because that was the way Lincolns had always made their living. The latter, an acting family, sought the rural life in order to restore mind and body.

The Lincoln family consisted of Thomas, his wife Nancy Hanks, daughter Sarah, and son Abraham. When Nancy died, Thomas remarried. His second wife, Sarah B. Johnston, came with three children of her own. Together with a cousin who lived with them, the Lincolns were a family of eight.

Junius Brutus Booth and Mary Ann Holmes had ten children. Four died of illnesses, but their beds were filled when Junius's sister Jane arrived from England with her husband and seven children. The Halls, a large African American family of hired servants who worked for the Booths, swelled the farm's numbers even more.

The Lincolns were frontier people through many generations. They worked hard, earned little, and moved on. Thomas Lincoln, poorly educated and rough at the edges, was a farmer, carpenter, and hunter. He was a simple man, popular with his neighbors. Nancy Hanks, whom neighbors believed more intelligent than her husband, was pleasant, thoughtful, and easygoing.

The Booths were easterners. Recently arrived from London, they were comfortable in the cities where Junius made his living on the stage. The father had a brilliant mind, a kind heart, and an erratic nature. Impossible to know, he was respected for his talent and intelligence. Mary Ann Holmes, his wife, was a homebody, seemingly as uncomplicated as her husband was complex.

Although they resided in the same country, the Lincolns and the Booths actually lived in different worlds. In a nation as physically vast as the United States, it seemed unlikely the families would ever connect among its millions of people. And yet they did. The son of one family killed the son of the other in the most infamous and consequential murder in American history.

ABRAHAM LINCOLN'S LIFE on his own began in earnest in 1831 when he was twenty-two and newly arrived in the village of New Salem, Illinois. Working a variety of jobs, he established himself there and was elected to the state legislature in 1834. After a winter spent studying law, Lincoln moved to Springfield, the new state capital, in 1837. His professional progress continued, placing him on track for a legal and political career. Never short of self-confidence, he told friends that he felt the future held something exceptional for him. At the same time, he believed it held something terrible, too.

In 1842 Lincoln married Mary Todd of Lexington, Kentucky. A bright and attractive woman from a prominent family, she shared the future president's interest in politics. To all appearances the groom was lucky to land her. He *married up*, as they said. But Mary had her own agenda. She wanted a husband who was going places. She said she would marry a great man, and she did, with all the glory and the grief that came with such an aspiration.

Lincoln opposed slavery, and he was stunned when the Kansas-Nebraska

Act was passed by Congress in 1854. This law opened (at least theoretically) the free lands in the west to slavery. Northern anger over the act led to the formation of the Republican Party, and Lincoln was its nominee for Illinois's senate seat in 1858. Although he lost the election, he gained national acclaim by his spirited campaign. Two years later, as the new party's candidate, he was elected president.

Few people cared less about these developments than the Booths. Junius felt that actors should stay clear of politics. It made no sense to alienate half the audience before the curtain rose by being a political partisan. For all his success, Junius didn't want his children on the stage. It was a punishing life. He recommended they do something else. Perhaps become undertakers.

The Booth sons turned to acting against his advice. Junius Jr. (called June), Edwin, John Wilkes, and Joseph all trod the boards. Billed as "The Father as He Lived," June was a modest success. Joe took one look at the audience, froze with fear, and was hauled off to the wings. Edwin and John were exceptionally talented, however, and they became stars. Their company was sought, their autographs collected, and their photographs sold in stores. By the time of the Civil War the two brothers were among the nation's top actors.

Lincoln never met either man personally. He did see them act in Washington, DC. The president attended eight performances by Edwin and an undetermined number by John. He liked meeting actors and once asked that John come out from backstage to visit him between acts. The young Southerner, who was passionately pro-Confederate, said coldly that "he would rather have the applause of a negro."

John's fear of a Lincoln dictatorship and his growing hatred of African Americans obscured the reality that he and the president had much in common. They were devoted to their mothers and ambivalent about their fathers. They loved children but had complicated relationships with women. They were extremely ambitious yet able to earn the affection and loyalty of others. They enjoyed poetry and the theater. They revered Shakespeare.

They also shared something else. Born in the first half of the nineteenth century, they lived in an era of remarkable progress. Advances in medicine brought forth anesthesia, the glass hypodermic syringe, and plastic surgery. Electromagnetic induction, absolute zero, and the cellular basis of plants were discovered. Propellers, vulcanized rubber, sewing machines, and the mechanical calculator were invented. Steel and petroleum came of age. Nature was being harnessed and rationality applied to life's challenges. As a benefit, people traveled faster, read more, ate better, and lived longer. Such progress was "the stride of God," wrote novelist Victor Hugo.

Regrettably, the new technology meant the end of the limited warfare of professional armies of the past and the beginning of the devastating world wars so familiar in the twentieth century. Rifled weapons, repeating rifles, land and river mines, ironclad ships, and hand grenades tore through soldiers in a manner unprecedented in history. Reconnaissance balloons (the first step in aerial warfare) spied on the armies, telegraphs carried their messages, railroad trains transported their soldiers, and photography documented their dead, while the first submarine raised its head from the deep and the first machine gun rewrote the nature of combat.

These advances changed the way people lived, thought, fought, and died. But would they change people? For all their progress, millions of Americans clung to beliefs that seemed irrational. They believed in ghosts. They studied omens, dreaded comets, and feared witchcraft. Apocalyptic writing flourished, and credence was given to visions, spells, and curses. Prophets and mystics abounded.

The Lincolns and the Booths were very superstitious people. Reaching high and hard in life, they sought to allay misfortune by gestures and beliefs for which they had no rational explanation. William Herndon, Lincoln's longtime law partner, said that the president's superstitions "ran through his being like a bluish red vein runs through the whitest marble." Mary Lincoln was equally affected. For example, she was fearful of Fridays, the day her "old slave mammy" told her the Devil made his weekly tally of her misdeeds. (Friday would be the day on which her son Eddie and her father-in-law Thomas died and the day on which her husband was shot.)

Edwin Booth, who was afraid of ivy vines and peacock feathers, was "an illogical person," thought a close friend, "full of genius, of perceptions and emotions, and cannot reason." And a contemporary journalist who studied John Wilkes's life wrote of the actor, "His mind was a haunted house."

Advocates of spiritualism, a new movement with a large following in this era, always insisted that such nonsense had nothing to do with them.

Spiritualism first appeared in 1848 when sisters Kate and Margaret Fox of Hydesville, New York, reported hearing rapping noises from the spirit of a murdered man buried in the basement of their home. The women became instant celebrities. Touring as intermediaries between the living and the dead, they gave séances nationwide. Soon they were joined by hundreds of other "mediums," a word indicating a position usefully halfway between the earthly and the spiritual planes of existence.

The movement of spiritualism was born. Its advocates asserted that it was a modern and scientific practice that rejected the finality of the grave. The dead simply progressed on through eternity. Only the departed's packaging changed as its soul went from one form to another, just as water can go from a solid to a liquid to a vapor and still be water.

Quasi-religious in nature, spiritualism held that the dead were nearby. They were "the discarnate," waiting to console those who mourned them. This was no delusion, believers insisted. How could it be when it produced observable effects in the physical world (like voices, movement, and noises)?

The Lincolns became interested in spiritualism upon Eddie's death in 1850. Their interest in the practice intensified when they lost Willie, a second son, in 1862. But spiritualism posed a problem for the president's admirers. That he might be attracted to charlatans and lamebrains of the hocus-pocus variety didn't fit well with his image as a man of wisdom. Mary Lincoln's public image suffered, too. Her interest in spiritualism, more profound than her husband's, made her appear a foolish person whose preoccupation with the spirit world placed yet another burden on her war-weary husband.

Mary was conventionally religious—more so than her husband. Unfortunately, she found little comfort for her sorrows in a pew. The reason was that she loved life and felt its reversals of fortune keenly. Her husband, on the other hand, expected bad things to happen. When they did, he suffered the pain of his losses acutely. But his fatalistic attitude about life and the relentless demands of the presidency on his attention made it easier for him to move on.

"Grief walks the Earth and sits down at the foot of each of us by turns," wrote the Greek author Aeschylus over two millennia ago. Nothing could be truer than these words, as the Booth family, too, discovered. John Wilkes, who would assassinate Lincoln in 1865, and his brother Edwin brought sorrows of their own to the séance table. Edwin lost his child-bride Mary Devlin in 1863. John had a close friend who was killed in prison the year before. Although the spiritualist movement was large, the number of distinguished mediums was not, and the Booths often sat with the same mystics as the Lincolns. Among others, they shared Charles Foster, a hard-living showman of mixed reputation, who conjured Willie for Mary, then days later produced Mary for Edwin.

No medium was more controversial than Charles J. Colchester. An English immigrant, this handsome mystic specialized in "blood writing," in which the name of an inquirer's deceased family member appeared on the medium's arm in red letters. Colchester was also a master at answering questions posed in sealed packets. Believers thought he was an extraordinarily gifted intermediary with the other side. Critics labeled him a talented trickster.

Introduced to Mary Lincoln by a mutual friend, Colchester gave her news of her dead son Willie. She was impressed and brought him to the White House, where he confounded the president by causing noises in different parts of a room. Lincoln was so intrigued with Colchester that he asked the medium to go to the Smithsonian Institution, where his powers might be studied.

Around the time Colchester sat with the Lincolns, he became intimate friends with John Wilkes. It was a very unsettling relationship. The actor, frenzied in his hatred of the president, planned to abduct him— or worse—and Colchester needed no psychic power to see where John's obsession might lead. Frightened, he salved his conscience by giving Lincoln repeated warnings to be careful.

IN THE HOUSES OF THEIR DEAD examines the common experiences of the Lincolns and the Booths with spiritualism. It is set in a time of political tumult and civil war with a cast of supporting characters further linking the principal families.

Lincoln, the most studied figure in American history, has been the subject of thousands of books and articles examining his views on slavery, his family, his politics, his mental health, and even his eyeglasses and footwear. The great president has been rightly depicted as a rational, careful, empirically minded man. But there was another dimension to him, a dimension he did not care to publicize.

This book is the first to examine in depth Lincoln's curiosity about spiritualism. It not only presents a more nuanced portrait of our most important president but also shows what the appeal of this strange practice was to Lincoln and his generation and how spiritualism shaped Americans' responses to the extraordinary upheaval of the era.

IN THE
HOUSES
OF THEIR
DEAD

1

IF THE FATES ALLOW

James Freeman Clarke was a young minister just starting his career in Louisville, Kentucky, in 1834 when he received a surprising letter. Junius Brutus Booth Sr. was in town at the United States Hotel and needed his help finding a burial place for a friend.

Recognizing Booth's name as that of the nation's greatest actor, Clarke quickly set out to see him. The minister had been unable to learn the price of a churchyard plot, but he thought he might at least try to comfort the bereaved. It was a night in need of cheer. The cold winter evening spread gloom in all directions. The feeble light of an occasional lantern, strung on a wire above an intersection, only accentuated the darkness around it. Clarke pulled his hat down on his head and hurried as best he dared over the icy streets to the hotel.

The minister found Booth in a suite of rooms near a brightly burning fire. The actor sat at a table on which were bread, cigars, and a decanter of wine. "He was a short man," Clarke wrote, "with a clear blue eye and fair complexion." Although Booth played larger-than-life characters onstage, he was smaller than Clarke had imagined—until his emotions were stirred. Then, as Clarke observed, he grew. "He became another man."

The minister asked Booth if the death of his friend had been sudden.

"Very," Booth replied.

"Was he a relative?"

"Distant," was the answer.

"Is the body in the house?"

Booth replied solemnly, "Will you look at the corpse?"

Clarke said yes, and Booth took a candle and led the way to an adjoining room. To Clarke's surprise there was no body on the bed. But, "spread on a large sheet on the floor, I beheld to my surprise, *about a bushel of wild pigeons!*"

Fresh from Harvard Divinity School, Clarke was only weeks into his first pastorate. He had found indifference, worldliness, and bigotry in Louisville. It occurred to him that this was some practical joke being played on the greenest Yankee in the slaveholding city.

But, no. Booth was deeply affected. The great actor took a pigeon in his hands and pressed it to his breast. "Poor little thing," he murmured. He seemed oblivious to Clarke's presence.

The astounded minister composed himself and stated that he didn't believe a bird needed a formal burial. "It is not a human. It has no soul."

"How do you know that it has no soul?" Booth snapped. "This is an innocent little creature that never injured anyone, that was kind and affectionate to its young, that knew nothing of wrong or injustice, and has been cruelly murdered. Why will you not pray for it?"

Booth knelt beside the birds. "You see," the actor continued, "these are victims of man's barbarity. I wish to testify in some public way against this wanton destruction of life, and I wish you to help me. Will you?"

"Hardly!" replied Clarke. "I do not look at it as you do. I must excuse myself from assisting you."

The men parted on friendly terms. "I was exceedingly astonished by the incident but also interested in the earnestness of the man," wrote Clarke. "A golden thread of human sympathy with all creatures whom God had made ran through the darkening moods of his genius. If an insanity, it was better than the cold, heartless *sanity* of most men."

Thinking about this many years later, the minister remained puzzled, but he drew—as preachers will—a moral from the encounter expressed in four lines from *The Rime of the Ancient Mariner*, Booth's favorite poem.

He prayeth best who loveth best
All things both great and small.
For the dear God who loveth us,
He made and loveth all.[1]

JUNIUS BRUTUS BOOTH immigrated to the United Sates in 1821 with his companion Mary Ann Holmes. Both were Londoners. He was a twenty-five-year-old actor. She was eighteen, the daughter of a Lambeth seed merchant. Her niece Eliza Ward said that Mary Ann met Junius while working as a flower girl in the theater district. As romantic as that would be, it is doubtful she was some Eliza Doolittle. But the niece was right in saying that "she possessed rare personal attractions and was, in fact, exceedingly beautiful."[2]

Junius sought a fresh start in America after a failed first marriage and trouble with English theater managers. He brought with him good looks, boundless energy, considerable brains, an amenable companion, and Peacock, a piebald pony he had purchased shortly before his departure. Piebalds were said to be good luck.[3]

Booth quickly established himself as a force on the American stage. At times he dressed inappropriately, insulted the audience, and annoyed fellow performers. He also tended to get bored and hurry through the tamer and less interesting scenes of a play. "But, in the representation of highly excited passion, bursts of frantic rage, or the agony of unutterable feeling, Mr. Booth was remarkable," wrote John Cooper Vail, a contemporary and author of *The Actor* (1846), an early biography of the tragedian. "In depicting violent rage or unrelenting hate, in the portrayal of bold and romantic villainy, in exhibiting the satisfaction of triumphant revenge or the terrific workings of despair, he never had a superior."[4] This ability to thrill audiences made him the nation's leading dramatic actor during the 1820s and 1830s.

No profession could have been more destructive to a person of Booth's sensibilities. He found a refuge from work in a tract of land off a rough

Junius Brutus Booth Sr. *Booth immigrated to the United States in 1821 with Mary Ann Holmes, his companion. The couple had ten children, including Edwin and John Wilkes. The father was a brilliant actor whose life was clouded by alcoholism and mental illness.*

coach road near Bel Air, Maryland, north of Baltimore. The Booths called this retreat "The Farm." Initially, it was no more than an open meadow surrounded by dense woods. A simple log house with small square windows was moved to the site and became their home. The structure had broad shutters and a front door, all painted red. Excellent water came from a nearby spring where an immense green bullfrog—believed to have lived for a century—serenaded the Booths each evening.[5]

Junius worried that Mary Ann would not be content with this type of living. She preferred cities and was so unprepared for rural life that Elizabeth Rogers, her nearest neighbor, found the couple eating hardtack out of a barrel. Mary Ann didn't know how to bake bread. Elizabeth laughed and pitched in, teaching her the basics. Since the husband liked it here, the new couple would stay. The price of being with Junius was doing what

Junius said. "Never did I hear her contradict Mr. Booth in my life," Elizabeth recalled, "and he was sometimes very eccentric."[6]

Ten children were born to Junius and Mary Ann between 1821 and 1840. They were—in order—Junius Jr. (June), Rosalie (Rose), Henry, Frederick, Elizabeth, Mary, Edwin, Asia, John Wilkes, and Joseph (Joe). Little is known about their births or infancies.

Frederick died in Boston in 1828, at the age of one. Junius was absent in New York at the time, and Mary Ann was terrified at what his reaction to the death might be. Since Frederick suffered greatly in his last illness, "she was not sorry for the death of the child for that she thought it was happy [now]," theater manager H. C. Charnock, with whom the Booths lived, wrote the husband. But Booth being so unpredictable, "the only thing she was afraid of was to meet you. She best knows the reason."[7]

Everyone realized that Junius was strange. The actor told journalist S. S. Southworth that he once "dug up a grave and carried home in a bundle a skull and bones which he used to sleep with." Junius also alleged that he and the Devil were seen together at night hovering over a grave in a Philadelphia cemetery and that he and a juggler named Peters, whose gimmick was walking upside down across ceilings, "bound themselves by an irrevocable and damning oath to the service of Beelzebub," drinking the oath in blood out of a horse's skull. Following this ceremony, the pair went to consult with a troupe of Romani (called "gypsies" in the newspapers of the time).[8] A prominent London newspaper reported, "It is well known to the public that this unfortunate gentleman is visited by paroxysms of temporary insanity, under whose influence he by turns puts on the characters which his profession leads him to personate."[9]

Daughters Elizabeth and Mary died in 1833 during a cholera outbreak. Elizabeth was an infant, not yet bonded with the father, but Mary was five and deeply loved by him.

"WHAT?!" he cried on learning the news of Mary's passing. He dug his long fingers into his temples as if attempting to steady the mind beneath. "My poor little child—my loved, my beautiful one!"

Junius was acting in Baltimore when the death occurred. Still dressed in his stage costume, he mounted Peacock and "galloped, galloped, galloped home, belaboring the little horse with the flat of his sword." Peacock snorted in pain as they raced through the dark forest along the Bel Air Road. Well past midnight Junius arrived to find not only a dead daughter, with her horribly sunken eyes and bluish skin, but June ill, too, and their mother teetering between the grave and the madhouse.[10]

When Frederick died, Junius had brought the body home from Boston and placed it in a cemetery on a hillside meadow west of the house. Elizabeth and Mary were now placed beside their brother under suitable markers. The lot was enclosed by a wrought-iron fence and a gate with handsome finials and the embossed name of "J. B. BOOTH." Yews and weeping willows were planted beside them.[11]

The effect of Mary's death on Junius's finely strung temperament was catastrophic. "Massa was druv clean mad," recalled a servant. Junius blamed the tragedy on his absence from home, broke his acting contract with manager Thomas Hamblin, accused him of eating pork, and challenged him to a duel—all in a letter signed, "Your brother in Virtue, Cholera!" "It was the culmination of his sorrow," wrote his daughter Asia, who published biographies of her father in 1866 and 1881. "His mind became entirely unsettled for a time, and a painful illness followed."[12]

To punish himself, Junius put hard peas in his shoes and walked all day, then fitted heavy lead plates to the shoes' insoles and marched to Washington. Later, growing frenzied, he took an ax and smashed Mary's gravestone to pieces. Digging her up, he brought her remains into the house, then he opened a vein in her arm and tried to suck out impure blood in hopes of reviving her. "Sometimes his mind would get a little off with wine," neighbor Elizabeth Rogers added charitably.[13]

As Junius recovered from these "spells," he worked the farm. It comforted him. Farming was practical and doable, unlike the artificial world of the stage or the vexatious life of the family. He labored contentedly in his bare feet and shirtsleeves, with a straw flap hat and a wet plantain leaf to cool himself. "Ignoring the superstition that iron poisoned the soil and only wood was safe for ploughing," he employed a newfangled metal plow. He was proud of the corn, oats, and turnips he coaxed from the soil, and the carrots, too, since local farmers said eating carrots made a person pretty. He and Peacock hauled the bounty to market.[14]

Peacock was a marvelous little creature with a striking coat of inter-mingled white and bay. "Being quite small and so singularly marked, almost every horse that met him on the road became frightened at his appearance," recalled W. Stump Forward, a local doctor. Peacock showed remarkable stamina carrying the actor, often drunk, back and forth to Baltimore, and Junius developed a parental concern for the horse. Peacock returned the affection, prancing in delight when his master came home from acting tours.[15]

EDWIN WAS BORN on the night of November 13, 1833. Fearing a physician might be needed, eleven-year-old June, his brother, started off for one.[16] The boy rode under a dark sky, the moon a scarcely visible crescent. Then, about an hour before midnight, the greatest Leonid meteor shower ever recorded commenced over his head. Meteors rushed in every direction, some with long shining white trains, others cascading over each other like falling water—all leaping, silent, tumbling apparitions. The torrent increased steadily until it disappeared into the dawn. No one who witnessed the spectacle could forget it. "I was awestruck," recalled Frederick Doug-lass, a teenage slave living across the Chesapeake Bay on Maryland's East-ern Shore. "The air seemed filled with bright descending messengers."[17]

"People who foretell the weather with a goose bone set great store in meteors," said one observer. "It can mean anything and everything in the way of a sign or omen."[18] Servants at the farm said it meant that Edwin had been born lucky as well as "gifted to see ghosts." As an added bless-ing, Edwin was born with a caul. A caul is a piece of the amniotic sac adhering to a baby's face or head. Perhaps because the condition happens so rarely—less than one in every 80,000 births—it is highly distinctive, and some thought that those born with it were divinely favored. Even clairvoyant.[19]

The Leonid Meteor Shower of 1833. *The greatest meteor shower ever recorded, this event occurred on the night of Edwin Booth's birth. Servants said it meant the baby was born "gifted to see ghosts."*

Ann Hall enjoyed talking about the night of Edwin's birth, although her voice grew uneasy when speaking of the portents. Ann and her husband Joe were African Americans who lived with the Booths. Joe purchased his freedom with Junius's help, then he bought that of Ann, and the couple were devoted to the actor and his family. Joe was a tall, dark-skinned man who boasted his descent from a Madagascan prince. He often wore a Turkish-style turban. Ann was a plump, serious-looking woman with long cheeks.

Ever-present on the farm, the Halls and their children became sub-ordinate family members. Ann nursed, cooked, doctored, and caretook black and white while Joe farmed, hauled, herded, and gabbed. Their large family included Young Joe, esteemed for his ability to make seven faces in rapid succession. Father and son could "tell stories heard among the old negroes, queer unreal tales that made us shiver and look behind us," neighbors recalled.[20]

Returning to the farm one evening, Junius found Peacock dead. He was frantic with grief and convinced himself that Mary Ann could bring Pea-cock back to life. "He had confidence in the prayers of Mrs. Booth," wrote Forward. Junius forced his wife to wrap herself in a sheet and lie on the horse's remains while he marched around her with a gun, reading from a book. Joe Hall ran for help. The Rogerses arrived, seized Junius, and led the terror-stricken mother to safety. Junius good-naturedly invited every-one in for a drink, then wandered off, only to be discovered seriously ill the next day. "The poor fellow," wrote his physician James Rush, "has for years kept his wife in misery and his friends in fear."[21]

Torments continued to bedevil Junius. On an acting trip to Charles-ton, he attempted suicide. Failing that, he tried to kill comedian Thomas Flynn, a close friend, in a midnight attack with an andiron. Flynn fought back, breaking Booth's nose.[22] "That Mr. Booth is sometimes mad, either from hereditary disease [alcoholism] or temporary aberration of mind, is sufficiently evident," wrote his biographer Vail. "He is a creature of impulse and passion . . . lost in the bewildering mazes of incessant reflec-tion. It would be a fruitless endeavor to solve the mysteries of Booth's eccentricities."[23]

John Wilkes Booth was born a few weeks after the attack on Flynn. Nothing is known about the event except its date—May 10, 1838—and the fact that Junius, drunk at a local tavern, was hauled home to greet the new-born. He was in a jolly mood.[24]

A portrait of Mary Ann by Thomas Sully reveals that she was afflicted with exotropia, a form of strabismus in which her left eye deviated out-ward. More than any other part of the body, the eye was the subject of folk

Mary Ann Holmes. *Shown in a portrait attributed to Thomas Sully, the mother of*
the Booth children was an emotionally positive counterweight to her erratic husband
Junius. She was given to dreams and visions.

beliefs. A walleyed person was believed to be gifted, able to look in two
directions at once and therefore to see more than the average person.[25]

Late in 1838, as the last leaves left the trees, Mary Ann pulled a chair
near the fireplace. It was "a ghostly night." The household was asleep,
Junius away, and Mary Ann alone in the silent hours to perform one of
those selfless acts of motherhood that—as her daughter Asia wrote—only
the angels observe. John was fretful and needed comforting.

As Mary Ann nursed the baby to sleep, she grew fascinated by his tiny
hand on her breast. An unexplained anxiety about him seized her, and she
prayed that God would reveal to her the baby's future.

Suddenly, the fire blazed before her in an unexplained flare. It was a
reply—a prophecy, thought Mary Ann, turned by Asia into these lines:

The flame up leapt
Like a wave of blood,
An avenging arm crept into shape
And *Country* shown out in the flame,
Which, fading, resolved to her boy's own name!
God had answered.[26]

THERE WERE PERIODS when Junius behaved normally, acted triumphantly, and earned real money. Success allowed him to purchase a two-story brick townhouse in Baltimore. Schools were better in the city and travel for his profession more convenient. The new home allowed the family to split its time between town and country.

Despite their peculiarities—and the father's exotic occupation of acting—the Booths were well regarded by their neighbors. Junius was considered an odd but honest person who paid his bills promptly and left others alone. Mary Ann was a loving wife and an indulgent mother. June, a handsome and big-hearted knockoff of the old man. Rose, a plain and peaceable homebody. Edwin, a thoughtful "boy with no boyhood" who attended his father. Asia, a proud and tempestuous belle. John, a happy little rascal, excitable but well meaning. And then there was Joe, strange and quixotic, an afterthought to his lively siblings.[27]

Richard Booth, Junius's father, died at night in a Baltimore tavern during the winter of 1839. The body of the retired London lawyer was kept in the receiving vault of undertaker John H. Weaver until the weather permitted Junius to bury it six months later. "Contrary to my advice, he had the coffin opened," Weaver later told Asia. "I drew off with the men, but from where we stood, I was able to see that he bent down and kissed the face of the dead. It was an unusual thing to witness and an unsafe thing to do."

Junius had come to accept that death was an irrevocable parting. The dead were gone forever. Any impression of contact with them was only a reverie of the bereaved. To Junius, the deceased were travelers departing an inn and ascending to the stars. Weaver, sexton of Christ Church, said that was not the proper Christian way to look at it. Life was no hotel and heaven no star.

Junius took a pair of scissors from a pocket kit and cut a three-inch lock of his father's hair, yellowish-white with stray black strands. He wrapped the lock in a strip of paper and secured it with a green silk cord. The cord, Weaver surmised, had "some Moorish or Arab signification." (Junius often wore an Islamic crescent broach on his coat.)[28]

With the passing of Richard Booth, death was finished with the Booths for the present. Trouble was not.

By 1840 a decade of heavy drinking, added to the stress of work, travel, and domestic woe, had taken a toll on Junius. He still drew good audiences, "but the laurel wreath of fame had withered on his brow, the once sonorous and musical voice fallen into a nasal utterance, the fine manly countenance disfigured" by his broken nose, wrote a friend in 1846. "We find him a splendid ruin. What might he not have been had time mellowed instead of blighting the fruit of that transcendent genius?"[29]

Mary Ann had difficulties, too. Not curious by nature, she followed Junius's dictum for "women to stay at home and hold their tongues." She knew her husband had been married before, of course, but always assumed he had been properly divorced and free to wed her. It never occurred to her that she was living in bigamy and her children were illegitimate.

To Mary Ann's astonishment a woman named Adelaide Delannoy appeared in Baltimore looking for Junius. The stranger claimed to be Junius's legal wife. She demanded her rights as his spouse and swore to "fall on his back like a bomb" to get them. Adelaide sought out Mary Ann. Often, when drunk, she waylaid Mary Ann at the city market and drove her from the street with curses. Nothing could have been more hurtful to the modest mother.[30]

While Junius arranged a tardy divorce, Mary Ann busied herself with the children. Despite Junius's wishes, June wanted a stage career. He had talent and enjoyed some success. Rose had a brief courtship with Jacob Driesbach, a lion tamer. Her father ended it, and she settled into her life-long role as companion to her mother.[31]

The younger children, shielded as much as possible from the marriage scandal, attended community schools. Asia did well, showing a flair for writing. Since Edwin was needed to assist his father on tours, his education was hit-or-miss. His schoolmates envied him for his independence, but they knew nothing of the lonely days and sleepless nights that were his life on the road. It was tedious and somber—and inappropriate—for a sensitive child to be guardian to an unstable parent. Edwin deeply regretted the absence of a decent education. Later in life he thought of himself as uneducated and felt intimidated by intellectuals. He reflected, "I grew up in ignorance allowed by an indulgent mother, who knew nothing more than that she loved her child, and a father who, although a good man, seemed to care very little about what course I took."[32]

There was nothing wrong with Edwin's mind. In fact, all the children were ready learners except John. That brother "had to plod, progress slowly step by step," Asia wrote in a memoir of his life. "He found it far from easy to keep up with his classmates. He possessed a tenacious rather than an intuitive intelligence. [But] what he had once learned remained, as he said, *stamped on the sight of his mind*."[33]

Asia never mentioned her brother's most troubling characteristic: John tortured cats. He chased them down alleys, across lawns, and through buildings. Nabbing two, he tied them together in a way that the movement of one produced pain to the other. He enjoyed their suffering. Stuart Robson, a playmate, once watched John climb across a remarkably steep roof in pursuit of a mouser. "If he had made the least slip, he would have fallen and probably killed himself. But he never stopped till he got that cat." At the farm John simply shot them. "He killed off almost the entire breed in his neighborhood."[34]

Some people hate cats. The animals are independent, sly, unpredictable, predatory toward smaller animals, and historically associated with evil (as the servants of witches). Ailurophobia—the fear of cats—is a more intense reaction than mere dislike. John's behavior was darker still. It was a lack of common compassion, and it boded ill. Repeated intentional abuse of animals by a child is a likely precursor of later violent behavior by an adult.

The connection had been observed more than a century earlier by Enlightenment thinkers like John Locke.

"A thief who takes property from another has it in his power, should he repent, to make a restoration," Junius believed. "But the robber of life never can give back what he has taken from beings equally capable of enjoying pleasure or suffering torture with himself." The father practiced that philosophy to the point of rescuing flies from drowning.[35]

John's actions were a grievous departure from his father's, but with limits. While he would torment cats, he had—oddly—strong feelings of empathy with other animals. He was kind to dogs, once saving a setter thrown into a river by its heartless owner. He loved horses, slugging a man he saw abusing one. He was even protective of insects, going out of his way to avoid injuring butterflies and lightning bugs. When Asia attempted to impale a katydid for her insect collection, John stopped her. "You bloodthirsty female," he teased. "Katy shall be free!" He returned the bug to its home in a sycamore tree.[36]

With his charm and buoyant personality, nothing John did cost him the friendship of others. "Wilkes was immensely popular," recalled George Stout, a childhood neighbor. "All the boys liked him." Stout joined John, Edwin, and Stuart Robson to form a theatrical troupe based in a latticework arbor in the family's backyard. They performed *The Shivering Idiot*. A seven-act play with an admission price of two cents, it was billed as the best bargain in Baltimore. In one scene John tied Edwin to a tree and "sawed off" his leg to the screams of a "packed house" of six boys and three girls.[37]

North Exeter Street in Baltimore, where the Booths lived, was a lively place. Its pleasant homes and boardinghouses were intermingled with stationers' shops and bakeries and churches. Cabs rattled along the rough stones, dodging the wagons of a busy woodyard nearby. (Once a heavy dray nearly crushed Asia.) The occasional fire engine hurried by, chased by throngs of children. The cries of grocers and milkmen mixed with the distant scream of locomotive engines at the Camden Station railroad depot. There was an energy along the street, and in the middle of it all was John.

He had a twinkle in his eye that seemed to say, "If I could only think of a good joke to play on you, I should be supremely happy."[38]

An incident on North Exeter revealed a curious self-perception of the future assassin—John's belief that he was unlucky.

One summer evening he and a group of friends played telegraph by stretching a line across the street. John fixed the wire from the maple in front of his house to the mulberry opposite. A passerby caught his tall hat on the line. Highly indignant, he fetched a constable. The officer burst onto the scene, scattering the children left and right. Everyone escaped except John. The officer seized him by the shoulders. But before John was hauled away, he asked permission to coil up the wire first as it might hurt a passing horse.

"To the Watch-house!" ordered the constable. Off they went, Asia trailing with her silk apron tied over her head for a bandanna. The street was deserted now, and when the constable finally released his grip on John, she took her brother's arm. Don't frighten mother, he told her.

They wound their way through a series of byways, mounted a worn staircase, and "entered a dim, filthy room, stifling with bad odors and heat." A few candles lit the unwholesome air. Beyond them three men sat on a platform. Despite their informal appearance, with linen coats half off their backs, shirts open, and collars limp, Asia gasped on seeing them. "They presented a terrible array for they were mighty men of the law." The aggrieved passerby was present, excited and demanding justice.

John removed his cap and looked directly at the magistrates as his misdemeanors were enumerated. Then he was ordered to give the names of the others involved.

"Must I?" Asia heard him say. The answer was yes, and he replied, "I refuse to give their names."

"How is it that only you were caught? This gentleman declares there were a dozen of you boys."

John looked at Asia and smiled. "Because that is my luck, sir."

The coolness of his reply frightened her, and she jumped to his defense. "No matter what game or mischief it is, *he* always fares worse than the others," she cried. "*He* is the one to be hurt or found out. All the rest get off clear."

The lords of the law gave her a kind look. Then, after lecturing John about "obstructing the pass-way," the bench dismissed him with the order, "You children go straight home."[39]

JUNIUS SAT WITH a half-dozen friends at a tavern in Petersburg, Virginia. He had concluded his engagement in the city and celebrated with dinner and drinks before the fireplace. "The snow was deep on the ground, and the night bitterly cold, and we determined to stay where we were for the night," he recalled.

Song and story flowed to which Junius contributed a recitation of Byron's "Epitaph to a Dog." Its beautiful lines were written in honor of Boatswain, Byron's Newfoundland who died of rabies in 1808.

The poor Dog, in life the firmest friend,
The first to welcome, foremost to defend.
Whose honest heart is still his master's own,
Who labours, fights, lives, breathes for him alone.
Unhonoured falls, unnoticed all his worth,
Denied in heaven the Soul he held on earth.

"We threw more coal in the fire," Junius said. Propping his feet on the fireplace jamb, the actor tilted his chair back and concluded the recitation. As he reached the final line of the poem, the lone candle in the room went out. At the same instant Booth's foot slipped down and accidentally struck a dog. It sprang up with a howl and bolted from the room.

Whose dog was it? No one knew. No one had seen it before. No one had any idea where it came from. No one professed to have noticed it until that very instant. "Perhaps you will smile at me, sir, and think me superstitious," Junius said to an acquaintance, "but I could not but think that the animal was brought there by *occult sympathy.*"[40]

The family got its own Newfoundland. Veto—named to honor President Andrew Jackson, who vetoed more bills than his six predecessors combined—was a handsome, lionlike creature with large hazel eyes. Never deceive him, the father cautioned John and Asia. "If we watch our dogs closely, we observe how anxiously they take note of our every look and movement," he said. It was almost painful to see their efforts to understand and to please.

Asia and her father were walking along the city dock when she felt herself being jerked backward. Veto had grasped her, tearing her frock and hurting her arm in the process. She leaped up yelling at him, but the father stopped her. Look around, he ordered. She had walked near a large pool of water covered thickly with bark, making the area appear as firm as ground. Veto had saved her a nasty experience, if not worse. A sailor who saw what happened came over to reward the Newfie with a piece of gingerbread. How did Veto, who was behind her, know what was in front of her, Asia wondered.[41]

Junius enjoyed spending his Sunday mornings on such walks. While Mary Ann headed for Christ Church, he preferred to stroll about the city, watching the splendor of a flight of birds or enjoying the stillness of a quiet cove. He was a free spirit, open to the best teachings of all religions. He admired the Koran, underscoring many passages in his copy of that book. He read the Talmud and joined the rabbis in their worship and in their tongue. Catholic fathers avowed that he was one of them. But, while he bowed his head reverently when passing their churches, he remained nonsectarian. He respected every person's quest for his or her own religious path. Junius seemed most at home at a shabby little sailor's chapel near the Patapsco River. "The congregation was of the humblest degree," wrote Asia, "and the ministry not at all edifying," but he liked it. His piety "did not show itself in Sunday clothes."[42]

At the farm Junius often sought peace in the deep woods. He discovered a cave (never since relocated) that he visited frequently. The cave was rumored to be full of evidence of his disordered mind. He also liked sitting by streams. A boy named Billy Harwood, hunting berries, chanced upon

him as the actor tossed pebbles into a creek. Just as Billy realized something was amiss with his behavior, Junius looked up and fixed the boy with
a stare. Billy stopped in his tracks.

People noticed Junius's eyes. They were blue-gray, the color of steel.
When he was excited, the eyes had "a scintillating gleam, like the green
and red slashes of an enraged serpent," wrote his friend James E. Mur-
doch, and he knew how to employ the look. Some years before John was
born, a deranged man came at Junius with an ax. The actor fixed his eye
on the maniac, who froze in fear, lowered the weapon, and backed away,
convinced the actor was a practitioner of the black arts. Billy felt no less
afraid. There was something "disturbing alien" in this encounter. He, too,
backed away and ran.[43]

Junius returned from his wanderings "silent, thoughtful, and completely abstracted, either unable or not inclined to give any account of himself," recalled Asia. She did not question him as to what happened. "I never
thought anything he did peculiar in those days, and I never commented
on what occurred."[44]

June, who managed a theater in San Francisco, came home in the spring
of 1852 for a visit. Between lessons teaching John how to fence and box,
June told his father there was a fortune to be made in California. Junius
and Edwin returned there with him that summer. The father was excited
but uneasy about the trip. Although his father Richard had lived well into
his seventies, Junius—now fifty-six—told neighbors that he felt his race
was nearly run.[45]

The results of the trip were mixed. Junius's fame drew many to the
theaters in California where they found the star, according to one critic, "a
splendid ruin, aged and crumbling but majestic and magnificent even in
decay." Exhaustion, illness, and drink—he fell twice onstage one evening—
wore away at him. Edwin knew his father was about to go on a drinking
spree by a peculiar motion. Junius would saw the air beside his head with
his right hand. When that happened, there was no stopping him. Once
Edwin tried, and the father exclaimed, "Go away, go away! By God, sir, I'll
put you aboard a man-o'-war, sir!"[46]

Junius Brutus Booth Sr. and Edwin Booth. *This striking photograph was taken about 1846, when Edwin was twelve years old. It is the only image showing the elder Booth with one of his children.*

After only two months of performances, the father suddenly announced his intention to return home. He gave the jeweled crown he wore as Richard III, his signature role, to June. This valuable piece of wardrobe was "an ornament that had been for years a treasure of considerable care." He told the son he no longer needed it.

Returning from the west, Junius fell ill while on a Mississippi River steamboat shortly after its departure from New Orleans. What was thought initially to be a cold worsened rapidly. There was no doctor on hand, so Junius drank river water. Locals believed that Mississippi sludge, as opaque as gruel, was wholesome. Over the course of several days, Junius became inarticulate and unable to move. He died of "consumption of the bowels" on November 30, 1852, on the river just below Louisville, Kentucky.[47]

Junius Brutus Booth's death was reported nationwide in the cities where he had earned his fame and fortune. Praise of his acting was universal.

So, too, were references to his eccentricities. His had been a complicated life, wrote admirer Walt Whitman, one that "illustrated Plato's rule that to the forming of the artist of the very highest rank a dash of insanity is indispensable."[48]

Junius's biographer Vail believed that few would understand this. "It is the peculiar characteristic of genius to find no sympathy [in this] cold and uncongenial world. The dull machinery of life, with all its petty annoyances, falls like a leaden weight upon its spirit." But, Vail wrote, if one could look into the heart of another, "no dark and damned spot" would be found in Junius Brutus Booth.[49]

2

HIS IMPERFECT SELF

Barnstorming across Illinois in winter was tough work, but actors must eat, so the Jefferson family troupe set out from Chicago as the year 1839 came to a close. The head of this itinerant enterprise was Joseph Jefferson Jr., veteran player and scenic painter. Cordelia, his wife, was their vocalist. Charlie Burke, Joseph's stepson, was their comedian. And Joseph Jefferson III—Little Joe—sang comic songs and danced. The child was born to the stage. No one knows when he first came before the footlights, but certainly whenever the plot called for an infant to be threatened by a lion, lost by a nurse, or stolen by a pirate, prop-baby Joe was handy. Now, at age ten, he was fast becoming a trouper, likely to be showered with small change from the audience.

The family traveled in a caravan of large open wagons. Joe sat on top of a horsehair wardrobe trunk, holding on tightly as the wagon jolted over the icy prairie. The bad roads occasionally jostled him off. He scrambled back up, and the actors pushed on. Smiling and smoking his pipe, the hopeful father walked ahead of them, dreaming of the fame and fortune just around the corner. Now and then, "he looked back with his light blue eyes," recalled Joe, "giving my mother a cheerful nod which plainly said, 'I'm all right. This is splendid. Nothing could be finer.'"

The Jeffersons discovered that frontier audiences, unaccustomed to stage productions, were as amusing as any performer. They munched their peanuts, read their newspapers, polished their boots, picked their teeth, and talked to each other and at times even to the actors. A hulking farmer became so involved in the tribulations of the hero and heroine in *The Lady of Lyon* that he warned the play's villain to stop interfering with them if he didn't want to get thrashed. His neighbor agreed, protesting loudly that she didn't see why the young lovers shouldn't be allowed to marry if they wished. On another occasion, during the scene in *Richard III* in which the wicked king woos Lady Anne, an audience member shouted to Anne that she should spurn him. Richard already had a wife in Texas.[1]

Springfield was the most promising stop on the tour. It had a population in the state second only to Chicago. In the big picture the town was small potatoes. Its entire population could have fit into the Bowery Theatre of New York with room to accommodate the residents of Memphis, Tennessee, as their guests. Pioneer times lingered here, with more log houses than brick or board, but it was the state capital and, as legislators gathered for their annual session, the town was full of people wanting entertainment. Jefferson partnered with Alexander McKenzie, his brother-in-law, for a short season here.

"The Illinois Theatre Company," as they styled themselves, decided to build a theater. It was a simple affair. "About ninety feet deep and forty feet wide," recalled Joe. "No attempt was made at ornamentation. It was unpainted, and the simple lines of architecture upon which it was constructed gave it the appearance of a large dry-goods house with a roof. I do not think my father or McKenzie ever owned anything with a roof until now, so they were naturally proud of their possession."

Unfortunately, in the midst of their rising fortunes, trouble appeared. A religious revival was in progress, and preachers began to sermonize against the company. It was the old hostility, dating back to Puritan times, of the church to the stage. The feeling was especially intense among the Methodists, Baptists, and Presbyterians, who were Springfield's principal denominations. They objected to the theater's risqué themes, coarse audiences, late hours, dancing, emotionalism, and exhibitionism.[2] The stage was "a school of vice, a hot bed of iniquity, and a pander to pollution and death," one writer complained to the local newspaper.[3] Unable to block "the wicked play-actors" outright, the religious element managed to get the city fathers to slap a prohibitively heavy license fee on their unholy calling.

To the theater folks the villains in this drama were the town's board of trustees, one of whose members now called on the Jeffersons. The visitor was tall—six feet, four inches—and somewhat stoop-shouldered. "His legs were long," said Robert Wilson, a local lawyer, "feet large, arms long, longer than any man I ever knew. When standing Straiht [sic] and letting his arms fall down his side, the points of his fingers would touch a point lower on his legs by nearly three inches than was usual with other persons." His eyes were bluish-brown, his face long and gaunt, and his look dull unless discussing an engaging topic. Joshua Speed, the visitor's best friend, loved him but acknowledged he was gawky and unattractive. The man was Abraham Lincoln.[4]

Abraham Lincoln. *The future president looks far removed from his frontier origins in this early likeness. His double-breasted frock coat with satin-fronted vest and a crisp white shirt whose starched bosom is fastened with metal studs show the hand of his fashion-conscious wife, Mary.*

Lincoln had been absent from the trustees' meeting when the fee was imposed. He was here, he told the Jeffersons, because "he desired to see fair play." He could try to get the council's decision reversed if they wished. The company hired him, he worked his magic, and on January 31, 1840, the trustees did just that, agreeing to suspend all future demands on the company.

The victory was a limited one, however. The Illinois Theatrical Company continued liable for the amount accrued before the reversal. And it owed five dollars to Lincoln. The Jeffersons thought the sum, as part of the larger culture war, was money well spent.

Back at his office the young lawyer pulled down a small octavo book with green papered boards and a calf backstrip. It was the fee book in which he recorded income of his partnership with John T. Stuart. He entered in it, "Notes on Theatre folks . . . paid [to] Lincoln 3.50, to Stuart 1.50."[5]

Lincoln's fateful link with the theater had begun.

ABRAHAM LINCOLN WAS not a native of Springfield. (Since the town had been founded in 1821, few people at that time were.) He was born on February 12, 1809, on a frontier farm near Hodgenville, Kentucky.

His father was Thomas Lincoln. A strong man with a boxy build, Thomas had black hair, gray eyes, and a nose large enough to draw comment. He was not as tall as his son but like him was humorous and good at storytelling. Thomas farmed and carpentered, but his passion was hunting. Calm and placid, he was an honest and social proletarian lump, well regarded wherever he lived. He was neither lazy nor dynamic. "Always doing but doing nothing great," recalled Nathaniel Grigsby, who grew up with Abraham. "He wanted few things and supplied them easily. Was happy—lived easy—and contented."[6]

Nancy Hanks, Lincoln's mother, was taller than most women. She had a sharp, angular face, light hazel eyes, and a high forehead crowned with black hair. "Her nature was kindness, mildness, tenderness, sadness, obedience to her husband," recalled John Hanks, a cousin of whom Abraham was very fond. "Abrm. was like his mother very much."[7] Minimally educated, Nancy was nevertheless highly intelligent. She had good judgment and a spiritual inclination. "She was superior to her husband in every way," said Grigsby. Despite their differences, "Lincoln and his wife were really happy in each other's presence—loved one another."

One of Abraham's earliest memories was working the family's seven-acre field with his father. Thomas planted corn and Abraham followed behind him dropping two pumpkin seeds in alternate mounds and rows. The next day a heavy rain soaked the rocky knobs above the patch. A flood resulted, washing away their corn, pumpkin seed, and laboriously prepared topsoil. So, this was farming, Abraham realized.[8]

Unable to secure a clear title to his land, Thomas Lincoln moved the family (which included Abraham's older sister Sarah, his one sibling) across the Ohio River to southern Indiana in 1816. Here they would live for the next fourteen years as Abraham grew up. The son told biographer John L. Scripps that the move was "partly on account of slavery." "This is untrue," said his cousin Dennis Hanks, who lived with the Lincolns in their new home. "He moved off to better his condition—to a place where he could buy land for his children. Slavery did not operate on him. I know too well this whole matter."[9]

Their new homestead was hacked out of a wilderness. Vines were pulled, timber cut, logs hauled, and fields cleared. Surrounding this hole in the forest were "Indians—wild bears—wolves—deer," recalled Dennis. He and Thomas hunted frequently, "and we were more or less depended on it for a living—nay, for life." A cabin was built. It had a sleeping loft for Dennis and Abraham, the pegs they used for steps creaking under their weight as the two ascended for the night. In time the farm was stocked with hogs, horses, and cattle, and a good crop of wheat, corn, and vegetables was produced. Nancy Hanks knitted their socks, Dennis made their shoes, Sarah fried their bacon, and Thomas built a table upon which to eat it. Abraham contributed what a child could, but as he grew into his teens it was apparent he had no aptitude for this kind of life. "Lincoln was not an industrious worker on the farm or at any other kind of Manu[al]

Labor," said A. H. Chapman, a family member. "He only Showed industry in attainment of Knowledge."[10]

In the fall of 1818, when Abraham was nine, his mother fell ill with what was called "milk sick." This strangely named illness was a vegetable poisoning caused by eating the meat or drinking the milk of animals feeding in the woods on the white snakeroot plant. Sufferers from milk sick did not slip quietly away; they died hard. There was repeated vomiting, abdominal pain, consuming fatigue, and a breath odor (produced by acetone) so offensive it could be detected upon entering a patient's cabin.

Nancy grew steadily worse over the course of a week and, realizing the end was near, she called for Abraham and Sarah. They had been taught to love other people and to revere and worship God, she reminded them. Now, in her absence, they must "be good & kind to their father—to one an other and to the world." Her death followed on October 5 at the age of thirty-four. "Abe never got over the mizble way his mother died," reflected Dennis Hanks. Nor did he. "Oh Lord, oh Lord, I'll never furget it," he said decades later. "Here, in this rude house, died one of the very best women of the whole [human] race."[11]

The following year Thomas married Sarah Bush Johnston, a Kentucky widow with three children. She was a tall woman with large bluish-gray eyes. Industrious by nature, she was plain, practical, and kindhearted. She brought to the Indiana farm some nice furniture, proper kitchen equipment—and soap. "Abe & his sister was wild," recalled Dennis. Thomas had no instinct for mothering. Sarah did, and "she Soaped—rubbed and washed the children clean so that they looked pretty neat. She sewed and mended their clothes & the children once more looked Human." She liked Abraham, probably more than she did her own son John, and the young Lincoln responded. Chapman remembered, "Her love for him was warmly returned & continued to the day of his death."[12]

She encouraged Abraham's education, as rudimentary as it was. Lincoln would later estimate his formal education amounted to a total of one year. The rest he learned on his own. His stepmother noticed that while her son John headed off to dances, Abraham lay his head near the fireplace and read. "He was a Constant and I may Say Stubborn reader, his father having Sometimes to slash him for neglecting his work," added Dennis. But, once "he got a new story—new book or new fact, he never forgot it." A teenage friend, Anna Roby, recalled proudly, "He was the learned boy among us unlearned folks."[13]

Abraham grew into a large and powerful adolescent. Sociable and fun to be around, he was intelligent, sincere, and honest. He liked children, loved poetry, and seemed happy most of the time. When the drinking started— as it always did in these frontier communities—he might not join in or, if he did, did so in moderation. He needed nothing to fire his natural witti- ness. He felt a burgeoning ambition; for what he did not know. He only realized, "I don't always intend to delve, grub, shuck corn, split rails, and the like."[14]

"He [had] great nerve when aroused," said Joseph Gillespie, a longtime friend. At the same time, he "was remarkably tender to the feelings of oth- ers." This compassion extended to animals. When his stepbrother John threw a terrapin against a tree, crushing its shell, Lincoln watched the ani- mal's broken body quiver to death in agony. He was appalled and rebuked John before the other children. "Abe preached against Cruelty to animals," said Matilda, John's sister, "contending that an ant's life was to it as sweet as ours is to us."[15]

He was no pacificist, however. When his sister Sarah died in childbirth in 1828, he was infuriated with Aaron Grigsby, her husband, for neglect- ing her. Lincoln decided to settle matters publicly in the frontier way—a fight between the families. It was no spontaneous melee. Announced in advance, it drew spectators from miles around. Due to Lincoln's superior strength, it was arranged for his stepbrother John Johnston to step in and take on William Grigsby, a brother of the despicable Aaron. "A terrible fight" ensued with Abraham standing nearby, seething with anger and excitement. When John was seriously injured, Lincoln broke the rules by jumping into the ring, seizing Grigsby by the heels, and hurling him off. Straightening up, "Abe swore he was the big buck at the lick," recalled Nathaniel, a third Grigsby brother. This was a deliberate provocation, and all hell broke loose. Lincoln's late sister, one hopes, was properly avenged in the edifying brawl that followed.[16]

In 1830 Thomas moved the Lincolns to Macon County, Illinois, in order to join the Hankses who were settling there. The move gave Abraham an opportunity to take a good look at his family and ask himself an important question: *who are these people?* In truth, he knew—commonplace country folk whose horizons extended only as far as their fences. He could not be like them, like his father, the Hankses, or the Grigsbys. There had to be a place in life for intelligence and ambition. He got a glimpse of that world by earning one dollar ferrying two men and their trunks to a steamer on the Ohio River. He looked in astonishment at the money. "I could scarcely believe my eyes," said Lincoln, accustomed to eight dollars per month as a laborer. "I could scarcely credit that I, a poor boy, had earned a dollar in less than a day. The world seemed wider and fairer before me. I was a more hopeful and confident being from that time."[17]

He moved to New Salem, Illinois, in 1831. Now twenty-two, he was on his own and spent the next six years in this little village. He was, at various times, a clerk, store co-owner, surveyor, pilot, rail splitter, militiaman, postmaster, and politician.

Lincoln signed on as a crew member on a flatboat bound for New Orleans. Also on board were his stepbrother John Johnston, his cousin John Hanks, and boss Denton Offut. Their cargo was corn and pork. The trip is undocumented except for two stories from oral history. Tradition said that John Hanks and Lincoln went to see "an old fortune teller, a Voudou negress" while they were in New Orleans. During the encounter she became excited and informed Lincoln he would become president and "all the negroes will be free."

Lincoln biographer Isaac N. Arnold, who knew the future president well, found the story unbelievable. He had never heard it before. Uncomfortable as he was with it, he printed the story after consulting William H. Herndon, who had been Lincoln's law partner. Herndon informed Arnold that he had a vague recollection that John Hanks told him about the fortune-teller. Other than that, Herndon wrote, "I do not affirm anything or deny

John Hanks. *Lincoln's first cousin, Hanks accompanied the future president on a flatboat trip to New Orleans in 1831. He was the source for the story that, on the trip, "a Voudou negress" told Lincoln he would one day free the slaves.*

anything." So the matter remains, with only Herndon's added insight that Lincoln had always said Hanks was a truthful individual. "Lincoln has stated this to me over and over again. Lincoln loved this man."[18]

Although Henry C. Whitney, another Illinois friend and biographer, alleged that Lincoln was eagerly attentive to the fortune-teller's prophecy, the future president was generally lighthearted about the supernatural. An acquaintance of his was afraid of ghosts. He asked Lincoln to walk him home one night. The future president agreed while secretly getting a friend to put on a white sheet and hide along the road to scare the man. This was successfully done, the man swearing he would never be out again after dark. Unbeknownst to all, however, Lincoln had stationed a second ghost nearby. Ghost two jumped out at ghost one, and pandemonium followed, with the man double-dipped and ghost one no less terrified.[19] "Lincoln was the drollest man I ever saw," wrote an admirer. "Never have I seen another who provoked so much mirth and who entered into rollicking fun with such glee. He could make a cat laugh."[20]

John Hanks said that it was in New Orleans that Lincoln first saw slaves chained and whipped. He also witnessed a slave auction. A pretty mulatto girl was pinched "and made [to] trot up and down like a horse" so purchasers might judge her soundness. Lincoln watched, saying nothing. Words couldn't express his emotions. "His heart bled," recalled John, "was sad—looked bad—felt bad. I can say knowingly that it was on this trip that he formed his opinion of slavery. It ran its iron in him then and there."[21]

RUSSELL GODBEY, A New Salem neighbor, saw Lincoln sitting on a woodpile reading a book.

"Abe, what are you studying?" he asked.

"Law," was the reply.

"Great God Almighty!" exclaimed Godbey.[22]

It wasn't as odd as it sounded. Lincoln found the study of law a natural progression from politics. After one failed attempt, he had been elected to the state legislature in 1834. He had made strong friends in his variety of occupations, and they supported him. Never lacking in self-confidence, he turned his mind to a long-standing interest in the law. After a winter of intensive study, he was admitted to the practice of law on March 1, 1837, and moved from New Salem to Springfield a few weeks later to take up his new career. New Salem was fading economically. It had no future. When Springfield became the new state capital in 1839, he was already in place, partnered with John T. Stuart, a mentor and veteran litigator.[23]

THOMAS LINCOLN HAD a dream. He was riding on an unfrequented road and came to a strange house. Going inside, he discovered a woman sitting by the fire and paring an apple. This woman, he realized, was destined to become his wife. Once awake, he could not shake the vision. It was too disturbingly real. It haunted him. Consumed by curiosity, he took the road and came upon the identical cabin placed precisely where it had been in his dream. Quietly opening the door, he found the same woman sitting there with her apple and paring knife. They met and were married.[24]

Whether it was Nancy or Sarah in the dream is not known—he was fortunate in both—but Thomas's natural sociability meant he would never be without female companionship.

Abraham, undirected by any vision, struggled socially.

An odd-looking young man with ill-fitting clothes, he didn't win the battle of first impressions. He lacked family clout, formal education, property, and, during the New Salem years, even a career. These things made him uneasy around women. He was alternately eager, shy, uncertain, or uninspired.

Anna Roby was a pretty girl of about fifteen. She thought Lincoln, who helped her with her schoolwork, was nice. She only wished he was more "sociable." One pleasant evening they sat together on the banks of Little Pigeon Creek. Bare-legged, they dangled their feet in the water. It was an idyllic moment, and she improved upon it by pointing out to him that the moon, sinking low in the sky, was about to go down.

"That's not so," he responded unromantically. "It don't really go down. The Earth turns from west to east, and the revolution of the Earth carries us under [it], as it were. We do the sinking, as you call it."

"Abe, what a fool you are!" she replied indignantly.[25]

"He was very reserved towards the opposite sex," recalled Jason Duncan, a New Salem doctor. Lincoln was aware his poverty and appearance held him back. But if his physical self wasn't attractive, his personality was. Sincerity, good nature, good habits, and a sense of humor were always prized, and if he got a second look, he made the most of it. He became quasi-engaged twice, but, unsure what marriage would entail, he both did and did not want to enter into it. He told one presumptive fiancée that not only was he poor but his profession of law required much travel—"a great deal of splashing and dashing in buggies" here and there—all of which she must suffer silently. She decided he lacked the attentiveness she required in a husband. The second would-be Mrs. Lincoln "flung him high and dry," considering herself, at sixteen, too young to be anyone's wife. Anyway, he didn't charm her. She thought of him as a big brother.[26]

Ann Rutledge was a different story. The daughter of one of New Salem's founders, she was the prettiest and most amiable young woman in the village. She had light auburn hair, a fair complexion, and expressive blue eyes.[27] Intelligent and unassuming like Lincoln, Ann was equally as plain and practical, content to work in her family tavern or take her turn at home on the quilt frame. Her homegrown charm and vitality attracted numerous suitors who jostled each other in a complicated romantic landscape. At first Lincoln was merely one of the crowd, a beau more interested in her than she was in him. In time her feelings caught up to his. This was fortunate as "she was a woman worthy of Lincoln's love," said William G. Greene, a New Salem friend. They studied together and walked in the evenings. They even sang together, although his efforts were painful to hear. Both in their twenties, they were no longer children and were capable of an affection more profound than either had before known.

Then, when everything seemed headed right, Ann fell ill, apparently of typhoid fever, and died on August 25, 1835.[28]

"The effect upon Mr. Lincoln's mind was terrible," recalled Robert Rutledge, Ann's brother. "He became plunged in despair, and many of his friends feared that reason would desert her throne." Lincoln secluded himself in grief, often wandering through the woods. Worryingly, he took his gun with him. He told Mentor Graham, the local schoolteacher who coached him in his studies, "that he felt like committing suicide."[29]

Graham, a fellow Kentuckian, was among those who helped walk Lincoln back from the ledge. Ann had been one of Graham's brightest pupils. He admired her and encouraged her promise. He and Lincoln talked about Ann's death. Friends noted that Lincoln—"from the commencement of his life to its close"—never asked anyone's advice. But he was a good listener and he turned an ear Graham's way. The teacher assured him that there was a divine purpose in what had happened. God's purpose. Abraham replied that he just couldn't see it. And yet, somehow—some way—that must be true.[30]

Lincoln's religious views were quite different from Graham's and most everyone else's. His family belonged to a fundamentalist Baptist church, but he didn't join. "Abe had no particular religion," recalled stepmother Sarah, "didn't think of that question at that time—if he ever did." A free-thinker, he could not buy into Christian orthodoxy. Hell, eternal punishment, human depravity, and the-whale-done-swallowed-me miracles seemed absurd to him. The bitter sectarianism of preachers also annoyed him, as did a sanctimonious "long face on Sunday and grind the poor on Monday" attitude. Skeptical and inquiring, he was willing to argue points most Christians considered beyond dispute, if not discussion. "He shocked me," said his law partner Stuart. The odd thing was that, in his conduct, he embodied many of the best values taught by the religion.[31]

The most distinctive feature of his home-brewed theology, thought Isaac Cogdal, to whom he spoke about his love for Ann, was "that Lincoln thought God predestined things, nothing going by accident." It was a comfort but of the coldest sort, expressed in a favorite maxim:

What is to be will be,
And no prayers of ours
can arrest the decree.[32]

WHEN THE ILLINOIS General Assembly gathered in Springfield in late 1839, more than politics was on the agenda. The three dozen or so legislators included a sizable number of bachelors and widowers. Matchmaking was in the air for these "rising men," recalled a resident, as "the pretty girls from all over the state flocked here under the care of fathers, uncles, brothers, cousins, any relation, however remote, who could be induced to bring them." Call them the "rising women," found at a flurry of balls, hops, levees, and parties.[33]

At the center of the whirl was the home of the socially prominent Ninian Edwards and his wife Elizabeth Todd. Central to that was Mary, Elizabeth's younger sister. Mary had come to Springfield from the Todd home in Kentucky, where she felt unwelcomed by her stepmother. Frances, a third sister, had married from the Edwardses' home the preceding year, and the expectation was clear that it was Mary's turn.[34]

If not as pretty as the kindly older sister who took her in, Mary had her charms. She was short with fair skin, rosy cheeks, light chestnut hair, and sparkling, long-lashed blue eyes. Well educated and fluent in French, Mary ruled any room as a skilled conversationalist. Witty, sometimes wickedly so, she was full of opinions about people and politics. Lincoln was charmed by her liveliness and intelligence. Having no idea of what to say in her presence, he sat and listened happily as she held court. Peeking into the parlor, Elizabeth observed how "Mary led the conversation, and Lincoln would listen and gaze on her as if drawn by some superior power—irresistibly so. He listened—never scarcely said a word."

Elizabeth grew fond of the awkward suitor over the years, but during the winter of 1839–40, as the couple talked of marriage, she realized he was a poor match for her lively sister. "He was a cold man, had no affection, was not social, was abstracted, thoughtful," Elizabeth realized. Nature and nurture had done a hard day's work on him. Ninian agreed. Differing in background, education, and temperament, Mary and Abraham were ill-suited.[35]

Law partner Stuart, who was also Mary's cousin, believed Lincoln was an emotionally detached and torpid person. He showed it in his lack of interest in community endeavors like the establishment of colleges, hospitals, and asylums. At his core Abraham cared for little except politics. "Lincoln was a kind of vegetable," thought Stuart.[36]

Nevertheless, the couple became engaged and a wedding was planned. Cakes were baked, decorations put in place. Then, suddenly, Lincoln backed out of the engagement. He told Mary he didn't love her, pulled her to him, kissed her farewell, and walked out the door.[37]

Over his shoulder he heard Mary stamping her feet and crying, "Go, and never, *never* come back!"[38]

Perhaps Lincoln had his own doubts about their compatibility. Perhaps he experienced the old anxiety about his inability to support a wife and family. Perhaps another woman had caught his eye. Or perhaps he had understandable anxieties about sex. Probably chaste until after Ann's death, he had the occasional sexual escapade thereafter. He was a man with strong sexual urges, but encounters appear to have been few and hardly ennobling. He did not enjoy the chase involved. "He was a virtuous man," recalled his friend Greene, "as much as any man—the sons of Adam."[39] Sex complicated life. It was "the harp with a thousand strings," as Lincoln put it. All of these reasons sound plausible, but who really knew what so private a man thought? Mary had it right when she said that what he felt the most he expressed the least.[40]

WHEN ELIZABETH EDWARDS started her day on Friday, November 4, 1842, she had no idea she would be hosting a wedding that evening. Unbeknownst to her, Lincoln and Mary had reconciled and were meeting secretly.[41] Family and friends learned of the couple's plan to wed only hours before the event and had so little time to prepare that a cake ordered for the reception was still warm when delivered moments before the ceremony started. It was simple gingerbread.

"Well, I suppose that will be good enough for plebeians," said Mary, mocking the Edwardses' poor opinion of her fiancé.[42]

The Reverend Charles Dresser, the local Episcopal minister, officiated. Lincoln looked dreadful, acting "as if he was going to the slaughter," thought groomsman James H. Matheny. He was finally face-to-face with his father's old adage: "If you make a bad bargain, hug it the tighter." The ceremony seemed appropriately solemn, if not tense. There were whispers and raised eyebrows and it seemed as if, given the secrecy, the history, and the haste of the couple, something untoward might happen.[43]

The tension was relieved by Thomas C. Brown, who stood directly behind Lincoln. The minister was cautioning the groom, in the ceremonial language of the Book of Common Prayer, that by marrying Mary, he endowed her with all his goods and chattels, lands and tenements. Judge Brown, a heavyset fellow with a reputation for saying whatever popped into his head, blurted out that the laws of Illinois were more than adequate to secure a wife's property rights! The guests burst out laughing.[44]

ON AUGUST 1, 1843—three days short of nine months—Robert Todd Lincoln was born. His brother Edward Baker Lincoln followed on March 10, 1846. Bobby was a headstrong child who wandered away from home, ate caustic lime from the privy, and seemed generally made for mischief. Eddie was more settled. A good-natured boy fond of his cat, he promised to be taller than his brother, although not as healthy. Abraham and Mary loved trotting their children out "to monkey around, talk, dance, speak, quote poetry, etc.," said William Herndon.[45]

"Let them run" was Lincoln's wish, and they were as free-range as possible. He indulged their antics, often to the annoyance of other adults. "His children literally ran over him, and he was powerless to withstand their importunities," said a friend. His defense: "It is my pleasure that my children are free, happy and unrestrained by parental tyranny. Love is the chain whereby to lock a child to its parents."[46]

"Mr. L. was the kindest, most tender, and loving husband and father in the world," Mary told Herndon shortly after Lincoln's death. The future president bought domestic peace by allowing her to have her way. "He gave us all unbounded liberty. Said to me always when I asked him for anything, 'You know what you want. Go and get it.' He never asked me if it was necessary."[47]

Lincoln was proud of his wife. He liked her looks and he liked her style. And, as for her mind, she was better educated than most women and many men. Early in their marriage she employed these assets as Lincoln's friend and adviser. The love they shared was evident.

Increasingly, however, periods of turbulence and anxiety intervened. Lincoln was the same predictable person day in and day out. With Mary, one never knew. She was sensitive, outspoken, and always worried about this or that. Emotionally, she was "either in the garret or cellar," thought Lincoln's lifelong friend Orville H. Browning. She might be needy or nervous, excited or depressed, angry or irrational. She loved her husband but struck him on more than one occasion. Browning thought she was occasionally "demented," making enemies among servants, friends, and townspeople. "Lincoln's wife was a hellion—a she devil," said one of those who disliked her. "Vexed and harrowed the soul out of that good man—wouldn't cook for him—drove him from home, etc. Often and often."[48]

"Jesus, what a home Lincoln's was!" exclaimed Herndon, who became Mary's bitter critic over the years. "What a wife! His domestic life was a hell—a burning, scorching hell." Hell has a devil, as Elizabeth knew, and she told Herndon that "the devil was in play and *did* play his part in Mr. Lincoln and Miss Todd's affairs, nay, during their lives." Mary required a deeper, more tender and consuming love than Lincoln could provide. He could only offer his imperfect self.[49]

MARY BELIEVED THAT Fridays were unlucky. Her old nurse Mammy Sally had told her that on Fridays the jaybirds flew to Hell and told the Devil Mary's weekly misdeeds. While a top lieutenant wrote her failings in a book, the old demon himself listened happily, bellowed, sharpened his horns on the ground, shook his head, and flicked his green tail. Terrified, Mary put her fingers in her ears rather than listen to the nurse.[50]

At six o'clock on the morning of February 1, 1850, Eddie Lincoln died. It was a Friday.

The younger son, two months shy of his fourth birthday, had pulmonary tuberculosis. The brutal illness ran its course with the exhausted child for fifty-two days. The weight loss and paleness attendant to the disease gave the sufferer the appearance of wasting away, hence the name consumption as the illness seemed to *consume* the victim. Dangerously high fevers, chills, and recurrent acute coughing with hemorrhaging and choking announced the end.

Eddie's funeral service was held at the Lincoln home. Reverend Dresser being away, James Smith, the town's Presbyterian minister, officiated. He offered his faith's traditional consolations, but few could doubt that the future—with its gift of hope—had been robbed.[51]

Desolate, the bereaved parents went to see "three good women who were in touch with the spirit world," said Mariah Vance. Or did she say that? Vance was an African American resident of Springfield hired by the Lincolns as a washerwoman in 1850. Her recollections, published nearly a century and a half after the events they allege to describe, are so compromised it is impossible to know what she said and what others added to it. One accepts only that she was fond of Robert, whom she described as a quiet, serious, and often lonesome youth, and found Mary erratic, impulsively generous, and "powerful odd."[52]

The parents erected a memorial stone measuring two feet by four feet at Eddie's grave. On it the dates of his short life were presented below a dove winging its way heavenward. "Of such is the kingdom of Heaven"

Mary Todd Lincoln. *A mother of two in her late twenties, Mary Lincoln still looks youthful in this early likeness. She wears a silk satin day dress with pleated bosom and armscyes low over the shoulder. Her hair is pulled back to form a chignon with a small shell comb ornament.*

appeared at the stone's foot. The words were proper and traditional. Unfortunately, Mary didn't feel the peace that they were meant to convey. Three years later she wrote, "Our second boy, a promising bright creature of four years, we were called to part with several years ago, and I grieve to say that even at this day, I do not feel sufficiently submissive to our loss."[53]

Abraham felt a heavy loss, too, saying that if he "had twenty children, he would never cease to sorrow for that one." But he had a career to pursue and ambitions to attend. He recovered from his grief more quickly than Mary and tried to console her in his practical way. When Mary Stuart, the wife of his first law partner, brought over breakfast one morning, the afflicted mother just sat there, staring. Lincoln said to her, "You must eat, Mary, for we must live."[54]

"I ALWAYS WAS superstitious," Lincoln acknowledged to his friend Joshua Speed.[55]

It would have been strange were it not so. The communities in which Lincoln grew up were rife with odd idiosyncrasies. "They performed various matters according to the phases of the moon; planted esculents by the dark of this luminary and products of the vine by its light," wrote Henry C. Whitney. "They dug for water by the guidance of the hazel fork in the hands of the water-witch and had a general belief in witchcraft. They believed in dreams, signs, and omens. They would commence no journey or undertaking on Friday." An accident, assigned by most people to bad luck, had a darker origin to them. The prevalence of such notions exercised a great influence on Lincoln as he grew to adulthood.

Dreams—thought of as visions when one sleeps—might forecast the future, Lincoln believed. "The near approach of the important events of his life were indicated by a presentiment or a strange dream," he told intimates, "or in some other mysterious way it was impressed on him that something important was to occur."[56]

There were some things, alarming to others, that he dismissed with a shrug, like the time he was awakened by his New Salem landlord shouting,

"Arise, Abraham, the day of judgment has come!" Lincoln looked out the window to see the 1833 Leonid meteor shower. (It was the night Edwin Booth was born.) While observing the amazing sight, he noticed that the constellations behind the meteors remained fixed. The world would linger after all, he concluded. At other times, however, he might be embarrassingly superstitious. For example, the number thirteen worried him. He refused to become the thirteenth person at a table once, leading one of those present to declare he would rather die than be so foolish. "His mind was readily impressed with some of the most absurd superstitions," recalled Herndon.[57]

Lincoln found it amusing when a bulldog latched on to his father, but he didn't laugh when a small mutt bit his older son Bobby. Mary was convinced that the animal was rabid, and Lincoln and his son hurried off to Terre Haute, Indiana, for Bobby to be treated with a famous madstone.

A madstone was generally a petrification of vegetable matter found in an animal's intestines. It was porous and, when applied to a wound, was said to draw out poison and impure blood. About the size of a walnut cut in half, the Terre Haute madstone was as light as a pumice stone and dirty white in color. It was owned by Robert Murphy and had come with his family from Virginia to Kentucky and then to Indiana. The earlier history of this mysterious object was unknown.

"The use of the madstone has been considered one of the vulgar superstitions of the credulous and ignorant," stated an Indiana editor. Still, Lincoln had faith in it. "He could give no reason for it and confessed that it looked like superstition," recalled friend Joseph Gillespie, but Lincoln reasoned that if the people in Terre Haute constantly resorted to it for treatment and were convinced of its power, that meant something. He would have been gratified to know that Bobby would live to the age of eighty-two.[58]

LINCOLN SERVED AS a Whig congressman from Illinois for one term from 1847 to 1849. He was unsuccessful, and he did not seek reelection. When he failed to receive a suitable appointment from the incoming administra-

tion of Zachary Taylor, for whom he had campaigned, he left elective politics to concentrate on his law practice.

Still, he was too political an animal to lose his interest in the slavery
debate. Stuart recalled an exchange between the two of them during this
period. It was one of those occasions when a conversation was so striking
that Stuart remembered precisely where they were when it occurred—in
this case, coming down a hill northeast of Delavan, Illinois. The men were
discussing North-South tensions, and Stuart observed, "The time is soon
coming when we shall all have to be abolitionists or all democrats."

Abraham replied, "My mind is fixed on that question—when it comes."
"So is mine," responded Stuart.[59]

Both men were as good as their word. In 1865, fourteen years later, Lincoln, as president, oversaw a shrewd campaign in the House of Representatives to win approval for the Thirteenth Amendment abolishing slavery.
Stuart, then a Democratic congressman from Illinois, voted nay.[60]

Although Lincoln had fantasized about high political office, he would
have been as astonished as Stuart that day near Delavan by his election as
president on November 4, 1860. True, he won acclaim with his eloquence
and doggedness in a losing race against Stephen Douglas for the Illinois
Senate seat in 1858. But there were other presidential aspirants from the
new antislavery Republican Party more experienced, better financed, and
better known. Unfortunately for them, it was time for a fresh face.

Backed by a strong political organization, Lincoln advocated powerful ideas. Slavery was a crime against humanity. African Americans,
like everyone else, were included in the promises of the Declaration of
Independence. Unless Northerners understood these facts and restricted
the spread of slavery, the institution would become national and establish itself in every part of the United States. These views appealed to vot-
ers whose patience with the demands and peculiarities of the South were
exhausted. In expressing them, Lincoln struck few as brilliant, said an
associate. In fact, there was something ordinary about him. But what he
had in terms of ideals, determination, and exalted language, he had to an
extraordinary degree.[61]

Before leaving for Washington, he visited Coles County, Illinois, where his parents had settled. Thomas had died in 1851—on a Friday—and was buried in a country churchyard. A small boulder was all that marked his resting place, so Lincoln took out his pen knife and cut the initials "T. L." on an oak board and placed it at the head of the grave. Then he rode over to see Sarah, his stepmother. On the way he told Augustus H. Chapman, his traveling companion, that "she had been his best friend in the world, and that no son could love a mother more than he loved her." Their meeting was touching. When it was time for him to leave, she cried. "His mother was very affectionate," said Chapman. "She embraced him when they parted and said she would never be permitted to see him again—that she felt his enemies would assassinate [him]."

"No, no, Mama," he replied, "they will not do that."[62]

3

SO OLD WHEN HE
WAS YOUNG

Junius Brutus Booth's body lay in state in the parlor of his Baltimore home for three days in early December 1852. The walls of the room were draped with white. Mirrors were covered, pictures were shrouded, and all ornaments were removed except a marble bust of Shakespeare.

Booth's coffin was an airtight cast-iron case with a closed glass plate that revealed the deceased's head and shoulders. "The face was very clear and beautiful," wrote his daughter Asia, "and the brown hair more thickly strewn with white than when his family had seen it last. The eyes were partly visible between the half-shut lids, and the lips, retaining their lifelike color, were smilingly closed." Junius appeared just as he did when he napped. He looked perfectly normal. Too normal, in fact. Was he really dead? Perhaps he was just in a trance. About to be buried alive! Frantic at the thought, John and Asia ran screaming from the house. A physician arrived to confirm that the father was indeed dead. After all, he had been embalmed.[1]

On December 11 a funeral procession wearing crepe on their left arms wound its way through the city streets and up the long hill to Baltimore Cemetery. It was a bleak winter afternoon with snow on the ground. At the door of the mausoleum a minister conducted a traditional Episcopal service before several hundred mourners. As he spoke, the wind whipped the priest's long dark robe about him. Stray flakes fell on the mourners, and the sun threw its final beam of the day on the treetops.[2]

BIG CHANGES WERE at hand for the Booths. Their breadwinner was gone, and they had debts to contend with as well as a lawsuit over the father's estate brought by Richard Booth, a son by his first marriage. Mary Ann decided that in these circumstances it would be prudent to rent out the Baltimore townhouse and move back to the country. There she could join forces with the Halls and farm.

Before he left for California in 1852, Junius had started construction of a Gothic Revival cottage as a more suitable residence for his family than the old log house. "Tudor Hall" was now the family's home. The area was rural, quite a change from Baltimore, and it compounded the social isolation an actor's family always felt, but at least there, if they were lonely, they could be lonely together, wrote Asia in a family memoir.[3]

As compensation, the daughter enjoyed more freedom here than she had in the city. She spent mornings walking in the forest or pondering the "fairy rings" near the pond. One day she came running back to the house, grabbed her guitar, pulled John from his hammock, and took him to a remote stream. The pair sat on a springy moss cushion near a mass of tangled bushes, and Asia began to play. One by one small brown heads with goggle eyes emerged from the water. It was an audience of frogs. They appeared engrossed in her performance. When she concluded the concert, a tremor of sorts ran through them. Each took a gulp of air and vanished.

Brother and sister laughed, and John said it reminded him of the toad-stone. This mythical gem, purportedly found inside the head of a toad, was believed to be an antidote to poison. Shakespeare mentioned the toadstone in the play As You Like It. Whatever the truth of that claim, John told her he did not believe the legend that a frog's croak cursed those who heard it. Asia agreed.[4]

They discovered an old Native American footpath through the woods. Arrow and ax heads were found there, and even more flints were on the hillside beyond the orchard. Some of these were dull slate in color; others, milky white. John and Asia began to dig, hoping to find "a dead Indian

Asia Booth. *Sister of Edwin and John Wilkes Booth, Asia adored the former and believed his marriage to Mary Devlin, a poor actress of Irish-American ancestry, would disgrace the family.*

chief." The smell of turned earth, Asia wrote, was nothing less than "the odor of good men's bones rotting, so pleasurable and sanctifying." They discovered no body, but she found what she believed were elfshots, missiles fired by elves to which were attributed sharp pains (like cramps) when they hit their victims.[5]

THE HALLS WERE a godsend. Typically for her time, Asia insulted them as a troop of silly layabouts who dozed, loved candy, and sang the livelong day. In truth, it's hard to see how the farm could have managed without them. Ann was constantly busy in the kitchen and garden, her children in the barn and henhouse, and Joe in the field with John. Joe was getting on in years, however, and John was in his mid-teens. There was a limited amount of work that they could do.

Joe was honest, knowledgeable, faithful—and voluble. He had an ear-catching tone of voice, and "his fund of ghost stories, legends and ill omens never knew exhaustion." John was inherently superstitious, and Mary Ann worried that these tales resonated too deeply with him. She was displeased with Joe's gruesome retelling of the night Junius dug up the body of little Mary. The old fellow talked too much.[6]

John enjoyed teasing the Halls. Trying out his budding acting chops, he dressed up as Meg Merrilies, a Scottish Romani who lived on the Moors. Meg had been immortalized in a poem by John Keats in which

Her Brothers were the craggy hills,
Her Sisters larchen trees.
Alone with her great family
She liv'd as she did please.

His father's friend Charlotte Cushman played Meg onstage, so in her style John put on a red blanket coat and chip hat. Without warning Asia or anyone else, he prowled the edges of the farm as the half-mad wanderer, terrifying the household.[7]

Real Romani looked differently. First, there would be a forerunner—an oddly dressed man or woman—scouting through the fields for camping sites. Then, a day or two later, the main body would arrive at night. The morning sun disclosed a dozen covered wagons, black iron pots over cooking fires, clothes hanging on bushes, dogs and children milling about, and gaudily dressed men with mustaches and women with long black braids. "Had Jesus of Nazareth passed through the country, he could not have caused more sensation," said the local newspaper. "They are Atheists and, I believe, worship the stars."[8]

Since one of the visitors' sources of income was buying and selling horses, they often camped off a lane near the Booth farm at Woolsey's blacksmith shop.[9]

John wandered down to the caravan, where he found an old woman to tell his fortune. "Ah, you've a bad hand," the crone commenced. "Trouble in plenty everywhere I look. You'll break hearts. They'll be nothing to you. You'll die young and leave many to mourn you, many to love you, too."

Taken aback, John asked if this destiny was unchangeable.

"You're born under an unlucky star," she informed him. 'You've got in your hand a thundering crowd of enemies—not one friend—and you'll make a bad end, and have plenty to love you afterwards. A fast life, short but a grand one."

"It is a good thing it is so short as it is so bad a fortune. For this evil dose do you expect me to cross your palm?" asked John.

"Young sir, I've never seen a worse hand, and I wish I hadn't seen it, but every word I've told is true."

"How am I to escape it?"

"You'd best turn a missionary or priest."

He laughed and paid her, reassured when Asia said it was only tattle for money. Still. "In those days fortune-tellers held secret but undisputed powers," the sister wrote years later, "and many well-bred and intelligent people resorted to them. Who shall say there is no truth in it?" John took out a pencil and wrote down the fortune. "No need," he said. "It is so bad I shall not soon forget it." He showed it to Asia, then folded the strip of paper and put it away.

"The Gypsey said I was to have a grand life," he concluded. "No matter how short then, *so let it be grand!*"[10]

LIFE AT THE farm had been Junius's dream. The rest of the Booths endured it for lack of other options. The family had good times there—horseback rides, nights talking in the old porch swing, music around the crackling winter fire. But it was a challenging existence. Money was tight, and a serious tone prevailed. Mary Ann grieved her late husband for years, dressing in mourning black. Rose was becoming a recluse, suffering from an unspecified illness. Joe was susceptible to attacks of "melancholy insanity." And Asia was volatile, often falling into what the Halls termed "Missy's long sulks."

John struggled against this gloom all his life. He demanded that his bedroom window face east. "No setting sun for me," he declared. "Let me see him rise." When Asia made him a quilt in the Job's Tears pattern, he pretended to shiver and said, "Oh, take away that sorrowful canopy. I shall always see old Job shedding tears as big as these patches. I don't want to be haunted and made melancholy."

"How glorious it is to live!" John told her. "How divine! To breathe this breath of life with a clear mind and healthy lungs! Don't let us be sad. Life is so short, and the world is so beautiful."[11]

ON THE EVENING of July 20, 1860, a rare Earth-grazing meteor appeared over New York City. It dipped into the atmosphere and broke into a meteor procession, an eye-catching train of crimson, gold, and white fragments traveling together. The lights looked so bright and seemed so near that people initially thought it was a fireworks display. "Dazzling and clear, shooting over our heads," wrote Walt Whitman in *Leaves of Grass*. "Balls of unearthly light. Year of Meteors! Brooding Year!" Artist Frederic Edwin Church, who saw it while honeymooning in Catskill, New York, commemorated the meteor in a famous painting, and three illustrations of it appeared on the front page of *Harper's Weekly*, the nation's most widely read journal.

"It was the main topic of conversation in the office and counting room, at the hotels, at the saloons, and wherever three or four persons were to be found together," wrote a Manhattan journalist, "all of them looking upon it with unusual mystery." People were fascinated, and not a few were worried. Celestial fireworks meant dramatic changes, wrote Tolstoy later in the decade in his classic *War and Peace*. A similar visitor had been seen the night before Caesar's death, as Shakespeare wrote in his play on the Roman general, and all knew, "When beggars die, there are no comets seen."[12] Such an event announced momentous things.

Thomas Clingman of Asheville, North Carolina, had been too far south to see the phenomenon. But two weeks later, as the future Confederate general snuffed out his candle and went to bed for the night, he noticed a glare at his window. "It seemed like a sheet of flame," he recalled. Alarmed, he rushed to the window where the light was now an intense silvery white. So bright that one could see a pin on the ground. "It was greater than hun-

The Meteor of 1860. *A meteor procession over New York City on July 20, 1860, startled many people who believed that it was a bad omen. Nine months later the Civil War started.*

dreds of moons would have caused." Another meteor was overhead. It traveled north, then exploded.[13]

"There seems to be an unusual agitation this season of the earth, the air, and the heaven," wrote Hugh Pleasants of the *Richmond Dispatch*. "The Devil seems to be about, making everybody roll up their eyes and wonder: what are we all coming to next?" At least, Pleasants continued, this latest marvel showed itself over Dixie. It was fully the equal of any Northern meteor. Theirs disintegrated. The South's exploded. "We yield to no section of this country in great terrific prodigies." Yankees should be warned by this bolide heading in their direction, "giving its fire-eating tail a most defiant flirt over the city of Springfield, in Illinois, as much as to say, 'Honest old Abe, what do you think of that?' "[14]

"PROPHECIES! WONDERS!! MYSTERIES!!!" Yellow posters with screaming black type offered the services of Marie-Anne Le Normand, "the French Sorceress." This celebrated sybil offered to reveal the destiny of the nation as war clouds gathered. The former adviser to Napoleon I had been dead nearly twenty years, but like the trouper she was she never lost a step. Madame Le Normand's "gypsy witch fortune cards" (often compared to tarot cards and still in use today) offered cartomantic advice to the public. "My cards permit no one to dispute them," she boasted from the grave.[15]

Her reading, Nostradamus-style, ran:

> And I saw a man whose name in those days will not be known among
>   the nations.
> And that man shall be a native of one of the most beautiful countries of
>   the whole earth.
> And the Lord will choose that man to deliver his Brothers out of the
>   hands of the oppressors.
> He will be victorious in many battles, and the hand of the Lord will be
>   with him.
> And his name will be blessed in every nation where the sun of liberty
>   shall shine.[16]

Did Lincoln feel the hand of God upon him? He had been told repeatedly as a child that life held something special for him. His mother, Nancy, regaled him with stories of George Washington and reminded him that, like Washington, his father also came from Virginia. "Abe had jist as good Virginny blood in him as Washington," said his cousin Dennis Hanks, recalling her words. "Maybe she stretched things some, but it done Abe good." His stepmother, Sarah, said pointedly that he would be a great man.[17]

Lincoln listened. By the time he arrived in New Salem in 1831 he dreamed vaguely of a great destiny for himself. The idea "grew and developed and bloom[ed] into beauty," thought William Herndon, and then, one day in 1840, its flame "burst on him." It had the quality of a quiet religious fervor. Lincoln occasionally spoke of it to his partner in their law office. He was modest and indirect in his words, but his certainty was unshakable.[18]

Once, riding across the Illinois prairie with Ward Hill Lamon, Lincoln told the fellow lawyer that "he did not recollect the time when he did not believe he would someday be President."

"I will get there," he said confidently.

"Yet," added Lamon, "these extravagant visions of personal grandeur and power [mingled] with gloomy forebodings and strong apprehensions of impending evil. His imagination painted a scene just beyond the veil of the immediate future, gilded with glory, yet tarnished with blood. It was his destiny—splendid but fearful, fascinating but terrible. To him, it was fate, and there was no escape or defense."[19]

Of course, anyone as interested in politics as Lincoln was might fantasize about becoming president. It was the greatest public distinction. Yet the torturous path he took in the 1850s to reach the White House would have hardly made this future seemed foreordained. After his death, many claimed to have seen it, however. Typical was Samuel Haycraft, who knew Lincoln's father well and issued the license for his second marriage. Haycraft felt no one could have risen from such obscurity otherwise. He was Providence's favorite.[20] And, if God needed a hand, there was always Mary. "She had the most constant and enduring faith in Lincoln's political future, and tried by every means in the range of her unusually inspiring and vigorous personality to assist her husband."[21]

If Lincoln felt indebted to God for the presidency, he didn't show it in his inaugural address, delivered on March 4, 1861, before an estimated audience of forty thousand. His remarks—part legal brief, part history lesson—provided a lawyerly (and tepid) reassurance over slavery to seven states that seceded from the United States after his election. The word *God*, so prominent four years later in his second inaugural, was absent from the address. "The Almighty Ruler of Nations" appeared, as did "Him who has never yet forsaken this favored land," but that was it. The phrases seemed like political boilerplate. Mary recalled after his death that he "had no hope and no faith in the usual acceptation" in God.[22]

THE WHITE HOUSE that the Lincolns inherited from James Buchanan, the outgoing president, looked like "an old and unsuccessful hotel" according to visitors. The beat-up furniture, worn carpets, and faded wallpaper may have suited her husband's bachelor predecessor, but Mary recoiled at the place.[23]

She needed a proper home for her family. Bobby—now more properly Robert—wouldn't be around much. A Harvard student, he stayed in Washington only long enough to see Buchanan hand Lincoln the White House door key (in a ceremonial flourish) and then he departed for Cambridge.[24]

But Robert had two younger brothers. William Lincoln was born on December 21, 1850, late in the year of Eddie's death. A sweet-natured child, Willie promised to be the smartest and best-looking of the children. In the White House the eleven-year-old was a playful scamp who, when strangers sought an introduction to his father, might point them to someone else. "I wish they wouldn't stare at us so," he said. "Wasn't there ever a president who had children?" Thomas, the final child and the fourth son, was called Tad. Born on April 4, 1853, he had a large head and smallish body, and he

The Lincoln Family in 1861. *Mary Lincoln is shown seated near Willie. The president thumbs through an album with Tad while Robert stands nearby. Contrary to later belief, this engraving was not based on a photograph. Spiritualist Francis B. Carpenter painted the scene in 1865 from photographs of family members.*

spoke with a lisp. Fond of animals, Tad was lively, loving, and impulsive—just like his mother.[25]

FROM A WINDOW of the White House, Colonel Elmer Ellsworth spied a rebel flag flying atop the Marshall House, a hotel in Alexandria, Virginia. Lincoln saw it, too. It was so close—just across the Potomac River—that it seemed like a deliberate taunt. "That must come down," Ellsworth muttered. The war commenced on April 12, 1861, with the rebel attack on Fort Sumter. When Virginia seceded a few weeks later to join the newly formed Confederacy, Lincoln authorized the military occupation of Alexandria, and Ellsworth decided to bring the flag back to Lincoln as a trophy.

A former clerk in Lincoln's law office, Ellsworth lived in the Executive Mansion with the family before going to New York City to recruit firemen into the army. He brought back an extraordinary group of "vulgar and jolly gay blackguards," said John Hay, one of Lincoln's secretaries. They were formidable-looking men, drawn from New York's toughest neighborhoods, and, if the South wanted trouble, Ellsworth boasted, "We will teach them a lesson they will remember for many years."

Ellsworth drilled his recruits every day on the White House lawn. "He was a magnetic, brilliant young fellow, overflowing with dash and spirit," recalled Lizzie Grimsley, Mary's cousin. Like his men, he wore a Zouave-style uniform (fashioned after those worn by French colonial troops) of red cap, red shirt, gray breeches, and gray jacket. A sword, a heavy revolver, and a ridiculously long bowie knife completed his outfit.[26]

The occupation of Alexandria by Ellsworth and his men was uneventful. Rebel soldiers fled instead of fighting, and the little colonel took the opportunity to climb to the roof of the hotel and retrieve the banner. In the emotion of the day, it was a rash act, Lincoln said, though typical of the daring officer. As Ellsworth descended the stairs to the street, James W. Jackson, proprietor of the Marshall House, stepped from a doorway with a double-barrel shotgun and shot him in the chest. Death was instantaneous. The colonel became the first Union officer to die in the conflict.

"Lincoln loved him like a younger brother," Hay wrote of Ellsworth. Ambitious, self-educated, poor, and proud, the colonel had much in common with the down-to-earth president. "He is the greatest little man I ever met," Lincoln said. There had been times when the president seemed closer to him than to Robert, described as "porcelain" by a critic, and he was stunned by Ellsworth's death. Learning of it, Lincoln burst into tears before a group of White House visitors and hurriedly left the room.

"So, this is the beginning—murder!" Lincoln said. "What shall the end of all this be?"[27]

Ellsworth had had a strong premonition that he would not survive the day. The night before the march to Alexandria he had written his parents what amounted to a farewell letter. If he died, he told them, they must take comfort in the fact that "He who noteth even the fall of a sparrow will have some purpose even in the fate of one like me." He closed his letter with the telling expression, "My darling and ever loved parents, *goodbye*."[28]

THE NEARLY FOUR MILLION men mobilized in the North and South for war did not include the Booth brothers. As Border State Marylanders, they had conflicted political feelings. They also lacked military genes, being sons of Junius, who deserted the British navy during the War of 1812. There was no chance they would become the war's "Fighting Booth Brothers of Baltimore." June lived in far-off San Francisco and was happy to be there. Joseph, a medical student in Charleston, South Carolina, plied his skills as a volunteer for the rebels during the Fort Sumter attack. Then he traveled overseas before joining his oldest brother in California. The first year of the war found Edwin in London, trying his luck on the English stage. Urged to enter the army when he returned home, he replied that his incompetence would hurt the cause. "If it was not the fear of doing my country more harm than good, I'd *be* a soldier," he wrote a friend. "A coward always has an 'if' to shrink behind, you know."[29]

John was the only brother with political feelings and soldierly instincts. These may have started in 1851 when the father of a Maryland schoolmate was killed while attempting to recover several fugitive slaves who had fled to Pennsylvania, a free state. John was confused by the incident. Why had they run away, he wondered? In his opinion African Americans were lucky to live in the United States, even as slaves. "Witness their elevation in happiness and enlightenment above their race elsewhere," he said.

He felt that Black people were living in the wrong nation. "This country was formed for the white, not the black man," John wrote at the time of Lincoln's election. "And, looking upon African slavery from the standpoint held by those noble framers of our Constitution, I for one have ever considered it one of the greatest blessings (both for themselves and us) that God ever bestowed on a favored nation."[30]

John believed that those who wished to abolish slavery were wrecking the country by making North and South angry at each other. John Brown, hanged after a failed antislavery raid into Virginia in 1859, was just the first. Others would follow, John warned his friends. He was in Montgomery, Alabama, in 1860 when an aurora borealis, rarely seen that far south, lit the sky. He was certain abolitionists were setting fire to the city.[31]

"John Wilkes is crazy or enthusiastic about joining for a soldier," Asia wrote insightfully. "It has been his early ambition. Perhaps it is his true vocation."[32]

When he talked about going south to join the rebel army, Mary Ann panicked. His mother had already lost four children and couldn't stand the thought of adding to that number the child who was "the most pleasure and comfort to me of all my sons." Her fireplace vision when he was a baby had been followed more recently by a remarkably vivid dream in which John died an early and unnatural death. She talked so obsessively about the dream that everyone in the family grew alarmed. "We let our minds dwell on the possibility that Wilkes would be a soldier and die for his country," said Asia. John admitted that the old fortune-teller's words put the same thought in his mind.[33]

Nevertheless, he intended to go—and started packing. Loving son that he was, he needed his mother's blessing first. Mary Ann refused to give it, pelting him instead with tears, pleas, and prayers to stay home. He begged;

she refused. It was agony for both of them. In the end John simply could not hurt the person who had given him so much. "Ah," he sighed resignedly as he put his hands on her shoulders, "you are no Roman mother."

Mary Ann got her wish. He stayed clear of the war. The decision went against powerful instincts at the core of John's personality. Unhappily for the future, it gave birth to a dangerous sense of guilt and self-reproach.[34]

Edwin, who had remained behind in California when his father returned east in 1852, came home to Maryland not long before the fighting started. He took charge of the family, rented out the farm, moved everyone to Philadelphia, and got John an apprentice acting job in the city. Hard work and hard knocks had taught Edwin much while he had been away, and he was ready to claim his father's acting mantle. Playing Junius's staples of Shakespeare and melodrama, he toured widely—from New Orleans to St. Louis, from Charleston to New York. His black eyes, long locks, graceful figure, melancholy air, and earnest style won praise, particularly in Boston, where female fans threw floral bouquets on the stage.[35] "Hard is the fate of a man who is the son of an illustrious father," observed a critic, yet Edwin told friends his dead father actually spoke to him and offered encouragement.[36]

Edwin caught up with his friend Joseph Jefferson in Richmond shortly before the war started. "Little Joe" was little no longer. It had been twenty years since Lincoln tried to save the family bacon in Springfield. Joe's parents were dead, as was his beloved stepbrother Charlie, and he was now head of the clan, working as stage manager of the Marshall Theatre.

Not yet a star, Joe was a promising comedian. He had a look for laughs—large ears and a prominent nose on a small head whose face lit up in humorous moments. In his repertoire was a dramatization of Rip Van Winkle, a character in a short story by Washington Irving. Rip was a lovable ne'er-do-well who stumbled onto the ghost crew of the early Dutch explorer Henry Hudson, drank their magical purple brew, and slept for twenty years. The play was popular, but not the hit he hoped.

Joe was a good businessman, although he didn't look like it. His open look made him seem eager and credulous. He was, in fact, somewhat

Joseph Jefferson. *Comedian Jefferson as photographed in the late 1850s when he introduced Edwin Booth to Mary Devlin, whom Booth would marry. Joe was the best-known spiritualist in the acting profession.*

childlike. Browsing in toy stores was one of his delights. Even when he was elderly, he would hunt them up in the cities where he played and gaze at the dolls in the windows. They fascinated him. He even imagined them talking to each other. "We are only children of a large growth," he explained in his defense.[37]

With a pounding heart, a pair of tight-fitting boots, and a new lavender suit that cost him two months' salary, Joe married Margaret Lockyear, a pretty seventeen-year-old. A dancer and comedian, Maggie fit right into the family business. She understood its demands, and she loved Joe. Blessed in each other, they lost two of four children in quick succession, however.

Increasingly, the slightly built Margaret was ill, and Joe was down to one lung (or so he believed) as the tuberculosis that killed his stepbrother Charlie crept insidiously upon him.[38]

To act as a companion to his wife, Joe brought Mary Devlin to Richmond. This attractive teenager, called Mollie, came from a large Irish family in Troy, New York. Her father was a tailor who made theatrical costumes. Mollie helped deliver them, and before long, she was onstage dancing and taking small parts. The graceful youngster had thick dark hair, parted in the middle and drawn back in a heavy satin knot. Her large brown eyes were her best feature. She had an affectionate, eager manner, and she proved a good addition to the Richmond company. Mollie lived with the Jeffersons.[39]

Edwin met the petite young woman in 1856 when she played Juliet to his Romeo. Legend aside, sparks did not fly immediately. Mollie was quite young and Edwin not ready to settle down.[40]

Edwin swore never to marry an actress. He knew what went on in the property room after hours. Perhaps it was predictable that actors, working in the close physical and emotional proximity, indulged themselves backstage. If so, Edwin was no exception. At the time he was flirting with Mollie, he and fifteen-year-old contralto Josie Orton wrinkled the sheets in Boston. "My p—k into her," he told Josie stories about California, where she wished to move. Edwin wrote to June that if she came to him in San Francisco looking for work, "[I] can't brag on her acting so much as what we do in secret."[41]

Edwin assured June that Josie was no tramp. Six weeks later he informed his brother that he had "the clap," as gonorrhea was known. The situation reminded him, as he told artist Jervis McEntee, that he had been deprived of the companionship of the better sort of women for too many years. They steadied and improved a person. He needed that. He was twenty-five. It was time to get serious about life.[42]

He renewed his courtship of Mollie. She had already dismissed him once—a shock to a handsome star accustomed to being chased—but he persevered, and in July 1859 they became engaged.[43]

Hand in hand, Edwin and Mollie went to Joe. They fell, smiling, to their knees before him and said, "Father, your blessing." This was their *Romeo and Juliet* line before Friar Lawrence. Like the good priest, Joe had his doubts. He knew that often "young men's love lies not truly in their hearts but in their eyes." Earlier Joe had made Mollie return Edwin's gift of a turquoise bracelet (until Edwin was shrewd enough to present a matching bracelet to Joe's wife Margaret the following day). Joe was won over at last, and, catching the spirit of the moment, proclaimed, "Bless you, my children!"[44]

Mollie had changes in store. While her knowledge of the hardships of an actor's life might strengthen their marriage, Edwin insisted she quit the stage and address what he considered her major defect—a lack of education. It was arranged that while Edwin toured, she would enter a year of semi-seclusion. Since she was (in Edwin's words) "as innocent as a babe," she would live with her married sister Catherine McGonigle at the sister's home in Hoboken, New Jersey. During this time she would read, study French, practice music, and visit Manhattan's museums and art galleries across the Hudson. This would "improve her mind" and make her a proper companion.

Ten years Mollie's senior, Edwin seemed wise to her, and she agreed to these demands. "My future ambition will be to see you great and good," she wrote him. "I shall strive to make you happy—and, if I succeed, 'mine the joy, mine the bliss.' You will be everything that the world has predicted."[45]

Asia Booth was settling down, too. On Halloween night at the farm she and her friends performed the "Ceremony of the Mystic Bridegroom." Filing silently into the woods, they found the stump of a tree and bathed their foreheads in the water nestled in its hollow. Then, standing silently and apart, they waited. After a few suspenseful moments, those destined to marry, they believed, saw visions of their future husbands.[46]

Emerging from the mist—or, more accurately, sitting across from her at the Hyde School in Baltimore—was John Sleeper Clarke. A neighborhood boy whose mother ran a small hotel, he was a lively child with curly hair, thin lips, and bug eyes. As a member of the Booths' juvenile theater troupe, he was a regular at the townhouse and the farm, where his clowning won him welcome. He became Edwin's best friend. He wasn't a heaven-sent match for the beautiful and tempestuous Asia, but Edwin favored him, and Asia, adoring her older brother, acquiesced. The couple married shortly before Edwin's engagement to Mollie was announced. "I married to please him," she wrote her friend Jean Anderson. She wasn't kidding.[47]

Now, to Asia's astonishment, the brother she loved the best and respected the most ignored her with his choice of spouse. Mollie was entirely unsuitable. "I detest and despise that woman," she wrote a friend. The fiancée was "a deep designing artful actress, a bold-faced woman who can stroll before a nightly audience. She wants his money and his name—a grand position for a poor obscure girl from the lowest Irish class," she told Jean. Why couldn't Edwin see that he would end up supporting her and her entire foolish family? She knew her brother drank too much. That explained some of it. One could only hope that Mollie would try to swim in the whirlpool at Niagara Falls while on her honeymoon. Happy thought! For the present, "I will not write the curse that I invoke on her."[48]

TWO YEARS EARLIER, in 1857, Edwin had received a letter from a stranger named Adam Badeau. Dramatic critic for New York's *Sunday Times*, Badeau told Edwin that his performances were amazing. The actor was "the incarnation of passion and romance and poetry." He had godlike qualities, and, if he worked hard, "there are certainly no heights you may not attain." The critic offered to mentor him.

The letter was timely. Edwin was at a professional plateau of sorts. While his reviews were filled with praise, he was still young and occasionally uneven and crude. The prospect of working with an intelligent and influential critic was exciting. Edwin had never had anyone like Badeau in his life.[49]

The two met and spent a Sunday together. They were about the same age, they liked each other—or at least they both liked Edwin—and they began to study texts, costumes, sets, and the careers of the great actors. Joe Jefferson warned Edwin not to refine away his natural intensity in favor of some intellectualized finish, but Edwin knew he needed polish and plunged ahead. The result greatly improved the actor's performances. It also served Badeau well. He had found a hero and proudly wore a cameo portrait ring of Edwin that the actor gave to him. "Young and happy hours," the critic recalled as an old man.[50]

Redheaded, red-faced, with blue eyes set in a pale face, Badeau was—to his great chagrin—physically unattractive. He compensated by being a dandy. So correctly attired that he seemed less dressed than upholstered, he promenaded about town pulling on his mustache ends and arranging and rearranging his necktie. When the gruff old Irish actor Rufus Blake saw him across a parlor, Blake exclaimed to a friend, "By gad, sir, who is that very lady-like young gentleman?"[51]

Adam Badeau. *Unrequited in his love for Edwin Booth, Badeau, an author and critic, remained close to the actor and attended séances with him. What he experienced on one occasion shook him deeply.*

Edwin and Adam visited Tudor Hall, the family home on the farm, when the theaters closed for the summer of 1858. The place looked deserted, but old Joe Hall emerged from a weed patch with the door key and, saying something about how he had raised Edwin from an egg, led away their horse and buggy. The house was unoccupied. In fact, it did not appear that anyone had entered it for months. They brushed cobwebs away from the door, unlocked it, and went inside.

Rummaging through trunks and drawers, the pair pulled out and read aloud Junius's old letters and playbills. According to an old-age reminiscence by Badeau, it was like a treasure hunt, with shouts of excitement at each discovery. The documents summoned a vibrant world once as intensely present as their own. It was sobering to realize that that world was as gone as if it never existed. Our time will come, too, thought Badeau.

When it grew dark, Edwin lit a candle and, using an old shoe as a candleholder, they moved on to examine his father's library. Among books in seven languages was Junius's copy of the Koran. Its passages, Badeau joked, gave them permission to commit all sorts of wickedness.

About two in the morning, they gave up. Pulling a pair of sofas together, they made a bed. Old costumes were requisitioned as bedding. Badeau took Macbeth's ermine cloak for a blanket and Caesar's mantle for a pillow. He settled in, drawing close to Edwin's face. The sad-eyed actor was a beauty, the critic thought, although Edwin said he cared for his looks only as tools of the trade. The candle burned out, and they talked on. "'Twas dark," Badeau wrote, "and I couldn't see his eyes." Soon Adam fell asleep with his head on Edwin's arm. It was the happiest day of his life.[52]

Adam had romantic feelings for Edwin. These were not returned. Edwin was neither gay nor bisexual. Once, as Edwin sat smoking in his dressing room between acts, Adam made his move. He reached out and pulled aside the robes of the actor's Richelieu character. "How dare you!" Edwin screamed shrilly and shrank back.

He didn't like being touched. "An introspective, distant man," Adam lamented, "so old when he was young, so cold though gifted with every personal charm." Affectionate in words alone. That was why he made a poor Romeo.[53]

At Edwin's request Badeau visited Mollie frequently during her year in Hoboken. He found her gracious and dignified. She found him boring. Badeau was an overeducated know-it-all. He showed it by speaking in learned allusions. Badeau would never say, for example, that people romped playfully when he could say they were like Bacchus with Ariadne or Donatello with Miriam. "Bader," as Mollie teased, loved talking about who wore what at the ball or who sat where at the opera—"and positively he talks of little else"—unless Edwin was the topic of conversation. Then it was all praise and advice and plans for the three of them to visit Europe. When he spoke of Edwin, Mollie wrote, "I sometimes feel as though he were a love-sick schoolgirl."

"I envy her," Badeau wrote Edwin. "I'm afraid I must make up my mind that my most intimate friends are to be an actor and his wife. Dreadful, isn't it? Suppose you were to have children!! In a year from now I suppose there will be some squalling ugly little creature to interfere with the Coliseum and Venice. Hang it. Don't you call it after me. I won't be a godfather, I warn you!"

"He is not like other men," Mollie wrote Edwin. He laughed and sent Adam a fruit card. Although she knew Badeau would be indignant when he got it, Mollie laughed, too.[54]

Their marriage took place on Saturday, July 7, 1860. It was a warm, clear summer day in New York, when Edwin and Badeau arrived at the West 11th Street home of the Reverend Samuel Osgood. Popular with the literary and arts crowd, Osgood was an associate of James Freeman Clarke, the minister whom the elder Booth had summoned in 1834 to bury his pigeons.[55]

Mollie came with her sister Catherine and Catherine's husband Harry McGonigle. Asia was not present—no surprise given her attitude—but neither were Edwin's mother Mary Ann, brother Joe, or sister Rose. Perhaps they shared Asia's prejudices. John was the only family member there, rounding out the small wedding party of six. Badeau was instantly

drawn to the younger brother. "He was excessively handsome, even physically finer than Edwin," he thought. Bright, graceful, and manly, John
seemed less intelligent, however. The party moved to Osgood's study.

Although Mollie was a Catholic, the couple had a Protestant service.
Osgood was one of the nation's leading Unitarian ministers and held the
service in that faith. It resembled those in the Episcopal Church of which
the Booth family were nominal members. Attired in a black silk gown,
Osgood cut a solemn figure with his arching eyebrows and iron-gray beard.
His look alone made plain the weight of the day. Edwin and Mollie came
forward, knelt, and exchanged their vows at a quaintly carved prayer bench
adorned with an embroidered cruciform.

When the service concluded, John was joyous. He threw his arms
around Edwin's neck and kissed him.[56]

4

GOD'S MOST
PRECIOUS TRUTH

William Herndon had been mayor of Springfield and partner in the high-profile law firm of Lincoln and Herndon before the war. His correspondence was wide-ranging, his opinions valued, and his influence sought. Now it was 1886. Lincoln was long dead, and Herndon's days were shadowed by debt and drink. His dream of being the great president's biographer had faded. His book floundered due to the scale of the project, while his controversial speeches on Lincoln's religion and home life turned old friends against him. In financial distress, Herndon sold copies of his Lincoln research to another author. Other sections of his notes were stolen. Still others were lost in a fire. Herndon gave away most of the letters Lincoln wrote him. Even the inkstands and pencils from their office had been gifted.

Now Lincoln's walnut desk and table were going, purchased by John W. Keyes of Chicago. It was painful to see them hauled out the door. "You now own the same desk and table that Lincoln once owned," he wrote Keyes. "He gave me the desk and table, and what you have is genuine and true. They have never been out of my sight since they were delivered to Lincoln and myself. Please take good care of the sacred things— mementoes of this noble man."

Realizing that Keyes might appreciate some impressions of Lincoln to

William Herndon. *Herndon became Lincoln's law partner in Springfield, Illinois, in 1844 and remained so until the president-elect left for the White House in 1861. He and Mary Lincoln disliked each other intensely.*

go with the furniture, Herndon provided them. "Mr. Lincoln was a sad man—a gloomy man and an abstracted one, and hence he was not very social in his nature," the former partner wrote. "He seemed to me to be an unhappy man at times. As a friend, Mr. Lincoln was true—true as steel. He thought in his life and lived in his thought. He did not trust any man with the secrets of his ambitious soul. Mr. Lincoln was a cool, conservative, and long headed man. [He] could be trusted by the people. They did trust him, and they were never deceived. He was a pure man—a great man, and a patriot."[1]

FEW NEW RESIDENTS of the White House had less interest in what the place looked like than the sixteenth president. The previous occupant's choice of style—*seedy hotel*—suited Lincoln, and he would have been content if the mansion were an office. Mary had other ideas. Each incoming administration was allowed twenty thousand dollars for refurbishments (plus six thousand annually for repairs). Never having had her hands on that much money, she was ecstatic. Wisely, Lincoln stepped back.

The challenge of redecorating the White House, whose East Room alone was roughly comparable in size with the Lincolns' Springfield home, was immense, but Mary tackled it with gusto. In May 1861, she left for Philadelphia and New York, the first of eleven shopping trips she made while First Lady. Over the next few months Mary purchased carpets, rugs, curtains, chairs, sofas, glassware, and porcelain dishware. Lincoln called these "flub-dubs" and said he couldn't be bothered with such things when soldiers lacked blankets. Mary was on a mission, however, and would not be deterred. She spent sixty-five hundred dollars on French wallpaper alone. At this rate she burned through the entire stipend before the year was out.[2]

Cost aside, the results were astonishing. The public rooms were transformed into elegant spaces. The shabby private quarters—furnished by George Washington, joked Mary's cousin Lizzie Grimsley—were likewise tastefully redone. Mary did well. For those who had questions about her alleged "log-cabin tastes," she hurled those questions back in their faces.

The two younger Lincoln sons had updated bedrooms on the north side of the second floor across the corridor from their parents. Willie was "a noble, beautiful boy of great mental activity, unusual intelligence, wonderful memory, methodical, frank and loving," wrote Lizzie, whom the boys called Grandmother for her kindly ways. He was "a counterpart of his father, save that he was handsome." Willie was devoted to his younger brother Tad, "a gay, gladsome, merry, spontaneous fellow, bubbling over with innocent fun." If Tad wasn't crying over something, he was laughing at it and his noise rang through the house. "He was the life as also the worry of the household."

The two boys had a grand time in the mansion and might be found anywhere in it from cellar to dome. The White House teemed with interesting characters, and there was plenty of time away from their tutor for play and mischief. They rode their ponies and herded their goats and drilled their playmates in a juvenile militia called "Mrs. Lincoln's Zouaves." The First Lady presented them with a flag, and the president reviewed them from the south portico. The children enjoyed military things, like concerts by regimental bands and visits with the soldiers stationed on the south grounds. Although they picked up measles from them or at some other army camp in the city, they recovered and established on the White House roof a fort with logs painted to look like cannon, ready to repel any attack by Virginia.[3]

Four hundred yards below the soldiers' camp south of the mansion was a line of trees. Beyond it was the Washington Canal, now paved over by Constitution Avenue, dividing the National Mall from the White House and other government buildings to the north. This abandoned canal was "the grand receptacle of nearly all the filth of the city," wrote Benjamin B. French, commissioner of public buildings. Waste from hotels, homes, and offices drained into it and festered. "This immense mass of fetid and corrupt matter [imperiled] the health of the entire population and the lives of thousands." French informed Congress he had never seen the canal in worse condition.[4]

French's phrases—"offensive soil," "fetid and corrupt matter," "bed of filth"—were polite ways of saying that the canal was an open sewer contaminated by feces. Typhoid fever is caused primarily by ingestion of food or water contaminated with bacilli present in such places. There were no antibiotic treatments for typhoid fever at this time, of course, and as many as twenty percent or more of those infected died from complications of the disease.

Willie and Tad fell ill in early February 1862. The older boy, who was never robust, was the sicker of the two. He had a troubling intermittent fever. A grand ball, scheduled for February 5, was not postponed, however, as doctors assured the parents that matters were in hand and an early recovery likely. A crowd of five or six hundred—"very large and very brilliant"—partied downstairs as the fitful children, breathing laboriously, tossed and turned above. "Did anyone see a ghost of the future fluttering from room to room?" a guest would later wonder.

Mary slipped upstairs several times during the night to check on Willie. She found him worse. But, as he was well cared for and she could do nothing but sit and fret, she gathered the long train of her white satin dress and returned to the ball. The music and happy voices from the party below throbbed through the floor of the sickroom. Elizabeth Keckly, a former slave, seamstress, and confidante of Mary's who sat nursing the boy, thought it sounded like "the wild faint sobbing of far-off spirits."[5]

By February 8 typhoid fever was announced in both cases. Tad seemed safe, but Willie did not. His brown hair matted with sweat, his blue eyes bright with fever, he rallied, then faded, then rallied, then faded again. By the 16th he was delirious. His physicians, who were bystanders at this point, watched helplessly as he died at five in the afternoon of February 20. He was eleven years old.[6]

"Well, Nicolay," Lincoln said to his secretary, "my boy is gone—he is actually gone." Bursting into tears, he wandered off. In Willie's room, he found Keckly, who had just washed and dressed the boy and placed him back on his bed, covering his face with a sheet. Lincoln pulled the cover down to look at him. He gazed for a long time. "It is hard, *hard* to have him die!" he exclaimed. "Great sobs choked his utterance," Keckly wrote. "He buried his head in his hands, and his tall frame was convulsed with emotion. I stood at the foot of the bed, my eyes full of tears, looking at the man in silent, awe-stricken wonder."[7]

"Mrs. Lincoln's grief was inconsolable," Keckly continued. "The pale face of her dead boy threw her into convulsions." Mary's sister Elizabeth Edwards was urgently summoned from Springfield, and Rebecca R. Pomroy, an army nurse, was sent for to care for Tad and the mother.

Willie was embalmed on Saturday, February 22. The wind was fierce that night, and Charles D. Brown took the reassuring arm of his colleague Charles E. Lester as they set out for the White House. The tempest howled around the doctors, gusts pushed against their steps, and dead leaves leaped from the ground to slap their cheeks. It was very odd weather.

"Is it not among the strangest of things," asked Lester, "that this event should have happened now?" He meant that the day was George Washington's birthday—coming immediately upon Willie's death?

"No," replied Brown. "I do not so regard it." The White House was home to many ironic sorrows. President William Henry Harrison had entered it like a prince in 1849. One month later his corpse was hauled out of it like that of a pauper.

Brown used an embalming method popularized by French anatomist J. P. Sucquet. It employed a chemical infusion that turned Willie's body hard and marblelike in only a few hours. Before that happened, his face was arranged to show an expression of cheerfulness. Then the body petrified. "It becomes a statue," Lester said, "and changes no more for the ages."

Embalming was a science and an art but it was about people, too, and when he left the White House that evening, Lester said to himself, "God heal the broken hearts left here!"[8]

In the Green Room the frames of the large mirrors were covered with black crepe and the glass with white. Willie's remains were placed in the room in a metallic coffin of imitation rosewood. "The body was clothed in the usual everyday attire of a youth of his age, consisting of pants and jacket, with white stockings and low shoes—the white collar and wristbands being turned over the black cloth of the jacket," wrote a visitor from Philadelphia. He held a bouquet composed of a camellia with azaleas and sprigs of mignonette in his right hand. A wreath lay on his breast and flowers were placed about his body. "The little favorite" appeared peaceful after his ordeal. Lincoln came into the room several times to look at him.[9]

The body remained in the Green Room in a closed coffin while family and friends gathered in the adjoining East Room on Monday afternoon, February 24. The Reverend Dr. Phineas Gurley of the New York Avenue Presbyterian Church held the funeral service. After Gurley wrung fresh tears from the mourners, Lincoln and Robert accompanied the remains to Oak Hill Cemetery in Georgetown. The inexplicably strong winds of the last few days continued, buffeting the pallbearers who placed the body in a vault to await burial in better weather.[10]

THERE WAS A reason why Dorothea Dix, superintendent of army nurses, chose Rebecca Pomroy out of the 250 women available to her for duty at the White House. A New England widow whose broad face had a peaceful look, Pomroy knew all about domestic sorrow. Like the Lincolns, she had lost two children. Her own Willie, a teenager, had died three years earlier and, shortly before that, her daughter Clara, aged eight.

Pomroy arrived just after Willie's passing. After paying her respects in the Green Room, she made her way upstairs to Tad's sickbed and went to work. Lincoln came in several times to sit with them. Pomroy's devout demeanor drew him out, and the nurse and the president soon had the type of conversation Lincoln had with very few people. When he learned of her troubles, he marveled at her tranquility. "Did you always feel that you could say, 'Thy will be done?'" he asked.

"No, not at the first blow, nor at the second," she replied. "It was months after my affliction that God met me when at a camp meeting."

Seeing how attentive Lincoln was, she continued, "telling him my history, and, above all, of God's love and care for me through it all." As she spoke, he covered his face with his hands. Tears streamed through his fingers. He rose, walked about the room, spoke about Willie, and cried out, "Why is it? Oh, why is it?"

"It was given me to tell Mr. Lincoln in my poor, weak way how wonderfully the Lord sustained me and brought me out of the darkness into light. I bade him take courage in this his time of trial." Pomroy reminded him that he had the daily prayers of thousands to sustain him.

"I am glad of that," responded Lincoln, who broke out again in sobs.

"Pray for him," said the president, motioning to Tad, "and also for me."

The next night he returned and begged her to retell her story. Leave nothing out, he said. How did she obtain her faith in God? What was the secret of placing oneself in God's hands? He returned the third night, repeating the same eager questions about how belief was obtained. It was as if he sought to understand intellectually something that was anything but.

"I wish I had that childlike faith you speak of, and I trust He will give it to me," Lincoln told Pomroy.[11]

Tad improved, but the First Lady was now a concern. As Cousin Lizzie observed, Mary could always be counted on to collapse in a crisis. True to form, the heartbroken mother was ill with grief. Declining to attend the funeral, she took to her bed, leaving it only to check on Tad. Lincoln was greatly relieved to see Elizabeth Edwards come through the mansion door. "You have such a power and control—such influence over Mary," he said to his sister-in-law. "Come, do stay and console me."[12]

Lincoln had a fear of insanity in himself and in others. When he was sixteen and living in Indiana, Matthew Gentry, a schoolmate, went mad and attempted to kill his parents. Gentry became "a howling, crazy man," weeping, laughing, cursing, praying, fighting, and screaming—finally wrestled to the floor by neighbors. He lapsed into what Lincoln termed "a mental night" that never lifted. Years later Lincoln remained disturbed by the incident. He referred to Gentry in a poem he wrote containing the lines:

But here's an object more of dread
Than aught the grave contains—
A human form with reason fled
While wretched life remains.[13]

During one of Mary's paroxysms of grief, Lincoln gave in to his anxiety. Taking her gently by the arm, he led her to a window. "Mother, do you see that large white building on the hill yonder?" he asked. He pointed to the Government Hospital for the Insane, clearly visible through leafless trees on a ridge to the southeast. "Try and control your grief or it will drive you mad, and we may have to send you there."[14]

FRIEND AND BIOGRAPHER Henry C. Whitney wrote that Lincoln, "like Joan of Arc, heard phantom voices." Lincoln told Whitney that when he was a boy, he used to wander alone into the woods. "It had a fascination for me which had an element of fear in it—superstitious fear. I could see nothing and no one, but I heard voices. Once I heard a voice right at my elbow— heard it distinctly and plainly. I turned around expecting to see someone. No one there but the voice."

Lincoln and Whitney were walking in the "Big Grove" near Urbana, one of those distinctive tracts of forest that dot the Illinois prairie, and the setting triggered Lincoln's memory. What did the voice say? asked Whitney. Lincoln didn't reply. Deep gloom—"a look of pain"—settled on his face. The memory was too private, Lincoln lost in reflection, "and we trudged slowly on."[15]

Now Lincoln had daily conversations with Willie. Eleven weeks after Willie's death, he was with the army near Norfolk, Virginia. He called to an officer with the improbable name of Le Grand B. Cannon, who was working in the adjoining room, "You have been writing long enough. Come in here and sit with me and rest, and I will read you some passages from Shakespeare." Cannon sat opposite the president at a small round table and listened as Lincoln read several selections in *King John* where Constance bewails the loss of her son:

And, father cardinal, I have heard you say
That we shall see and know our friends in heaven.
If that be true, I shall see my boy again.

When he finished, he closed the book, laid it down, turned to Cannon, and asked, "Do you ever find yourself talking with the dead? Feel that you were having a sweet communion with him?"

"Yes, Mr. President, I have."

"That is my feeling toward my boy Willie. I catch myself talking to him as though he were with me." At the table Lincoln laid his head on his arm and sobbed. Cannon was so affected that he, too, broke down. Recovering, he slipped out of the room, leaving Lincoln alone.[16]

Willie died on a Thursday. For a part of that day each week Lincoln closeted himself away and indulged his grief. His sister-in-law Elizabeth was concerned. "To calm his mind—to cheer him—to inspire him with hope and confidence," she walked him over to the White House's glass conservatory west of the mansion.

"Oh, how beautiful this is—these roses!" she exclaimed as he followed patiently behind her. "And these exotics are grand! Gathered from the remotest corners of the earth and grand beyond description."

There was a moody silence that Lincoln finally broke. "I was never in here before," he said. "I don't know why it is so, but I never cared for flowers."[17]

Elizabeth continued Nurse Pomroy's good work, inviting the Reverend Dr. Francis Vinton to visit the White House. Vinton was a West Point graduate and a Harvard lawyer who had become an Episcopal minister. Tall, with dark hair and a dour look set on what contemporaries termed a massive face, Vinton served at fashionable Trinity Church on Wall Street (which George Washington attended and where Alexander Hamilton was buried). The minister had lost children—four in his case—but he had eight others at home, and life had not rattled his self-confidence or self-regard. George Templeton Strong, an unfriendly member of Trinity's vestry, when shown a portrait of the vain and theatrical clergyman, remarked that it had one great advantage over its subject: "It preaches not." Strong thought Vinton had missed his calling. "He might have been valuable as a captain of a whaler or as a chief of police."[18]

A man like Vinton, who acted as if he were God's associate, not his servant, was unlikely to win Lincoln's friendship, but the president was hurting and welcomed him. The grieving father sat patiently as the voluble minister recounted the family travails of Old Testament figures from Abraham to Moses.

How much of this Lincoln heard was doubtful. "The President listened as one in a stupor," Vinton observed.

But when Vinton said, "Your son is alive," Lincoln woke up. Leaping from the sofa, he exclaimed, "Alive! *Alive!* Surely you mock me."

"No, sir, believe me," responded Vinton.

"*Alive? Alive?*" the president repeated.

"My dear sir, believe this, for it is God's most precious truth. Seek not your son among the dead. He is not there. He lives today in Paradise! God has called your son into His upper kingdom—a kingdom and an existence as real—more real—than your own."

The head of any government was an agent of God, continued the minister. Lincoln was "the Viceregent of the Lord Jesus Christ." Therefore, "I told him that he must not allow his own tender heart to interfere with his public duties."

In a speech delivered shortly after Lincoln's death in 1865, Vinton told a New York audience that the president, in response to his remarks, lay his head on Vinton's shoulder and wept. "From that day forth, Thursday was no longer kept as it had been for his private griefs," the minister assured his listeners, "and he went forward sternly to his duties." Vinton had saved the Republic![19]

The minister left the White House convinced that Lincoln was a Christian despite the fact that the president never said so. Just as with Junius Brutus Booth Sr., the respect Lincoln showed the faith of others, together with his humanity, sincerity, and humility, led people to ascribe to Lincoln whatever beliefs they held. It was a happy aspect of his personality, but it was not done for political advantage. As Pomroy observed, "Mr. Lincoln was not a man to say things for effect."

Meanwhile, the nurse spent her days with Mary, who secluded herself in her room. Like her husband, the First Lady listened to Pomroy recount her own sorrows. Like him, she was bewildered. "She could not understand how I could be so happy under it all," Pomroy wrote, "and, bursting into tears, said she wished she could feel so, too." Although more conventionally religious than her husband, Mary drew little ready comfort from her faith. The death of a child was a theft from the future, as the First Lady knew, for Willie was the one whom she believed would have cared for her in her old age.

"Look up for strength," was all Pomroy could say.[20]

Back at her hospital, Pomroy received a visit from an elderly man whose long white hair and full white beard made him look like an Old Testament prophet. It was the poet John Pierpont. He settled himself on a trunk—she had no chairs in her tiny room—and handed her a letter tied with a white satin ribbon and sent from California. The writer purported to be her own dead son Willie. The boy wanted her to know that he was happy. He had recently met Willie Lincoln in the spirit world and they were often together. On Pomroy's visits to the White House, the two children hovered encouragingly nearby, but Pomroy was too cold and closed to receive them. Willie despaired to see her weep over a lock of his hair when he was present and eager to comfort her.

The First Lady, on the other hand, was more sensitive to their presence. Willie's letter had been found on Capitol Hill on the desk of a senator. It was known only that the recipient was a widow with dead children and that she worked in a local hospital. The letter made its way to Pierpont, who had consoled the Lincolns when Willie died. He showed it to Mary. The First Lady knew for whom it was intended and gave him a note of introduction to Pomroy. "Important business," she wrote to the nurse.[21]

SPIRITUALIST R. D. GOODWIN, a friend of Colonel Elmer Ellsworth, lamented the officer's death so much that he made a pilgrimage to the Marshall House in Alexandria to pull up a souvenir section of the blood-stained floor on which the gallant soldier had fallen. It was a sacred relic to him. Imagine Goodwin's surprise when there soon followed a letter from Ellsworth himself, written in the dead man's hand. "Go on to victory!" it ordered. "I can accomplish more now than if I had survived my fate. I was impressed of my end before it came."[22]

The spiritualist movement that Goodwin followed owed its rise to Margaret and Kate Fox, who allegedly communicated with the dead through a series of rapping noises in their home in Hydesville, New York, in 1848. The practice spread rapidly across the country. "No movement of mind or spiritual forces, within the limits of recorded history, is comparable with this, either in its moral or phenomenal aspects," wrote a believer.[23]

The movement soon reached Springfield. Herndon thought it likely that the future president attended séances in the city before moving to Washington in 1861. So said local spiritualist oracle John Ordway, a pump maker. Ordway, whose wife was aptly named Sybil, was living in Georgia at the time of Lincoln's election, but his secondhand claim sounded credible to Herndon. "Mr. Lincoln was in some phases of his nature very, very superstitious, and it may be—it is quite probable that he, in his gloom, sadness, fear and despair, invoked the spirits of the dead to reveal him the cause."[24]

There were many believers in spiritualism who worked for the federal government in Washington. John Pierpont was a clerk in the Treasury Department. Thomas Gale Foster clerked in the War Department, Cranston Laurie in the Post Office Department, and Chauncey A. Horr in Indian Affairs. In the executive and legislative branches, among the bosses of these civil servants, were more spiritualists, "but for prudential reasons, prominent people do not like to confess it," wrote William Henry Burr, a congressional reporter. "They prefer to call themselves *inquirers*."[25]

Isaac Newton was the most prominent Washington spiritualist in public life. He was a Pennsylvania farmer in his sixties who worked to secure the votes of his fellow Quakers for Lincoln in 1860. Newton's farm had a side business selling ice cream, pie, and fruit to railroad passengers going south. That drew him to Washington. Newton sent Mary six quarts of early peas. She acknowledged the gift with a note of appreciation. He promptly returned her thanks with a crock of fresh butter. "Thanks again—thanks from the White House—overwhelmed the old man," wrote a friend, and he deluged Mary with pumpkins, squash, melons, cabbages, lettuce, and arm-long strings of onions.[26]

"Why can't Isaac Newton have an office?" she asked her husband.

Lincoln joked that he would make the old-timer a brigadier general.

"No!" she replied. "I am in earnest!" Mary wouldn't drop the matter, so the president proposed to make him the White House gardener.

"That's not an office. It's only a place. I mean *a good office*."

To keep Mary happy—and for no other reason—Lincoln made Newton commissioner of agriculture. The comical Quaker quickly proved the old saying that one may occupy a position without filling it. "That Sir Isaac [as his critics labeled him in an unflattering comparison to Sir Isaac Newton] ever got an office was a wonder to all his friends and a wonder to himself," wrote a journalist. "He was entirely unqualified and should never have had it. He is a poor, ignorant, credulous man, [albeit] with a very good heart."[27]

Lincoln rebuffed Newton's critics, saying, "I think he's competent enough to attend to all the agriculture we will have till the war is over." Anyway, the president added, "I didn't appoint him and therefore I can't remove him. Mrs. Lincoln appointed him, and as long as he continues to send her fresh butter and vegetables and strawberries out of season, I don't think she will."[28]

Isaac Newton. *Mary Lincoln badgered her husband into appointing Newton as commissioner of agriculture. A kind-hearted Quaker seemingly out of place in wartime Washington, Newton accompanied the First Lady to séances.*

While Newton's lack of education may not have been his fault, it was his misfortune. His verbal gaffes and laughable logic enlivened the dreary wartime city. The story was told of a friend who, pointing to a certain woman, said that by her skin tone, he suspected that she was a quadroon. No, no, countered Sir Isaac. She was too light-skinned for a quadroon. She must be what was known as an *octagon*. Wits amused themselves by imitating his orthography. "Not a single paragraph of a single report sent out from his office has ever come from his pen. He could not write three sentences of English if his retention in his office depended upon the accomplishment." Lincoln, receiving messages from him, shrugged charitably and headed for the wastepaper basket.[29]

Congress was less indulgent. Criticized by a legislator for misspelling the word "sugar," Newton replied, "Well, if s-h-u-g-g-a-r don't spell sugar, what does it spell?" Shuggar now joined the Newton hit parade along with lettis (lettuce), inons (onions), and sausgee (sausage). These rivaled his declaration that birds did not have *plumage*. They had *foliage*, a remark that sent Lincoln into a painful fit of laughter. On another occasion, when called upon to explain his department's overspending, Newton boasted, "Yes, sir, the expenses have been very great—exorbitant, indeed, sir. They have exceeded my most sanguine expectations."[30]

An embarrassing incident added to his woes. A young woman from Ohio called at his office seeking a job. "So, miss, you want a clerkship, hey?" he said. Playfully, he poked his thumb in her ribs and quacked like a duck. She fled and fetched her senator, who returned with her to lambast Newton for his boorishness. The commissioner was mortified and apologetic, saying that he thought of the applicant as his daughter. Everyone agreed the white-haired old-timer meant no real offense, but his "hands-on" style of management was now on notice.[31]

"Artless old muff." "Laughingstock of the Capital." "Fossil." "Amiable blockhead." "Ignoramus." Let them carp. Newton survived every attempt to return him to his ice cream churn thanks to Mary. She loved him. While his assistants wrote the monthly crop reports (and he was a surprisingly able and energetic boss), he visited her almost daily with vegetables for her kitchen, flowers for her drawing rooms, and bouquets for herself. Newton made himself the unofficial White House chamberlain. It was impossible not to like the warmhearted, gossipy, and sociable old duff.[32]

Clambering into Mary's coach, he was a sight. His broad-brimmed Quaker hat framed a round and fleshy face. His shad belly coat struggled to accommodate a kettle-drum stomach. He was an amusing contrast to the birdlike Pierpont, his seatmate. Dressed in a drab frock coat and trousers, the poet had a glowing pink face, happy blue eyes, and a nervous manner. Approaching his eighth decade, Pierpont was tall and thin and had the step and manner of a boy, a fact he attributed entirely to the fact that he never drank or smoked.[33]

Mary and her companions were off to a séance. Pierpont, the maternal grandfather of financier J. P. Morgan, had quit the Unitarian Church to investigate spiritualism. He became a believer. "The facts were incontrovertible," he concluded. "The spirit survived the body in a state of intelligent activity." Pierpont knew this because he spoke regularly to his father James, who died in 1840, and his wife Mary, who joined her father-in-law on the other side in 1855.[34]

Newton's spiritualist origins were less clear. He was not a birthright Friend, having joined the Quakers only in his teens because of "a Religious turn of mind." His meeting was rural and conservative. It was the home church of Elizabeth Collins, a preacher celebrated for having visions. Collins was well known to Newton and his family. But whatever her influence on Newton, she had little in common with the radical New York Quakers who befriended the Fox sisters. She was orthodox, Bible-based, and pietistic. Like her, Newton had no history with reformers like Pierpont, a highly educated New England antislavery zealot.[35]

The party traveled to the two-story brick townhouse that Cranston and Margaret Laurie rented in Georgetown. Mary had expressed a desire to meet a trance medium—one whose mind and body were taken over by a spirit—and very shortly one walked through the door. She was a young woman with brown hair in delicate curls, brown eyes, a broad face, ruddy complexion, and receding chin. She was small and slight and, although in her early twenties, childlike. One instinctively wanted to reach out and touch her. She was Nettie Colburn.[36]

Nettie was from Albany, New York. She was in town to secure a medical furlough for her brother Amasa, a private in the 16th Connecticut Volunteer Infantry, who was suffering from the dreaded typhoid fever. Nettie had been buffed and rebuffed from one army office to another in her efforts. Her eyes, swollen from tears of frustration and worry, caught Mary's attention. When Nettie's problems were explained to her, Mary snapped, "Don't worry any more about it. Your brother shall have [a] furlough if Mr. Lincoln has to give it himself."

Her words calmed Nettie. "I was in a condition to quiet my nerves long enough to enable my spirit friends to control me," she said. "Some new and powerful influences obtained possession of my organism and addressed Mrs. Lincoln with great clearness and force." When Nettie came to herself an hour later, she had no idea what she had said while under. She never did. Everyone around her was talking excitedly, however, about her important message on "matters of state."

"This young lady must not leave Washington," exclaimed Mary. "I feel she must stay here, and Mr. Lincoln must hear what we have heard. He must hear it."

Nettie explained that she couldn't stay. She made her living as a speaker and must travel, as there were no opportunities for her in Washington.

Turning to Newton, who sat on her right, the First Lady asked pointedly, "You can give this young lady a place in your department?" It was a question that wasn't a question, and Sir Isaac understood. He bowed and replied, "If it pleases you."

Amasa got his furlough two days later, apparently without Mary's help. It took Nettie three weeks and twenty-two supplicating visits to various government officers, including nine to Assistant Secretary of War John Tucker, together with all the money she had. But there was a surprise at the end. Cranston Laurie handed her an envelope. It contained one hundred dollars and a note reading, "From a few friends who appreciate a sister's devotion." Nettie wrote a quarter-century later, "No name anywhere to tell who were the generous donors. I do not know to this day whence came this most welcome tribute."

Her brother left for home shortly after Christmas 1862. The next day, Margaret Laurie received a note asking her and her husband to come to the White House that evening at eight and bring Nettie. The young woman trembled at the prospect, but she gathered herself and joined the party in the mansion's Red Room, which Mary used as a sort of living room. Belle Miller, the Lauries' daughter, came along. She had gifts as a physical medium, a person through whom the spirits could do manifestations in this world.

Mary greeted them graciously. The First Lady looked younger than her years, Nettie realized, surprisingly so for the mother of four children. "Mrs. Lincoln was a pre-possessing woman with an abundance of rich, dark-brown hair and large and impressive eyes, so shifting that their color was almost undecided," she observed. "Her face was oval, the features excellent, complexion white and fair, teeth regular, and her smile winning and kindly. A handsome woman."

Belle seated herself alone at the grand piano. A general conversation ensued around her. Suddenly, Belle's hands, under the control of the spirits, fell on the keyboard with force and hammered out a grand march. "As the measured notes rose and fell, we became silent," said Nettie. Then, "the heavy end of the piano began rising and falling in perfect time to the music."

The rocking stopped when Lincoln entered the room. "So, this is our 'little Nettie,' is it, that we have heard so much about?" he asked. He led her to an ottoman. Sitting down nearby, the president questioned her about her mediumship. "I think he must have thought me stupid," she later wrote, as all the awestruck young woman could stutter in reply were yesses and noes.

A circle was suggested. "Well, how do you do it?" Lincoln asked. While the matter was being explained by Cranston, Nettie felt herself losing awareness of her surroundings and slipping under control. One hour later she realized she was standing in front of the president, who sat back in

Belle Miller. *Spiritualist Miller, the so-called Georgetown Witch, held séances in the White House, once allegedly levitating Lincoln as her spirits sent a piano skyward during one of her performances.*

his chair, arms folded upon his breast, staring appraisingly at her. Nettie stepped back in surprise. She had been speaking to him but not by her own volition. As with all her messages, she felt she had been made to say the things she said and had no idea what they were.

Friends told her she had urged Lincoln not to delay signing the Emancipation Proclamation, scheduled for January 1, 1863. Conservatives in Congress and the army urged him to postpone it, aware that it would make the South fight more desperately. Do not, she warned the president. "He must stand firm to his conviction and fearlessly perform the work and fulfil the mission for which he had been raised up by an overruling Providence. It was to be the crowning event, the spirits said, of his administration and his life."

Feeling that the only source of moral authority was internal to each individual, spiritualists like Nettie were adamantly antislavery. Her message, therefore, was not unexpected. But she did not put the proclamation into his head, as was later claimed on her behalf. In fact, it wasn't clear what she actually accomplished. Lincoln had no intention of delaying the act. Nevertheless, he seemed grateful for her encouragement.

Laying a hand on Nettie's head, he said, "My child, you possess a very singular gift. That it is of God, I have no doubt. I thank you for coming here tonight. I must leave you all now, but I hope I shall see you again." The president shook her hand, bowed to the rest of the party, and left the room.[37]

ONE EVENING ELIZABETH took Lincoln for a walk through the park near the White House. She had some unhappy news for him. She needed to return to Illinois.

Elizabeth had opposed Lincoln's marriage to her sister. They were simply incompatible. "His habits, like himself, were odd and wholly irregular. He would move around in a vague, abstracted way, as if unconscious of his own or anyone else's existence. I have seen him sit down at the table absorbed in thought, and never, unless recalled to his senses, would he think of food. But, however peculiar and secretive he may have seemed, he was anything but cold. Beneath what the world saw lurked a nature as tender and poetic as any I ever saw.

"He was a man I loved and respected. He was a good man, an honest and true one."

Lincoln, his eyes filling with tears, begged her to stay. Elizabeth replied that she just couldn't. Her own family needed her. "The picture of the man's despair never faded from my vision. Long after my return to Springfield, in reverting to the sad separation, my heart ached because I was unable in my feeble way to lighten his burden."[38]

5

LOVE'S SACRED CIRCLE

Edwin Booth and Mollie Devlin honeymooned in a cottage on the Canadian side of Niagara Falls. After a week, Edwin allowed Adam Badeau to join them. The critic was so hungry for the actor's company that it seemed cruel to exclude him. Edwin did order Badeau to stop calling him "The Prince," a reference not only to his role as Hamlet but also to his lordship over Badeau's feelings. The critic complied, realizing Mollie now owned Edwin's affections. "I suffer ten times worse than I can make you feel," he wrote the actor, "but I vow you always give me good cause for my naughtiness and my exacting, jealous, ridiculous behavior. I wish to God I'd never seen you. It's a frightful thing to live out of one's self, to be buried alive in somebody else. To depend on that body for your own happiness. Damnation, damnation, damnation, damnation. Hell! Damn you. God bless you."[1]

When the Booths returned to New York, they took a suite at the Fifth Avenue Hotel. The most elegant hotel in the city, the Fifth Avenue was a new five-story building with an Italianate brick-and-marble exterior so impressive that English visitors conceded it was more handsome than Buckingham Palace. The interior was a showcase of gilded wood, crimson curtains, and damask carpets. With private bathrooms and fireplaces in every room, the hotel's luxury and comfort were unparalleled. Its small army of servants were masters of boot-blacking, coat-brushing, cork-drawing,

Mary Devlin Booth. *The first wife of Edwin Booth, "Mollie" was devoted to her husband and encouraged his career at a critical moment. The delicately built young woman died in 1863, an event that plunged Edwin into the world of spiritualism and mediums.*

plate-changing, and bed-making. "Everything about the establishment is gorgeous, fairy-like, and enchanting," wrote a visitor. Few guests knew that when the hotel's foundation was being dug, dozens of skeletons were unearthed. The opulent Fifth Avenue was built on an old charity cemetery for the poor, the unknown, and the unwanted.[2]

Lillian Woodman, a teenager living down the hall from the Booths, caught a glimpse into their apartment. It looked cozy—a table set for two, several well-filled bookcases, a black bearskin rug on which lay a cushion and an open book. Nearby was a guitar, a gift from Badeau. Heavy curtains covered the windows. A blazing fire lit the room, glimmering on picture frames.

Lillian had recently seen Edwin play in Boston. Entranced, she came home and informed her family that her fate would be somehow entangled with his. She called it a prescience. "The turning point has come to my life," she announced. Her family laughed since neither she nor they knew Edwin or any other actor, but now here he was, living just down the corridor.

One day, as the gong sounded for lunch in the dining room, Lillian met the newlyweds. Tables were shared at busy times, and two chairs were unexpectedly pulled up to hers. Edwin and Mollie took them. Lillian gasped in excitement. They were close enough to touch. It was unreal.

Edwin had a "fine bearing and natural grace, magic charm of face and figure, melodious voice and an ever-changing expression in his eyes. A deep expression of melancholy. The strange magnetic quality of his nature was almost perceptible to the touch." His wife was "slight but with lovely lines; honest and straightforward eyes, brown and tender; and an ineffable grace that made even strangers love her."

Suddenly, Mollie's greyhound bounded up to the table. Edwin was angry that the dog handler had let the leash slip. Mollie was amused. The incident humanized the pair for Lillian. While Edwin sat silently, stuffily, and annoyed, the young women giggled and talked excitedly over ice cream. They became instant friends. Many years later Lillian realized why. Although a wife, Mollie was still a girl.

"It was not decreed that Mr. Booth in his life of gloom and glory should know much of happiness," Lillian wrote in *Crowding Memories* (1920), her autobiography. "Doubtless the first year of marriage brought him nearer to it than he had ever been before. No hermit in his cell, or nun in her cloister, was more secluded from the world than this happy pair. Daily on their table were laid letters, cards, notes of invitation—all read and courteously declined. They went nowhere, saw no one." Lillian witnessed their happiness with a peek through their door. Mollie, accompanying herself on the guitar, was singing the madrigal *The Passionate Shepherd to His Love*:

Come live with me and be my love,
And we will all the pleasures prove,
That valleys, groves, hills, and fields,
Woods, or steepy mountain yields.[3]

There was always time for Badeau, of course. Edwin was eager to show him "that his marriage made no difference in his feeling toward me," the critic recalled, "and his wife was quite as anxious that I should perceive none." As the actor lay on the bearskin rug, face down and propped up on his elbows, Mollie and Adam would go over his lines with him. Then the wife withdrew for the night, leaving them alone, and it was old times anew as they sat up late smoking and talking.[4]

Badeau wanted Edwin to be embraced socially. That meant confronting the old prejudice against actors that Lincoln and the Jeffersons had experienced in Springfield. It was a bigger battle than any one player could win, but Edwin had the looks, talent, and innate dignity to strike a blow. The actor didn't share Badeau's enthusiasm for society, but he wanted his profession respected and he knew that the friendship of prominent individuals could be useful to his career, so he joined the Century Club with Badeau as sponsor. There he met poet William Cullen Bryant, historian George Bancroft, Senator Charles Sumner, author Julia Ward Howe, artist Winslow Homer, and other celebrities. Most became good friends. They liked Mollie, too. He was grateful for their attention, but, aware of his lack of education, he was uncomfortable when the spotlight at their gatherings swung his way.

"I'd rather be off in some quiet corner telling stories with a few kind souls," he remarked.[5]

Edwin and Badeau continued their studies, ascending the thirty-six broad marble steps of the Astor Library to its main sanctuary. They found the elderly Joseph Cogswell standing guard behind a rail over his trove of 100,000 books. At ten in the morning he lowered the rope. Books did not circulate, not even what librarian Cogswell called the trash of Charles Dickens, but admission was free and the collection unique, so the two men settled in to study the large color-plate books of costumes of the Classical, Tudor, and Renaissance eras that formed the principal time periods of Edwin's plays.[6]

Cogswell expelled his readers at five and locked the library doors. Nevertheless, he told friends that he found insurance broker Austin L. Sands loitering at Shelf B-30 on multiple occasions late at night. This was disturbing because Sands was dead. It was his ghost in the stacks.

Cogswell explained to the apparition that the Astor, like any well-run library, had strict hours. As librarian, he must enforce them. The ghost replied that the streets were cold and dreary and the theaters closed. Being dead, he was no longer occupied with business and therefore in need of diversion. Cogswell was sympathetic but repeated his demand that the rules be obeyed. Sands must depart. The ghost, having no plausible reply, gave him a stern look and vanished.[7]

FAMILY FRIEND JOE JEFFERSON visited the Booths with news that his wife Maggie continued unwell. She had had six children in nine years. Two died and a third, dropped in infancy by a nurse, required constant care. It was too much for the delicately built woman, and she was chronically weak and tired. Joe felt ill, too. Something continued amiss with one of his lungs, yet nightly he had to project his voice over fifty rows of seats and up two balconies. Joe feared it was tuberculosis, the family curse. Whatever it was, it was so serious that he could not buy life insurance.[8]

At the same time critics were attacking the comedian's performances at the Winter Garden Theatre. They felt Joe was strictly a second banana over his head in starring roles. The *New York Times* complained, "It is one of the misfortunes of our drama that the moment a good stock actor contributes to the success of a piece in which he plays, eaten up with a ridiculous self-conceit, he sets up at once for a star. We have only to hope that Mr. Jefferson may be disenchanted of the delusion that because an actor shows himself a good stock actor and plays two or three parts well, he is able to carry alone the weight of attraction of a first-class metropolitan theatre. There are, in fact, but three or four artists at the outside fairly entitled to the position of 'stars.' Among these stands preeminent Mr. Edwin Booth, who, at his last engagement, made the most legitimate success within our recollection."[9]

Joe was thirty-two years old. He had been on the stage his entire life. If he wasn't yet ready to star, when would he be?

Jefferson remained intrigued with the dramatic possibilities of Rip Van Winkle, the ne'er-do-well villager who slept for twenty years. On a rainy fall day in 1860 he reread Washington Irving's *Sketchbook* (1819), in which the character of Rip first appeared. It was delightful. But the challenge for Joe was that Rip doesn't speak ten lines in Irving's text. The actor would have to turn a short story into a three-act play. Joe knew he could do it, however. He actually *saw* himself as the character so clearly that he went out and created Rip's wardrobe before he wrote a single line of the script.

Versions of Rip had been performed for decades, including several by his own family. These played but they didn't pay. Jefferson's idea was to refashion Rip's encounter with the crew of ghosts into a dramatic center-piece. Joe believed that the earlier versions in which the ghosts spoke and even danced made them seem mortal. What if they were mute and no char-acter spoke for an entire act except Rip? It would be almost unprecedented onstage but rivetingly suspenseful. Audiences already inclined to believe in the supernatural would love it if Rip, lost in the forest, were surrounded by odd-looking creatures who stared and gestured and crawled about him in deathlike silence but said nothing.[10]

Maggie Jefferson died on February 18, 1861. Loving, intelligent, artistic, orderly, gracious—and gone. The official cause of death was asthenia, a diagnosis that covered a variety of problems but generally meant a wasting away. Simply said, Maggie wore herself out.[11]

Journalist Henry Watterson saw Joe shortly afterward. "He was passing through Washington with the little brood of children she had left him," wrote Watterson. "The young father was aghast by the sudden tragedy which had come upon him. It made the saddest spectacle I had ever seen, a scene of silent grief, of unutterable helplessness with a haunting power."[12]

The war intruded on everyone, even widowers, and Joe discussed it with friends. The comedian believed that William Seward, Lincoln's secretary of state, was dead wrong to think the war would be brief. Joe believed that "war between men of such courage and determination as his countrymen would last for years, and that for himself, he would have no part or share in it. He would not fight with brother against brother."[13]

"I am not a warrior," he confessed. "I cannot bring myself to engage in bloodshed, or to take sides. It may seem to you unpatriotic, and it is, I know, unheroic. I am not a hero. I am, I hope, an artist. My world is the world of art, and I must be true to that. It is my patriotism, my religion."[14]

Joe had taken a beating over the past year. "I felt myself growing very old," he recalled, "an old young man." His heart broken, his health failing, his career sputtering, he needed a change. He needed a place where he could restore mind, body, and spirit and escape the war as well. The answer came to him in a word. Australia.

On November 6, 1861, the day Jefferson Davis was formally elected president of the Confederacy, Joe sailed from San Francisco for Sydney. He did not return to the United States until the war ended.[15]

JOHN WILKES BOOTH was not the only family member to have his fortune told. Edwin and his manager Ben Baker were traveling to Wheeling, Virginia (now West Virginia) for an engagement when their coach broke down. Seeing a Romani camp nearby, they wandered over. The requisite "old hag" read Edwin's palm. She predicted "all sorts of good things" for him. Pleased, Edwin joined the travelers for a supper of the uncertain contents of their black pot.[16]

Edwin knew that things *were* going well for him. Mollie was a loving and supportive wife. Badeau continued a devoted friend. Together, they helped him to stay clear of liquor. The critic's advice? Drink water! "For God's sake, don't desert so true a friend," urged Badeau.[17]

Wife and friend also helped him seize an opportunity. After Junius stumbled in the 1830s as the most brilliant star of the dramatic profession, Edwin Forrest took over. Forrest was a tall and powerfully built actor with good looks and a beautiful voice. He owned the stage as a gladiator, rebel leader, or Indian chief. But times change, tastes change, and Edwin Booth's more sensitive characterizations found receptive audiences.[18]

Acting was learned, not in a school, but through an apprenticeship of small roles. "Muffins," as novices were called, moved up if they had the right stuff. Edwin had his first lessons as a child while serving as companion of his father. It's wrong to say he studied with him. More properly, he *studied him.* "It was while standing in the entrance, waiting for him to come off the stage, when I was to hand him some property or make some change in his costume, that I learned most of the parts I am now playing," he told fellow actor William Seymour. "Watching my father, I imbibed the lines of the great characters I act."[19]

In the theatrical year following his marriage—from September 1860 to June 1861—Edwin played sixteen individual roles. Half were major Shakespearian characters, half standard melodramatic heroes. Cutting back on touring, he confined himself solely to Boston, New York, Philadelphia, and Baltimore. On occasion he went head-to-head with Forrest in the same city, once in the same role on the same evening. "Good voice, good eyes, and his father's name," grumbled the aging rival.[20]

Reviews were excellent in Boston, and he was fond of that city. New York opinion was mixed, as some found him too sentimental. "He is a Hamlet to please schoolgirls and very young men," complained *Frank Leslie's Illustrated Weekly.*[21]

"Nearly all the women are in raptures about him," playgoer Emilie Cowell confided in her diary, "and I heard many expressions such as, 'Well, now, ain't he pretty' and 'Oh, there he is again. I don't care for anything when he is not there.' "[22] But Edwin's acting was intelligent and believable. At times he performed as if there were no audience present, and he was alone with the other actors onstage. That was a great achievement. "Fortune has placed me in (for my years) a high and, many think, an enviable position," he wrote a friend. When it lays out such a path, that path must be followed.[23]

IF FORREST FELT Edwin at his heels, did Edwin feel John Wilkes? After an unsuccessful first year in Philadelphia, John moved on to Richmond. John T. Ford, a fellow Baltimorean and family friend who managed the Marshall Theatre in the future Confederate capital, hired him for the resident acting company. This company of about two dozen actors, dancers, and singers played in support of traveling stars whom Ford contracted to visit. John was the theater's "Second Walking Gentleman." As such, he was not the theater's young lover and hero; he played that actor's butler, groom, or delivery man.

John was young—only twenty—and had a lot to learn. "A country-looking boy," recalled Harry Langdon, the Marshall's leading man. "His clothes, style, and everything were countryfied." The Maryland farm clung to him. So did a mediocre education. Langdon saw promise, however, and helped him study his lines. He also got John a grammar book and had him memorize and pronounce a certain number of words from it each day. There was progress, but John's roles continued to be small. He was eager for better.[24]

In this period John played under his middle name of Wilkes. It was a family name, made famous by a distant cousin John Wilkes, a political radical of the 1760s and lord mayor of London. John was proud of the Wilkes connection, but he used it as a stage name to avoid burdensome comparisons with his father and brother. He also intended to be his own person. Ford felt that John had a sense of individuality so intense it was irrational at times.[25]

Edwin came to Richmond in the fall of 1858 for three weeks of performances. The visit meant better supporting roles for John. On October 5, he played Horatio to Edwin's Hamlet. Horatio was Hamlet's best friend, so this was an important part that kept the younger brother onstage for much of the play. When the curtain fell, playgoer Ned Alfriend and the rest of the audience clamored for Edwin to come forward and be acknowledged. The curtain ran back up and the star came downstage. He brought John along with him, holding him by the hand. Pointing to his brother, Edwin said, "I think he has done well. Don't you?" Cries of "Yes! Yes!" sounded, "and thunders of applause."[26]

Edwin was handsome, Alfriend thought, but John more so. He was taller, stronger, and possessed "marvelously intellectual and beautiful eyes, with great symmetry of features, an especially fine forehead, and curly black hair." He was a fine elocutionist and his voice was as beautiful as Edwin's. John had chosen the right career, Alfriend concluded. "His ability was unquestionable, his future assured."

The brothers' father had commenced his American career in Richmond in 1821, so the family had a generation of friends in the city. Edwin, in earlier visits, added more. But even if John's name had been unknown, he would have flourished here. He had what Alfriend termed "a quality for social success." "With men," the friend explained, "John Wilkes was dignified in demeanor, bearing himself with insouciant care and grace, and was a brilliant talker. With women, he was a man of irresistible fascination by reason of his superbly handsome face, conservational brilliancy, and a peculiar halo of romance with which he invested himself."[27]

Many young professionals like Alfriend were members of Richmond militia companies. Theatrical life precluded John joining. Like the militiamen, however, he was outraged by John Brown's antislavery raid at Harpers Ferry, Virginia, on October 16, 1859. And, like them, he was pleased when Brown was captured and sentenced to hang on December 2. The day before the execution, the *Richmond Dispatch* editorialized a common feeling: "Old Brown says he is ready to die. The abolitionists say they want a martyr. The conservatives think he ought to be hung. And the Virginians will swing him off with great gratification. We never heard of a public execution which promised so much satisfaction to everybody concerned."[28]

When it appeared that Northerners might try to rescue Brown, militia rushed to secure the jail where he was held. John left the theater to join them. He was welcomed and was made a noncommissioned officer.[29] On the morning of the execution he marched with Alfriend's Richmond Grays under its flag depicting the Virginia state seal, showing a fallen tyrant and the phrase "Sic Semper Tyrannis" ("Ever thus to tyrants"), the slogan he later shouted after shooting Lincoln at Ford's Theatre.

Stationed thirty feet from the gallows, the young actor had an exceptionally good view as the old abolitionist dropped to his death. The sight sickened him. Though satisfied the execution was just, John found the hanging difficult to watch. He grew pale and said, "I would like a good, stiff drink of whiskey."[30]

If anger is a political philosophy, John's bedrock principle was a hatred of abolitionists like Brown. He was not, at this point in his life, a classic "negrophobe," one whose every thought was characterized by a fear and hatred of Black people. Just as he had with the Halls, the African American tenants at the family farm, John might treat individual Blacks well enough, but he dismissed the race as insignificant. They were the chips on the table; they were not the game.

Slavery had been around for hundreds of years. What was new and unsettling to John was the sympathy for slaves in the North and rhetoric about them that threatened the nation's unity. Adding knives to words, Brown was the worst Yankee in the bunch. He was a freak and a fanatic. And yet John admired him. The old radical had lionlike courage and an indomitable will. He made the entire country stop and take notice of him and his cause. He fought his fight and stared at death with the grit of a dime-novel hero. John believed one could be a murderer (as he labeled Brown) and also be "the grandest character of this century."[31] What that meant for the future can be imagined.

John returned with the other soldiers to Richmond two days after Brown's execution. When he showed up at the theater, big trouble waited. He had left the cast without permission. Caught up in the excitement, the young actor simply took off. George Kunkel, the manager, was furious, and he fired John on the spot when he reappeared. Word of the dismissal reached the soldiers returning from the execution. A large number of them gathered, marched through the city streets, called out the manager, and *demanded* he reinstate John. Startled, Kunkel complied.[32]

John's Richmond years were the turning point of his life. He made good progress in his profession. He was popular onstage. He was admired off it for "a life that seemed so full of joy and promise," as a friend phrased it. Politically, he was at home. "John was always an intense Southerner in all his feelings and thoughts," recalled Alfriend. The camaraderie and sense of purpose he experienced during the Brown crisis led to a strong identification with the people of Richmond.

John had never lived or acted north of the Mason-Dixon line except for the one unsuccessful year in Philadelphia. Knowing nothing else, he was remarkably insular compared to his well-traveled father, or even to his brothers June and Edwin.

"He was in absolute sympathy and harmony with his [Southern] surroundings," wrote Edwin's friend Francis Wilson. "Indeed, it would have been strange had it been otherwise."[33]

In Richmond, John liked to say, he had been reborn.[34]

"I GO PRYING into all sorts of places and frequent every corner of Manhattan," wrote Adam Badeau. "I am likely to find out whatever there is of the queer, quaint, or passing strange. I may tell you of things that some of you would otherwise rather dream not of." Under the pen name "Vagabond," he contributed essays to the *Sunday Times*. He wrote about authors, composers, dramatists, preachers, orators, artists, and male dancers. His essays presented Badeau as a sophisticated man-about-town. In one piece he confessed to a fondness for skinny-dipping in the ocean where a water nymph embraced him. Three articles dealt with Edwin. Their language led one reader to speculate that "Vagabond" was a woman.[35]

The war offered a chance at greater things, but Badeau fretted about enlisting. He had poor vision, attributed to excessive reading as a child, and he was dependent on his glasses. With his nearsightedness he might not fare well at the front. Then there was Edwin to consider. How would his friable friend carry on without his presence and advice?[36]

Edwin had plans that did not include Badeau, however, and he urged his friend to head to the sound of the guns. When a Union expeditionary force captured Port Royal, South Carolina, during the first winter of the war, an opportunity appeared. Badeau went to Port Royal and became editor of *The New South*, a weekly newspaper for Northern soldiers and sailors. Its goal, he wrote, was "to strengthen the hands of the government and to incite the courage and fortify the endurance of its defenders. The one great object of us all is the suppression of the Rebellion." His first issue contained a notice of Willie Lincoln's funeral.[37]

Meanwhile, Edwin developed an important new friendship. Richard

Cary was a broad-shouldered young man with deep-set, hooded eyes placed in an egg-shaped head. He had a moat of brown curls below a balding dome, a handsome beard, and a warm smile. He was three years Edwin's junior.

Cary had been a commission merchant in New Orleans. His business failed with the outbreak of the war, and he came home to Boston. His family were city blue bloods. His sister Mary was married to Professor Cornelius C. Felton, a future Harvard president. Sister Lizzie, later the first president of Radcliffe College, was married to Louis Agassiz, a world-famous naturalist. Some money attached to the family, but not great wealth, and it distinguished itself instead by education, civic-mindedness, family affection, and strong personalities.[38]

To Edwin, viewed from the rough precincts of the Booth family history,

Richard Cary. *"In my heart there is no man holds a prouder place,"* Edwin Booth *wrote of Bostonian Richard Cary. After Cary was killed at the battle of Cedar Mountain in 1862, Booth sought his spirit at séances.*

the Carys were amazing, and he and Mary happily joined them for a holiday in Nahant on Massachusetts Bay. The family had a stone cottage there with a broad piazza overlooking the water. The house's rooms were crammed with Agassiz's marine specimens. Edwin was intimidated by the celebrated scientist and by Felton, a brilliant Greek linguist, and anxious about meeting them. "Dear boy," laughed Cary, "they're just like other men."[39]

Edwin and Richard seemed mismatched as friends. Edwin was slim, dark, and domestic. Richard was solid, fair, and footloose. The Bostonian's life had been one of adventure among Southern slave owners and Western miners where the stakes thrown on the table were often one's own physical self, and he lived full-bore, come what may. Edwin, embarrassed by his father's excesses, was naturally cautious. But they were alike younger sons in large families. Both had cheerful mothers who were generous and kind and down-to-earth fathers who were intelligent and ambitious. Moreover, Richard and his wife Helen had recently had a baby while Mollie had just told Edwin she was pregnant.

An intimacy quickly developed between the two men. It was said they were like David and Jonathan, a pair of biblical characters knit soul-to-soul. "In my heart there is no man holds a prouder place than Richard Cary," Edwin wrote him.[40]

They spoke of establishing a model theater with a modernized stage and historically accurate productions. Cary would handle the business end of things while Edwin would control the acting, producing, and directing.[41]

Then came the war. Within weeks of the rebel attack on Fort Sumter in April 1861, Cary was wearing blue as captain of Company G, Second Massachusetts Volunteer Infantry Regiment. One hot summer day Edwin and Mollie drove out to visit him at Camp Andrew, a training facility located south of Boston. Oddly enough, the camp was on a farm owned by James Freeman Clarke, the minister whom Junius Booth had asked to officiate at the pigeon funeral in 1834. At the outbreak of the war Clarke offered the site to Lincoln, and the president eagerly accepted.[42]

The Booths had trouble finding the place. They got lost on the way, and when they finally arrived—sunburned, dust-covered, and headachy—they learned that Cary had already left for the front. Edwin wrote him of his disappointment and worry. "I cannot tell you how sad I feel at your going away without bidding you goodbye. There is no need of protestation, I trust, on my part, to assure you of the regret, the anxiety, the hope, the fear I feel for you."[43]

Changes were in store for Edwin as well. Theater managers felt that the war would ruin their business. The public would have little appetite for make-believe and tinsel amid war's grim reality. It seemed almost obscene to seek amusement in a time of suffering, and no one would pay to see the pretend sorrows of actors when real ones were free in the streets.

Maybe it was time for Edwin to fulfill an ambition: go to London and try his luck there. Every actor dreamed of starring in the large and lucrative mother-city of the English-language stage. Success there would open every stage door in America. "It is the grand turning point of my career," he believed.[44]

The trip would also allow Edwin to escape the war. He was just as apolitical as Joe Jefferson—he had never even voted—and like Joe he intended to put some miles between himself and trouble.

"My dear Dick," he wrote in a farewell letter to Cary. "How I long to grasp your hand ere I go, but fate has ordained it otherwise. I hold you proudly, Dick. I am proud of your friendship. God bless you, my boy! God bless you! Adieu. May God protect you!"[45]

On August 7, 1861, as the nation lapsed into war, he and Mollie sailed from Boston on the Royal Mail Ship *Arabia* for England.

JOHN WAS NOW the only Booth left on the American stage. He starred in the Deep South and small Northern cities before the war broke out. Results were mixed and complications many. In Columbus, Georgia, he was accidently shot in the thigh by his manager. In Montgomery, Alabama, he was threatened for opinions considered too Northern. In Albany, New York, he was threatened for opinions considered too Southern. He fell on his stage dagger, slicing the muscle under his right arm. Then he was stabbed in the forehead by an actress with whose affections he trifled. Was John truly the darling of misfortune, as unlucky as he feared?[46]

In Albany, John had his first encounter of sorts with Lincoln. He was playing an engagement at the Gayety Theatre where he so resembled his father that local spiritualists (like Nettie Colburn) swore they saw old Junius hovering above him, showering the son with conception and soul. About four in the afternoon of Monday, February 18, 1861, Lincoln and his party arrived in Albany en route to his inauguration in Washington. An immense crowd greeted him. Artillery boomed, flags waved, and cheers sounded along the streets. Lincoln was escorted about the city, passing the Stanwix, John's hotel, before settling in at the Delavan House on Broadway. Since Albany had not voted for Lincoln in the election, John was confused by his reception. "Is this not a Democratic city?" he asked Jacob Culyer, the Gayety's treasurer. "Democratic? Yes, but disunion, no!" Cuyler replied.

That night, while Lincoln received citizens at his hotel, John played the villain Pescara in *The Apostate* at the Gayety eight blocks away. The two men did not meet. They were on different tracks. "How little did either then dream of the tragedy that was to link their names together in all coming time," wrote Culyer's friend Henry Phelps.[47]

Honoring his promise to his mother to stay out of the rebel army, John spent the summer of 1861 improving his acting. The rewards were immediate. Over the ensuing fall, winter, and spring—the 1861–62 theatrical year—he starred in St. Louis, Chicago, Baltimore, and New York to increasing acclaim and receipts. His three-week Manhattan engagement featured *Richard III*, and he was declared better at the role than Edwin or anyone else in America. "The American stage still has a Booth," proclaimed one critic. "The reputation of his father, and of his brother, now in England, will—we predict—be equaled by his own. In word, look, gesture, tone, motion, and position, the youngest Booth reminded us of the high-toned actors of days gone by."[48]

The doomsayers had been proven wrong about the war ruining the entertainment business. In times of crisis people crave escape, and they flooded into the theaters. "While at Antietam dead men lay rotting in the fields," wrote Edwin, "the theaters were crowded to their flag-draped roofs."[49] Managers had never made so much money, nor had John.

Across town at the Old Bowery Theatre, Dan Bryant and his brothers were raking it in as minstrels. White entertainers, they blackened their faces and did musical and comic routines poking fun at Black Americans. (Minstrelsy was so popular and successful that T. D. Rice, who had dumped three-year-old Joe Jefferson out of a bag onto the stage to "jump Jim Crow," wore twenty-dollar gold pieces for jacket buttons.) Dan Bryant was a dancer, singer, actor, and manager. His numbers included "Shoo Fly," a song-and-dance piece, and "Dixie," written expressly for his company in 1859 and a favorite with Lincoln.

Gentle and congenial, Bryant was inexhaustible fun. Like John he was an antiwar Democrat. The actor loved being around him.[50]

John gave the merry showman a beautiful silver pocket flask, shaped to fit the hip and gracefully ornamented with a grapevine design. It was inscribed "J. Wilkes Booth to Dan Bryant, April 8, 1862." In return Bryant gave him a diamond stickpin, which the actor wore on his undershirt. Detectives found it there when John was shot to death on April 26, 1865, and it was one of the means by which they identified his body.[51]

Bryant and his fellow minstrels loved jewels. When Pony Moore, the London showman, traveled to America, he paid his way by bringing stones for sale to his burnt-cork brethren. He once brought a large emerald ring set with diamonds that shone in the light like a chandelier at an evening dinner party. Moore sold it to Luke West. West fell gravely ill and gave the ring to Matt Peel in remembrance of their friendship. West recovered after giving the stone away, but Peel died. Then West died. Peel's widow Mag sold it to Hiram Rumsey, a man of remarkable health. Rumsey went to England, lost a fortune, returned home, and died.

The Gravestone, as it began to be called, was just getting started. George Christy, who bought the stone from Rumsey, had it made into a scarf pin. He sported it up and down Broadway, had an epileptic fit, and died. Sher Campbell took it in payment for a loan and brought it to Bryant's theater. From time to time he lent it to Bryant, Jim Unsworth, and Nelse Seymour to wear onstage. All three died, as did Campbell, who never even wore the stone.

"That's an accursed bit of property," exclaimed Seymour's brother Harry. Tony Pastor replied, "Its work is finished!" Together the men placed the death-dealing Gravestone on the kitchen hearth, smashed it to pieces, and fed its glittering shards to the fire.[52]

"IT IS HARD to leave the comforts of a home," Richard Cary wrote to his wife Helen, "hard to part from mother and sisters, and harder yet to leave behind a loved and loving wife and child, to go forth battling for one's country [only] to find a sudden and bloody grave. Yet I, who have felt the pains of all except the last (and God may spare me that)—I am more than ever convinced that in coming as I did, I did what was simply my duty. What I would do again with alacrity. If the truth were told, most men set too high a value on this life."[53]

He was ordered to deliver to Illinois a detachment of sailors drawn from the regiment and assigned to Mississippi River gunboats. Naturally, each company captain took the opportunity to dump his biggest headache into this unit, and Cary had his hands full with them. The men drank, fought, stole, and disobeyed him. On occasion he ordered them around at gunpoint. They were so unruly he needed help from the Baltimore city police to handle them. While he was in the city, John was acting at the Holliday Street Theatre, and the captain caught his performance. He walked out after an hour. The younger brother had received favorable notices in the press, but Cary was Edwin's friend and showed it. "He rants," complained the officer. "His face has no more expression than a board fence." He found John's voice very much like Edwin's, however.[54]

Back with his company, Cary was swept up by events. After a Union threat to Richmond eased in the summer of 1862, rebel forces moved north in the state. Stonewall Jackson and A. P. Hill were two of General Robert. E. Lee's top lieutenants in the Army of Northern Virginia. Opposing them was Nathaniel Banks, commander of a corps to which Cary's

Second Massachusetts belonged. These forces collided near Culpeper at Cedar Mountain, a forested knob from which the rebels enjoyed a view of the countryside. "At the foot of this picturesque mountain the freak of fate or the madness of man located a frightful scene of carnage and despair," wrote George Alfred Townsend, war correspondent for the *New York Herald*.[55]

Saturday, August 9, 1862, was intensely hot. Cary—too sick to march—was determined to go with his men, and he caught a ride in an ambulance. Noon found him and his company near the edge of a wood on the right wing of the army, the mountain before them. They stopped to rest. Some soldiers made coffee; others slept. In midafternoon an artillery duel opened, a sign that things were serious. The rattle of musketry grew louder.

At about five o'clock orders came for the Second to move out and disable the rebel guns that were doing the devil's work from their elevated placements. The men marched rapidly down a hill, across a clearing, through a bog, over a ravine, and into a wood before finally emerging onto the edge of a wheat field. The field had recently been cut, and shocks of wheat stood about it erect as sentinels. Cary halted here and stationed his men—red in the face, gasping for breath, and exhausted—behind a low rail fence.

Concealed on densely wooded hillsides nearby were great numbers of the enemy. They unleashed a torrent of slug, buckshot, and bullet from the front and side of Cary's position. "The storm tore through them," recalled General George H. Gordon, Cary's brigade commander. "A terrible, dreadful, remorseless fire that came like a whirlwind. The crash was terrific. It was indescribable." The regimental colors were shot through, shaft shattered, and flagstaff eagle blown away. The line withered. Amid roar and smoke Cary was struck in the leg and collapsed. He was dragged to the cover of a nearby oak tree. His command clung to the fence and fought on. "I have witnessed many battles during this war, but I have seen none where the tenacious obstinacy of the American character was so fully displayed," wrote journalist Townsend.

Darkness put an end to the fight. Thirty minutes had done butcher's work to the regiment. Of the twenty-three officers in the Second who went forward, only seven came back unhurt. Enlisted men suffered heavily, too. "Never in the entire history of the Second Massachusetts had its percentage of loss been so great," wrote Gordon. "Not at Winchester, Antietam, Chancellorsville—not at Gettysburg, Resaca, the Atlanta Campaign, or the March to the Sea—was the sacrifice so large."[56]

As the shattered Second withdrew from the field, Cary was left behind along with the other gravely wounded men and the dead. The moon was full that night and the sky clear. It was as easy to see as if it were daylight. Cary took out his miniature of his wife Helen. She was a small woman with delicate features set in an oval face. Light brown hair. Striking gray eyes. Lovely. Cary had been lucky.[57]

The captain heard a noise nearby—someone crawling toward him. It was Roland Williston, the company's first sergeant. Williston had a frightful wound in the thigh and another in the hand, but when he saw Cary's condition he decided to stay with him. He would not let his captain die alone.

Cary seemed more concerned about his wife than himself. "If anything should happen to me, it would kill Helen," gasped Cary, his last words.

Shadowy figures appeared among the wheat shocks. Confederate soldiers crept slowly over the field to collect their wounded and to take prisoners and supplies. There were weapons to be had under the oak, but no prisoners. Cary was dying and Williston too hurt to haul off. The rebels stripped the captain of his valuables. Williston begged them to leave Cary's ring and locket in order that he might get the items to the dying man's wife. "Their hearts melted," Williston later said, and they agreed. A second group of rebels gave Cary water and found a piece of wood upon which he could rest his head.

A truce on Monday allowed burial parties onto the field. Gordon and his aide Robert Gould Shaw (later colonel of the all-Black 54th Massachusetts Infantry Regiment) found Cary among dozens of other corpses. His pockets were turned inside out and his papers scattered around him among the leaves. Cary's hands were folded over his chest, his head turned to the right. He looked like he was asleep. Williston told them he had died the preceding afternoon. "The expression of his face was as sweet and happy as an angel's and my first feeling was that I wanted to stoop down and kiss him," wrote Shaw. "I could have stood and looked for a long time."

Shaw clipped a lock of Cary's hair and gave it, along with the ring and locket, to Eugene Shelton, Helen's brother and a fellow officer in the Second Regiment. Shelton sent them north with a note: "Tell Helen Richard died without a murmur and without pain."[58]

EDWIN WAS IN London on the day of the battle. At breakfast with Benjamin Moran, an American diplomat, "he complained, as all American actors do, of unfair treatment at the hands of the profession in England." Scheming managers, stage rivals, and bad feeling over the war against the South made this the wrong time to make a mark. Moran believed that Edwin, "a pale young man," had the tools to succeed—"a wonderfully intellectual face, a fine marble forehead, long raven hair, and an expression of great beauty."[59]

He was ready to return home and return "a poorer but a wiser man," as he had written Cary. With Edwin and Mollie came Edwina, their baby, born shortly before Christmas 1861. Edwin had draped an American flag over the birth bed so that the child could be "born under the stars and stripes."[60]

The couple sailed from Liverpool on August 16, 1862. News of Cedar Mountain passed them going in the other direction. Upon arriving in New York on the afternoon of August 27, they went immediately to Philadelphia to see Mary Ann, Edwin's mother. Returning to New York, they checked back into the Fifth Avenue Hotel, where Mollie learned of Cary's death in a letter from his sister Mary Felton. When she shared the news with Edwin, "he wept like a child."[61]

"Richard was always in my eyes the noblest of men," Edwin wrote the Carys, "and his conduct in the face of death proves that I was right in my judgment of him. He was a hero born. He acted as Richard Cary only could act—nobly, unselfishly, bravely. I knew it would be so. I knew that he would be loved by all about him. And I knew that if he fell, he would be found contented—grand in death. With dearest love for you all, believe me ever your friend and servant, and your brother's lover, Edwin."[62]

Cary was a rare exception to a hard fact. Edwin meant more to his friends than they did to him. It was terribly frustrating. "While he yearned for intimates, he was disqualified by nature to choose or attract them," wrote an old acquaintance. "A desire for confidants ever possessed him but insurmountable buttresses, inherited from an erratic father and a shy mother, always stood in the way. There was a heritage of queerness."[63]

Delighted to have the Booths home, Lillian Woodman noticed they had changed. Mollie had a child, a French maid, and less time for those fun little whispered confidences. She was also less deferential to her husband and therefore less influential upon him, particularly on the old problem of drinking. Edwin was displaying quite a taste for wine. The Booths remained friendly to Lillian, despite the changes, and evidently didn't share the opinion of a mutual friend that he could not stomach her "except on a raft at sea with no other provisions in sight."[64]

She was in their apartment when Edwin gave Mollie a beautifully painted miniature of himself.

"When Death takes you, my best beloved," she said to him, "nothing will be more solace than this. I shall wear it eternally upon my heart."

Lillian found it odd that Mollie, who was only twenty-two, thought of death. "She had all that the world could give, yet her look held more of longing than of joy." And why was she certain Edwin would die before her? "Death could not be so cruel as to take me from him," was her answer. "He needs me."[65]

Edwin and Mollie attended a party at the home of Richard Henry Stoddard and his wife Elizabeth. Richard, a poet and editor, and Elizabeth, a novelist, dispensed cakes and ale at a literary salon in their shabby rooms on Tenth Street. The company was distinguished. Among those present were Bayard Taylor, famed travel writer whom Lincoln appointed to the American legation in Saint Petersburg; Fitz Hugh Ludlow, journalist and author of *The Hasheesh Eater*; Edmund Clarence Stedman, poet and amateur scientist; and Launt Thompson, a promising sculptor. These were talented and creative people who accepted Edwin as a fellow artist, not just an entertainer.[66]

Edwin was so pleased with the evening that he invited everyone to a soiree of his own later in the month. Mollie asked Lillian to help her get ready. The young friend dove in and was so busy that day that she didn't have time to braid her long blonde hair. When the guests arrived, she felt very drab in her plain mouse-colored dress, and she shrank back.

The Stoddards came with their crowd and were joined by Albert Bierstadt, the most talked-about artist in America. He had a painting trip to the Rockies in mind and was taking Ludlow along with him. Everyone was talking about that or about Richard Stoddard's new narrative poem, *The King's Bell*. Not outdone, Elizabeth Stoddard had recently authored *The Morgensons*, the story of a young woman's struggle for autonomy against the social and religious norms of the day. Edmund Clarence Stedman was at work on a new book of poems dedicated to Richard Stoddard, and Launt Thompson had just finished a portrait medallion of the poet Tom Aldrich, who was also present, from which a frontispiece would be engraved for Tom's latest book. Socializing with these people, the city's cultural avant-garde, made Lillian's head spin.[67]

For the soiree, Mollie wore a light silk dress of subdued color. It was fastened high at the neck with a beautiful broach. The ornament contained a large opal Edwin had given her. Friends shuddered. An opal boded the early death of the wearer.[68]

GHOST KISSES

"Gould! Coming up!" exclaimed the elder Booth, running into Edwin's room. "Say I'm out." Without another word the father dove under the bed.

Gould was sculptor Thomas Ridgeway Gould. Idolizing the great actor, he had become a pest. Edwin greeted the visitor warmly, lying as best he could, while Gould, who had seen Junius rushing up the stairs, was puzzled not to find him. Nevertheless, the two talked for several minutes, then the conversation lapsed. When the silence continued, Junius thrust his head out from under the bed and asked, "Is that infernal bore gone yet?"[1]

It was Junius who was gone, dying shortly after in 1852, and Gould who lived on to become Edwin's friend. Gould turned to sculpture in midlife when the war swept away his fortune. Poorer but happier than he had ever been, he set to work. He is best known today for his bronze of Kamehameha I, the first Hawaiian monarch, a casting of which stands in front of the ʻIolani Palace in Honolulu. His *Ghost in Hamlet*, chiseled in high relief on an oval sunk into a square, is haunting, while his *Satan*, depicting a face with snake-like coils of hair and a cruel mouth, made the evil one appear a greedy Wall Street speculator—the very type of person that caused the sculptor's business misfortune.[2]

Gould called on Edwin one day not long after the actor's return from

England. The artist was creating a bust of Edwin and had a second commission from him for a Michelangelo, but this visit was about something else. Gould was a spiritualist. At a séance, the spirit of the elder Booth had contacted him. Friends like Gould believed that the father had "presentiments which sometimes seemed to link him with the Far Beyond." Now that Junius was stationed there permanently, he was a font of information for the living. The dead actor informed him that Joe Booth, youngest of the sons, was in Australia. Gould was guileless and sincere, but it seemed impossible to the Booths that Joe was on the other side of the world.[3]

Until it didn't. Joe Booth actually *was* in Australia. He had been John's agent when the latter played in New York in March 1862. They quarreled, and Joe disappeared. He was depressed at the time, and John feared he might attempt suicide. Joe had, in fact, sailed to England to join Edwin. Then, without telling anyone, he left for Australia. While the family looked anxiously for him, he was at work as a clerk at a sheep and cattle station in the northern part of the country. Later, he traveled to San Francisco, where older brother June, acting and managing in the city, got him a job carrying letters for Wells Fargo.

"I would not say so to Mother, but I am afraid he is not sound in mind," June wrote Edwin. "Mind, I do not say positive insanity, but a crack that way—which Father in his highest had and which, I fear runs more or less thro' the male portion of our family, myself included."[4]

Sister Asia's husband Clarke was in London at the same time as Edwin and Joe. Failing to find his fortune there, the comedian returned home. Life struck Clarke as a joke, and he put that observation to work onstage in the buffoonish characters of low comedy. When he bobbed about as a drunk in a red fright wig or, dressed as an absentminded cook, placed food on dining room chairs where guests were about to sit, playgoers roared with laughter and dollars poured in.

Clarke and Asia had two small children, and John loved playing with them. "He lays on the floor and rolls over with them like a child," the sister wrote. "He laughs outrageously at me for having babies. He can't realize it, he says, to think that our Asia should be a mother." John disliked Clarke, however, once choking him when the comedian lambasted Confederate president Jefferson Davis.[5]

Asia had not been wedded to Clarke long before she wondered if she had made a mistake. Maybe she should have become a nun. "All my life some loving hand has seemed beckoning me there," she confided to her friend Jean Anderson. Asia had attended a school run by the Sisters of the Carmelite Convent in Baltimore. The nuns, dressed in their coarse brown woolen habits, lived a demanding life of fasting and prayer. They practiced vegetarianism, slept on straw mats, and kept, Asia observed, "a small wooden skull in their cells to keep Death, if not in their dreams, at least in their bed-rooms." Under their influence she became a Catholic. It was a way of dealing with the shame and embarrassment of her father's bigamy and the knowledge that she and her siblings were born out of wedlock. "I have tried so hard to keep free from all taint of that which is low and vulgar," she wrote Jean.[6]

She may have given John the Catholic medal he was wearing at the time of his death. It was said to be an Agnus Dei token blessed by the pope. To him the small copper medal, worn on a ribbon, was little more than a good-luck charm since, like his father, he was a freethinker in religious matters. "He tied himself down to no one dogma or creed," said Robert Brigham, a friend. "He believed in an all-powerful head and master of the universe, but reserved for himself the right to think and live according to the teaching of the Bible and of nature, as he himself understood it, and to draw his own conclusions as to the meaning and intent of the Almighty."[7]

John was an original. He was generous, ardent, impetuous, and proud. Wild at times, he was not vicious. Like Junius, he drank; unlike his father, he didn't drink to the point of acting bizarrely on the streets or the stage. He was charming and authentic and had an army of friends in and out of the profession. One of them, Joseph Howard of the *New York Times*, wrote, "He was as lovable as he was bright and beautiful. He had more brains in his little finger than the rest of the Booth men put together. He was a chip off the old block, with the fire and enthusiasm and lack of balance that characterized the father."[8]

Other traits were displayed during a summer jaunt in the New England countryside. In the village of Fitzwilliam, New Hampshire, John joined a party forming at the village hotel to climb nearby Mount Monadnock. The mountain is a prominent peak, dominating the landscape, and was a popular hike. Because of the summit's remoteness, the hotel provided transportation to a jump-off point, box lunches, and a guide.

As the group ascended through the maple and birch lower forest, John fell in with a young woman wearing a Parisian-made Alpine climbing dress. Talkative and energetic, she was good company as the hardwood gave way to spruce and the spruce to open boulders and rocky slopes. The trail grew steep, and John complimented his companion on her stamina.

When everyone gathered near the broad open summit, the guide cautioned them that the previous week a rattlesnake had been killed at a slab farther up. John laughed and christened the spot Rattlesnake Peak. The young woman instantly desired to have lunch there. John was game, so the two scrambled on.

At the top they could see much of southern New Hampshire as well as parts of Vermont, Massachusetts, and Connecticut. The spot was ideal for a picnic. Out came the sandwiches, chicken, pickles, and cold coffee. It was warm and sunny, and, although they could hear voices, they couldn't see the other hikers. They were quite alone.

The young woman, who recalled this adventure in an 1876 interview, never gave her name. She was a semi-professional singer of about John's age. Having spent several years in Europe, she was cultured, and the two talked knowledgeably about literature and art. Then the conversation drifted, as it always did with him, to politics and slavery. "His Southern proclivities [were] very sharply defined." She did not share them but was happy to let him talk. After all, "he struck me then as the handsomest man, without a single exception, I ever saw."

Realizing the hour, John suggested they start down. To their surprise, the other hikers, believing the couple were enjoying more than the scenery, had left without them, taking the guide. As if that weren't enough, the sky grew suddenly dark, and a blinding rain hit the mountain. Stumbling along, the pair emerged from the cleft of a gigantic boulder to realize they were lost.

"It thundered and lightninged, and the falling torrents had swollen the little mountain brooks and made the path we were on a tumultuously rushing stream," she remembered. "Our position was now one of no little peril, taking into consideration the electric discharges rattling about us, the danger of the rushing currents undermining rocks above our heads and beneath our feet, and the wind, which blew a perfect tempest, whipping off the dead branches of the immense trees that came crashing down around us."

John put his jacket over her shoulders, and they staggered on as best they could. "My escort treated me with all possible consideration and delicacy." Shaking with exhaustion, the couple reached the hotel at ten that night.

John took with him a souvenir of the day. His companion had picked up a gray stone with an odd streak of white. The streak looked like a snake. She gave it to him, and he had the stone set into a seal ring that he wore on the little finger of his right hand. He spoke mysteriously of his snake ring, saying it possessed a near-magical power over him.[9]

"I know some very precious things are hidden from common sight," he remarked.[10]

"BADEAU WAS A modest, slender, and delicate man of agreeable manners and high intelligence," wrote Lieutenant James H. Wilson. To his credit, Badeau wanted to be closer to the war than an editor's chair and became a field correspondent for the *New York Express*. Critics complained that the *Express* was little more than a throwaway read by commuters on trains, but it got Badeau to the front, where he made a favorable impression on Wilson, a topographical engineer based at Daufuskie Island, South Carolina. "He deservedly became a prime favorite with the staff," the officer recalled.

Wilson invited Badeau to tag along on a reconnaissance of rebel-held Savannah. Commandeering a large rowboat from a nearby plantation, Wil-

John Wilkes Booth's Ring. *The future assassin attributed an occult power to a ring he had made from a stone found on a hike of Mount Monadnock in New Hampshire. It had the pattern of a snake.*

son manned it with ten fugitive slaves as sailors and set out at night up New River. By sunrise they reached Hog Marsh, then waded three miles through its muck to a point where Wilson could observe the city's waterfront. After studying its defenses for several hours, he started back.

Unfortunately, the tide came in. It climbed and climbed and soon was waist high. A pocket compass kept them headed right, but the marsh flooded deeply, the reeds massed obstructively, and the men had not gone a mile before Badeau gave out. He simply couldn't take another step. Wilson and a fellow soldier put their shoulders under his arms and hauled him forward, "exhausting work, tiresome to the corporal and myself, but killing to Badeau, who cried piteously for water and even for a morsel of tobacco." They had none to give.

At one point the soldiers had to swim with him. Wilson pushed Badeau forward; the corporal grabbed him and paddled on. Too weak to care, Badeau told the men to leave him. Save themselves. Let his life close in this God-awful place and his body float down to kiss the ocean as a sacrifice to their cause. Shut up, replied Wilson. They struggled on, discovered their boat, and were rowed safely back to camp.[11]

Despite the misadventure, Badeau was ravenous for comradeship and wanted more. He wanted a commission. That was problematic. Badeau was short and stoop-shouldered, he was nearsighted, and he was unfamiliar with horses. A city boy, he also lacked the bush savvy essential to life in the field. "He hardly knew how to buckle a trunk strap," laughed Wilson. On the other hand, Badeau was well-educated, an able writer, and knew important people. He was certainly competent enough to fill out muster rolls and game enough for someone whom a strong wind might blow away.[12]

John Hay, the president's assistant secretary, arranged an interview for Badeau with Lincoln one morning before breakfast. Hay ushered him into the presidential office. Lincoln sat before a fire, "one of his long legs thrown over the arm of his chair and the other coiled and twisted in some extraordinary fashion as if there was more of it than he knew what to do with."

Badeau had seen Lincoln once before. On February 20, 1861, as the president-elect passed through New York on the way to his inauguration, the critic attended a performance of *Un Ballo in Maschera*, a Verdi opera, at the Academy of Music where Lincoln was the guest of honor. A hard-core Democrat, Badeau was not an admirer of the man from Illinois. In the 1860 presidential election the young New Yorker voted for the most conservative candidate, John C. Breckinridge, who became a Confederate general. That night he sat "with a party of men and women bitterly opposed to republicanism." But when the orchestra played "The Star-Spangled Banner," he rose and cheered for Lincoln with everyone else. "The scene showed that New York would subordinate politics to patriotism," said Badeau. It would support the Union, and so would he.

It was poignant to recall the evening, Badeau realized. *The Masked Ball* (in English) foreshadowed Lincoln's fate. It was about the assassination of an American political leader.[13]

Badeau handed the president letters from Wilson, General David Hunter, and others that detailed his service as a volunteer without rank or pay during the capture of Fort Pulaski, Georgia. "He looked over my papers wearily, as if he had such things thrust at him every hour of his life."

"Well," Lincoln asked, "what do you want me to do?"

"I want to be made a captain," replied Badeau.

Lincoln took his pen and wrote on the recommendations, "Let Mr. Badeau be made a captain. A. Lincoln."

Badeau tried to thank him, but the president had turned his attention elsewhere. The newest officer in the Union army left the room without another word.[14]

He ended up being given the rather attenuated title of "Additional Aide-de-Camp." Nevertheless, Badeau was exultant. "I trust we'll laugh and cry and live and fight and maybe die—brothers in arms," he wrote Wilson.[15]

Unfortunately, Badeau was assigned to Brigadier General Thomas W. Sherman. Called Tim by his friends, this officer (not to be confused with the more famous William Tecumseh Sherman) was an experienced and able commander. He possessed "a voice that startled you like an electric shock" and flashing blue eyes that followed up like a saber slash. Leading an army of mindless helots, he would have been the best general of the age. Commanding volunteers from a democratic society, Tim struggled, alienating everyone. "He turned out to be a martinet of violent and ungovernable temper," wrote Wilson. "Too exacting, too impatient, and too violent to get on with his troops."[16]

A born soldier like Tim took one look at Badeau and despised him. "Badeau was short and so were his legs. He wore spectacles, his hair and beard were trimmed in a style unfamiliar in the camps, and there was a freshness about his toilet and a general nattiness about his whole appearance regarded as marks of effeminacy and pretension," recalled an officer. "He was what we would term a 'dude.' He was, in fact, the laughingstock of our officers. Sherman frequently remarked to me that all he was good for was to entertain Southern ladies."[17]

NATHAN W. DANIELS was a former colonel of the 2nd Louisiana Native Guards, an African American infantry regiment in the Union army. Dismissed by General Banks for misuse of government property, he joined the hundreds of others who loitered in Washington in search of their next job. In short order Daniels became friends with Nettie Colburn and "Father Pierpont," fellow spiritualists evidently unconcerned about his checkered past.

The First Lady knew (or cared) little as well. She invited Daniels to the White House for an evening with herself, Tad, and their cousin John B. S. Todd. He brought Wella and Lizzie Pet Anderson, a husband-and-wife team of spirit artists. Lizzie Pet, born with second sight, supplied the emotional "battery" for her husband's trances. Wella supplied a Faber No. 2 lead pencil with which he drew rapidly, seemingly unconscious of his actions. Mary was delighted with the result. The couple were also full of news from Willie. Lizzie Pet told Mary the dead boy was present in the room. He was nearby, holding a vase of beautiful flowers for her. When the medium described the vase, the First Lady said it was one that her son had in his room at the time of his death.[18]

What was this? What actually happened here? Could those who indulged in such practices call themselves Christian? Or were they flirting with the unscriptural and the unholy?

"I hate spiritualism," said the Reverend T. De Witt Talmadge, an army chaplain. "It finds its victims in the troubled, the bankrupt, the sick and the bereft. Spiritualism takes advantage of a moment of weakness when the house is so lonely, the world so dark, and the separation so insufferable.

"Spiritualism says, 'We will open the future world. Your loved one can come back and talk to you.'

"What does God think of these delusions?" Talmadge asked. "He thinks so severely of them that he never speaks of them but with livid thunders of indignation." Adapting verses from Deuteronomy and First Samuel in the Bible, Talmadge continued, " 'There shall not be among you a consulter of familiar spirits, or wizard or necromancer, for thee that do these things are an abomination to the Lord. The soul of those who seek after such as have familiar spirits, and who go whoring after them, I will set myself against them and he shall be cut off from among his people.' "

God's commandment was plain, concluded Talmadge. "Be a spiritualist if you dare!"[19]

Mary was unconcerned by such warnings. She thought of herself as an entirely proper Christian. Raised in her parents' Presbyterian faith, she attended church throughout her life. As a child she went to the Second Presbyterian Church in her hometown of Lexington, Kentucky. Later, in Springfield, she attended the First Presbyterian Church and then, in

A Spiritualist Circle. *Séances were family affairs according to this 1853 cover title page for a song. A grandfather (his long hair denoting eccentricity) summons the spirits who push his grandson's chair off the floor.*

Washington, the New York Avenue Presbyterian Church. (The latter was formed from an earlier church established by the Reverend James Laurie, the grandfather of spiritualist Belle Miller.)[20]

The First Lady went to church nearly every Sunday. She attended services because that was what decent people did, just as they said grace before meals and prayers before bed. Church was a place to display one's respect for morality and higher things. It was also a place to be seen. This point was brought home to Mary early in life. There was no slipping in the back of her family sanctuary in Lexington. One had to enter the building facing the entire congregation as it stared forward from pews placed on ascending rows like seats in a theater. Church members formed a sort of audience to watch new arrivals come forward like players on a stage.[21]

Mary took care to look good on such occasions. Bettie Stuart, a cousin, recalled the Sunday in Springfield when Mary came to church exquisitely gowned in an ashes-of-roses silk dress "with satin bayardere [sic] stripes in rich folds spread over a voluminous hoop skirt." She wore a black lace shawl, secured at each shoulder with small gold pins, and a white bonnet decorated with white plumes. Her ensemble was completed with a collar of point lace and white kid gloves. Even when she was in mourning, fashion reigned. Her black flounces were of the highest quality and style.[22]

Unfortunately, Mary lacked a religious turn of mind to go with the finery. Proud, and unshakably sure of herself, she had none of the inborn humility of acquaintances like Fanny Henning, wife of Lincoln's intimate friend Joshua Speed. Mary loved life too much. Passionately attached to this world, she spent little time thinking about the next—until something like a death in the family stopped her short.

Then she floundered.

Her Christian faith taught her that her sons Eddie and Willie were in a better place now than when they were with her. Free of earthly suffering, they nestled in the arms of God. In this vein Mary wrote a friend, "The only comfort that remains to us is the blessed consolation that our beloved ones are rejoicing in their Heavenly home." But Mary was saying words whose comfort she didn't feel. She told Rebecca Pomroy, afflicted similarly with the loss of two children, that she would happily live on bread and water if she could only feel as accepting of God's will as the nurse did.[23]

Struggling with her losses, Mary seemed ready to argue with God. Her half-sister Emilie observed that the First Lady did not believe in "a passive acceptance of fate." She attempted "to divert predestination into more pleasant channels." The idea of a reunion in Heaven with her sons had limited appeal to her for a simple reason—she couldn't wait that long.

Mary turned to her own resources, like the ability to attune to things she couldn't possibly know or see. Emilie recalled an occasion in Springfield when the Lincolns attended a party, leaving the children home with a maid. During the evening, Mary grew anxious.

"Mr. Lincoln, we must go home!" the wife exclaimed. He brushed her off, but she insisted, and they left.

Arriving at home, "they found the house on fire, the maid fast asleep, and the children's lives in danger." That was an example of Mary's clairvoyant powers, felt Emilie.

Equally impressive was the First Lady's ability to beckon Willie's spirit. Sometimes the boy brought his brother Eddie with him. Twice he came with Aleck Todd, Mary's half-brother. The most popular of the Todd clan, Aleck was a Confederate officer killed early in the war near Baton Rouge. Willie told his mother that he loved this redheaded uncle, a likable young man only twenty-three when he died, and he spent much of the time in the spirit world with him. This was supernatural stuff, Emilie believed.[24]

Mary was no passive host to these ghostly visitors. She seemed to summon them, bringing herself into a trance state just like a medium. Through this ability and through her dreams, Mary was able to achieve what professional spiritualists termed "the unconscious celebration of somnambulist visitations."[25]

TWO BOOTHS, ONE nation. Since the brothers were trying to rob the same train, as it were, opportunities appeared limited, but things worked out after all. In the two theatrical years between Edwin's return to the United

States in 1862 and John's retirement from the stage in 1864, they never went head-to-head in the same city. Both traveled, but John, being younger and less established, had to tour more extensively. He acted in twice as many theaters as his brother, some in the Midwest like Chicago, Illinois, where Edwin never went, and some in small towns like New Haven, Connecticut, which Edwin disdained to visit. The war made it impossible for either to visit Richmond or act on a Confederate stage.

Edwin customarily opened with *Hamlet*; John opened with *Richard III*. In the former play Hamlet was buffeted about, tormented by conscience and indecision. In the latter Richard *was* decision, buffeting and tormenting others as he drove forward with no conscience at all. The brothers' choices of these roles revealed a lot. As with all fine acting, the parts channeled their personalities. A Boston critic caught it: "Edwin has more poetry, John Wilkes more passion. Edwin has more melody of movement and utterance, John Wilkes more energy and animation. Edwin is more correct, John Wilkes more spontaneous. Edwin is more Shakespearian, John Wilkes more melodramatic."[26]

In November 1862 Edwin and Mollie moved to the Boston suburb of Dorchester. She was pregnant again, and, as her health was poor, she was put under the care of Dr. Erasmus Miller, a specialist in obstetrics and gynecology. The young wife looked only half-present. "She was one of those exquisite women who charm us because their ethereal natures seem to have so little of earth about them," wrote Florence Howe. The friend believed that such a person did not have a very strong hold upon life.[27]

"I have been suffering where almost all women suffer," Mollie wrote Emma Cushman, niece of Charlotte Cushman, the first great tragedienne of the American stage. Despite embarrassment, discomfort, and fear of the result, she consented to a pelvic exam by Dr. Miller. He was cheerful, confident, and quick, and he had good news. Her condition was serious but not alarming. As was his way, he preferred a conservative treatment. Rest for four to six months and all would be well. Mollie was encouraged but puzzled as to why she always felt so weak. "I wonder if I will ever be well and strong."[28]

While Mollie was not entirely housebound, she rarely made or received visits. That set tongues wagging. "Boston is a fearful place for small talk," she confided to Lillian Woodman's sister Mattie. "They have us divorced and had our darling baby [Edwina] dead a dozen times. As for me, I am, according to the seers, living in a state of misery (conjugal) the like of which is unparalleled in modern times."[29]

There *had* been cross words and hurt feelings between her and Edwin as he prepared to leave for a New York engagement. The actor was peeved that she had argued with him over household matters. Nevertheless, she minimized her own feelings and put on a happy face with smiles and blown kisses when he departed.

Edwin arrived in New York in a dark mood. He told Badeau that at such times "it was like a veil shrouded him from other mortals, and he walked behind it, apart." "It was appalling to witness," wrote the friend, "and must have been still more appalling to endure."[30] Edwin was notably silent and sad and experiencing a sense of dread, "a feeling that evil was hanging over him and that he could not come to good." The fact that he had lost his birth caul, an omen of good luck, enhanced his fears.[31]

The star opened at the Winter Garden on February 9, 1863, and went through his repertoire with no interest in what he was doing. He simply didn't want to be there. The plays were poorly produced (Ophelia wore crinoline) and the company so-so. Moreover, he felt unwell. Edwin begged to be let off, but the managers wouldn't hear of it. Sick or well, he was money to them. They were mean, dirty people, he told a fellow actor, and he disliked them, particularly A. W. Jackson, a pinchpenny whom Edwin called "a hog Jew." Edwin hurled this disparagement at anyone who he felt cheated him, whether the individual was Jewish or not.[32]

Edwin moderated his drinking in Mollie's presence, but she wasn't around now and he had demons to banish. He drank like he was a bachelor again. One evening he stumbled about onstage, confusing his lines as Hamlet. As deliberate comedy it would have been amusing. As a display of personal failure, it was disturbing. The audience laughed at him while Jackson prepared to bring down the curtain.

"Ned at his old wild ways," sister Asia wrote with satisfaction. Apparently, little Miss Mollie Devlin's "wonderful influence [over him has] wonderfully ebbed." It was an unkind remark about a brother's struggle with the same curse that bedeviled their father. And curse it was. "No one can image the call of that desire," Edwin said. "When it engulfs me, I could sell my soul—my hope of salvation—for just one glass."[33]

Alarms went off at the Stoddard salon. Tom Aldrich, Launt Thompson, and Dick Stoddard agreed to take turns watching him. They would see what friendship, affection, and kind words could accomplish. The poet, the sculptor, and the critic became Edwin's inseparable companions, trying to keep him either at the theater or at the Stoddards' on Tenth Street—and at no other place. Edwin would wander about the Stoddard apartment after a performance, excited and nearly deranged until he collapsed on a bed. Elizabeth Stoddard slept on a nearby sofa, and Tom on the floor. The routine exhausted everyone. Elizabeth said that, although she was a professional writer, she didn't have words to describe the scenes they endured.[34]

One day an attendant brought a glass of spirits to the dressing room where Edwin and Tom sat. The actor reached for it. Tom grabbed the glass first and dumped its contents out the window. "The two men looked at each other, and the subterfuge was over," wrote Lillian. "Neither spoke, nor was the incident ever alluded to between them."

Edwin worried everyone. His eyes flitted, his thoughts darted about, his psyche wandered. On February 19, at about two in the morning, he was in bed when he felt a brush of wind strike his right cheek twice. "It startled me so that I was thoroughly aroused," he wrote Badeau. "I turned in bed, when I felt the same on the left cheek—two puffs of wind—ghost kisses. I lay awake wondering what it could mean when I distinctly heard these words—'Come to me, darling. I am almost frozen.'—as plainly as I hear this pen scratching over the paper."[35]

Mollie died on the morning of Saturday, February 21, 1863. Her daughter Edwina, only fourteen months old at the time, would be told that her mother, having gone into Boston, found the trolley home running late due to bad weather. Standing in the cold and snow, she was chilled and caught a cold that developed into a fatal case of pneumonia. The actual cause of Mollie's death was inflammatory bowel disease. Dr. Miller brought in the vastly experienced Dr. John Ware, a president of the Massachusetts Medical Society, but nothing could be done for the sufferer.

How odd was life. When forty-five-year-old Louisa Miller, the doctor's wife and nurse, was ten, she met Junius Brutus Booth Sr.—the hard way. The great actor, rushing to Boston for an engagement, smashed his buggy into her family carriage, overturning it. Louisa was knocked unconscious. She recovered and here she was decades later, holding the hands of his dying daughter-in-law.

Mollie's hair was dark and limp. Her eyes, very black, stood out in a deathly pale face. As she slipped away, Dr. Miller placed her head on his shoulder. The contrast of her face against the doctor's massive locks of white hair became one of Louisa's lasting memories.

"It's a shame you have to do all this for me," Mollie whispered. Then she leaned back on the doctor and just stopped breathing.[36]

When Dr. Miller realized Mollie was sinking, he summoned Edwin from New York. The actor and Dick Stoddard caught the express train from the 27th Street Station in the gray dawn of that Saturday morning. It was eight-plus agonizingly slow hours to Boston. Looking out of the car windows at the bleak winter landscape, Edwin later told Badeau he was startled to see his wife, lying dead in a coffin with a white cloth tied around her head and under her chin. He had this vision at least a dozen times.

In Boston the artist Walter Brackett met him at the depot. As Brackett came forward, Edwin raised his hand. "Don't tell me," the actor said. "I know."[37]

"LOOK OUT, YANKS!" read a sign on the road north of Baton Rouge. "This is a hard road to travel."

Northern soldiers marched on, unconcerned by the warning. Although many of their officers were experienced, the majority of the enlisted men were nine-month volunteers who had never been in a battle. They had no idea what was in store. They sang, laughed, and joked as they tramped forward in the warm spring weather.[38]

Lincoln, whose bond with the Mississippi River dated back to his youthful flatboat days, wanted the North to control the river for political, economic, and strategic reasons. "We need the Mississippi," he told General Daniel Sickles. "It ought to flow unvexed to the sea." Lincoln's army had already bitten off New Orleans to the south and Memphis to the north. But two strongholds between those cities secured the central section of the river for the rebels. One was Vicksburg, Mississippi. The other, 240 miles downriver, was Port Hudson, Louisiana. While not as famous as Vicksburg, Port Hudson was that city's proud little sister, strongly fortified and filled with veteran troops led by able and determined officers.[39]

Free the Mississippi! That was Lincoln's mandate to Major General Nathaniel Banks, whose Army of the Gulf would make the attack on Port Hudson. Hopefully, Banks would have more success than he had had the previous year at Cedar Mountain. (Lincoln hoped so, too.) Banks's XIX Corps consisted of four divisions, one of which was led by Brigadier General Tim Sherman. Tim's division was comprised of three brigades, each with its own artillery batteries.[40]

Superbly uniformed and mounted, Sherman was in his element. His blood boiled at the approaching campaign. "He is untiring; he never sleeps; his power is despotic," wrote Charles McGregor, a noncommissioned officer in the 15th New Hampshire Regiment. "Nothing can move fast enough to suit him." Badeau and the other staffers bore the brunt of it. Sherman barked and they flew, like birds scattering in a field. "They are other eyes and hands of his, and dart hither and thither, and reach and see all things."[41]

Service with Tim had not turned out to be a form-filling sinecure for Badeau. True, he got his own tent, his own servant, and his own horse. But the general's division consisted of almost seven thousand soldiers. Daily responsibilities for these men were huge. And, in critical moments,

Badeau could not falter due to fear or uncertainty. Too many faces turned to him for orders or inspiration. Danger was frequent as Sherman reconnoitered the enemy positions boldly. "He had a way of riding up in full sight of the enemy's batteries, accompanied by his staff," wrote Captain Wickham Hoffman, Badeau's colleague. "Presently, a shell would whiz over our heads, followed by another somewhat nearer. 'They are getting [our] range now. You had better scatter,' Sherman would remark quietly." Badeau did not linger to hear the suggestion repeated.[42]

Banks held a council of war with Sherman and his other commanders on the evening of May 26, 1863. He had decided to attack Port Hudson the following day. The advantages were all theirs, he explained. They outnumbered the fort's defenders three or four to one. They had more and better artillery. And, from the river, they had the added firepower of four steam frigates, three gunboats, and an ironclad. Sherman, together with generals C. C. Augur and Godfrey Weitzel, advised against Banks's plan. The fort was entirely surrounded. It couldn't receive supplies, reinforcements, or even messages. Starve the place out. It would fall without fighting in a matter of weeks. Wasn't that better than attacking a bastion whose defenses were imperfectly known?

Banks should have listened to these men—all West Point graduates—but the stubborn politician and former governor of Massachusetts had made up his mind. Major General Ulysses S. Grant, attacking Vicksburg upriver, might need their help, countered Banks. There was no time to waste here. Besides, he added, "The people of the North demand blood."[43]

By midnight Sherman was back with his command. It was warm, and his tent was thrown open, revealing a candle burning on a table. The general was too anxious to sit, however. Badeau watched him pace up and down in the darkness outside. Officers and messengers came and went. Knowing what pended with the sunrise, Badeau found the alternating hush and bustle intensely dramatic. *I've seen this before,* he realized. Life was imitating art—Edwin's tent scene the night before the Battle of Bosworth Field in *Richard III*.[44]

At dawn on the 27th Weitzel attacked along the right section of the line.

His force included two regiments of African American soldiers, the first instance of their use in heavy combat. By late morning Weitzel had stalled below the enemy walls. Banks heard nothing from Augur in the center or Sherman on the left, however, except cannonading. No roar of battle signaled a ground assault.[45]

The major general had made a rookie mistake. Banks had failed to give his commanders a specific time to attack, saying only that it should be "at the earliest hour practicable." He felt it was as obvious as it was essential that all divisions move simultaneously. But Augur was waiting on Sherman. And Sherman was waiting on lunch.

Banks galloped to Sherman's headquarters, where he was astonished to find Tim's soldiers lying at rest on their arms and his horses tethered to ropes with their saddles off. Inside the command tent he discovered Badeau, Hoffman, and their boss enjoying a bite to eat.

A very ugly scene ensued. Banks exclaimed that Sherman was criminally negligent in failing to attack. *Criminal*, Tim shouted in reply, was wasting lives by assaulting defenses not fully understood. Where were Banks's engineers who were supposed to come and designate the point of attack?[46]

Banks stormed out. Sherman, stung by the major general's rebuke, ordered his division into immediate action. Badeau rode forward and looked again at the terrain before the fort. The farm of planter William Slaughter, it was mostly cleared land. A half-mile-plus of this broad plain must be crossed before they could even get a good look at the enemy. Then they would meet an abatis of downed trees, then a ditch some fifteen feet deep and twelve feet wide. Above the ditch were the imposing ramparts of Port Hudson. Behind them, thousands of battle-hardened rebels.

General Neal Dow, who commanded one of Sherman's brigades, formed four assault lines, numbering about 2,500 men. While garden trees gave them a bit of cover, shells from the fort were already finding them. The soldiers remained calm, but Dow worried as they were little more than well-trained militia. "Could [such] men be held up to a hopeless, foolhardy charge?" Dow wondered. What genius thought of this? "The undertaking would be without the slightest prospect of success. The attack would be worse than folly. Utterly hopeless." It was not his job to make such decisions, however. He was there only to execute them.[47]

The attack began with an extraordinary sight. Bursting from the smoke of Sherman's field guns were 300 African Americans. They ran—unarmed—straight for the fort with long poles to lay over the ditch. With them came 170 soldiers carrying planks to lay over the poles, bridging the moat for the assault. A murderous fire from sharpshooters and artillery shredded both groups, and the survivors dove into a nearby ravine.

Badeau joined Sherman at the head of the brigade, ready to execute any orders, and Dow gave the signal. Bugles sounded, drums beat, flags flew, and the brigade advanced past the smoldering remains of the plantation house, through a garden, and onto the ominously named Slaughter Field. It was a clear, bright, breezy day.

The men marched forward double-quick. Four fences obstructed them; these were broken down and scrambled over. Meanwhile, an increasingly severe crossfire greeted them. The fort's defenders had trained for this moment and had the attackers' exact range. They laid shells above, around, and among the soldiers while rifle bullets slammed into their ranks or struck at their feet, popping like raindrops hitting a dusty street. The noise was deafening.

Stunned, the men hesitated. Then the brave headed on to the front, the coward on to the rear, and the rest had no idea where to go. Their courage would not let them advance, their pride would not let them retreat, so they leaped into the gulch with the pole carriers.

At last Lieutenant Colonel Henry Blair rallied a vanguard and asked Sherman what to do. Despite his rank, Blair, too, was a beginner. Ten months earlier he had been a small-town lawyer.

"Lead them ahead—straight ahead!" the general shouted. "Dead on the enemy's works!"[48]

As Sherman turned toward his second brigade, a shot hit his horse. The animal lurched backward ten yards and fell into a farm ditch, landing

The Battle of Port Hudson, Louisiana. *Adam Badeau, then an army captain, was seriously wounded in a May 27, 1863, assault on the Confederate fortress of Port Hudson. Recuperating at Edwin Booth's New York home, he was nursed by John Wilkes Booth.*

on the general and pinning one of his legs. Major John Aldrich managed to extricate Sherman from beneath the horse. The general was severely shaken, but, when Aldrich handed him his hat that had been knocked off, he seemed to recover. Scrambling through the blackberry bushes that lined the ditch, Sherman faced the enemy, pulled his sword, and charged them on foot.

Now the storm. "I turned my eyes to the silent rebel rifle pits," wrote one of Dow's privates. "Suddenly, above them, appeared a dark cloud of slouched hats and bronzed faces. The next moment—a sheet of flame." A grapeshot (one of dozens of metal balls fired in a hissing spray from a field gun) smashed into the general's right leg. It fractured the bones, and he collapsed. Something struck Aldrich on the hip, toppling him back into the ditch with Sherman's horse. Shot in the arm, Blair staggered backward. A round tore through the cheek of Herman Stork, Sherman's orderly, and a second ripped into his groin. Spurting blood from his mouth, he dropped to the ground.

Lieutenant Colonel Abel Smith of a nearby Zouave unit seized the United States flag Stork carried. Mounting a tree stump, he waved the banner to rally the men, but his baggy red breeches made him a perfect target. He was shot in the chest. When his men saw this, Badeau observed, "they were demoralized and scattered like scared sheep."[49]

In the midst of the carnage, Badeau didn't flinch. "He showed himself as brave as a lion," said an eyewitness. Riding to the head of Smith's 165th New York, he ordered it forward. There was cheering. Turning to see why, he was astonished to realize *they were cheering him!* Badeau had always sought the hero in books, onstage, in life. Improbably, this sheep in wolf's clothing had become one.[50]

Badeau felt a blinding pain in his left foot. At the same instant a powerful wallop struck his horse. They fell to the ground together. The horse was dying. Badeau feared he was, too. His foot felt as if it had been sawed in half. Four Zouaves threw him in a litter and hurried to a field hospital in the rear.[51]

Dr. Eugene Sanger, brigade surgeon of the XIX Corps, examined him. The doctor, with piercing look and crisp commands, told Badeau a bullet had entered the outside of his foot. It traveled straight through, smashing the cuneiform and metatarsal bones before exiting on the medial side of the ankle. Sanger cut away one inch of each of the damaged bones, washed the wound clean of boot and sock debris, and marked his patient for evacuation to New Orleans. Badeau's civil war was over for the present.[52]

Nearby, other doctors worked on Sherman, who shouted wildly that he would never let them take off his leg. "They pulled out the loose pieces of bone with pincers, taking hold and yanking every end that showed," said medical orderly Lawrence Van Alstyne. "Then they ran their fingers in and felt for more." Finally, they stuffed the wound with cotton to stop the bleeding and bound it with long strips of muslin.[53]

Badeau hated Sherman for belittling him and had sought a transfer for months. Fate had now arranged one. When the doctors told him they feared the general would die, Badeau confessed to Harry Wilson, his South Carolina friend, that he had one thought: go right ahead.[54]

WHEN MOLLIE DIED, Edwin wrote Badeau what the latter characterized as the saddest letter he ever received. "He was crushed," the friend recalled, "and saw no hope, no reason for living." He hated his profession, found no happiness in his daughter, and drew no solace from his friends. "He turned to me in his bereavement, and I did what I could to comfort him. At least I could grieve with him."[55]

Edwin learned of Badeau's wounding from a list of Port Hudson casualties published in the *New York Herald* on June 6, 1863. The injury was described as serious but hopefully not life-threatening. The actor immediately sent an encouraging note, but revealed his own depressed state of mind by urging Badeau, if he died after all, to pay him a ghost visit.[56]

No specter showed up, but the invalid did. Badeau arrived on medical leave to convalesce at Edwin's house on East 17th Street. He was unable to walk, so John scooped him up in his arms and carried him upstairs to bed. Over the next week the younger brother dressed his wound, gave him his medicine, and hauled him downstairs for meals. He proved a tender nurse—and a good actor. John never displayed the intense hostility he felt toward Lincoln.[57]

Edwin's late soldier-friend Richard Cary had feared what would happen to Edwin if Mollie died, and, sure enough, the widower seemed in peril. "My heart is crushed, dryed up, and desolate," he wrote Badeau. "Nothing on earth can fill the place of her who was to me at once wife, mother, sister, child, guide and savior. All is dark. I know not where to turn, how to direct the deserted vessel." Taking their marriage license, he tied it to the key of her coffin.[58]

But was she really lost? Mary Ann, his mother, saw his father twice in the weeks after the old man's death. She said that Junius stood at her bedside. When she tried to speak to him, he vanished. He stayed and spoke to Mollie, however, giving her advice about how to have a happy marriage.[59]

These stories were eagerly told and readily believed by everyone in the family except Edwin. He laughed at them, doubting Mollie would ever manifest herself to him. "I don't think I am worthy of it," he told the Stoddards.[60]

He wasn't laughing now. Edwin's vivid imagination made him receptive to the inexplicable. Like most actors, athletes, and gamblers whose profession involved performing under pressure, he was highly superstitious. Edwin feared broken mirrors, peacock feathers, and ivy vines. He hated brushing up against people on the way to the theater or touching anyone once there. Shaking hands robbed him of something vital. If he could avoid that, he had to pace three times across the green room and tap three times with the heel of his shoe at his entrance mark. A draft of wind might trouble him, deranging his thoughts and sending his mind tumbling. "Edwin is a man strangely constituted of exquisite susceptibilities. His mind is not trained in any logical fashion. He is a man of genius, of perceptions and emotions, and cannot reason," said Badeau.[61]

LAURA EDMONDS WAS a personable New Yorker in her early thirties. She lived with her father, John Worth Edmonds, a former State Supreme Court judge. There were rumors that the father drank excessively and used drugs, but, if so, he remained well regarded as a lawyer and prominent as an advocate of spiritualism. A devout Catholic, Laura was frightened by her father's beliefs—and she should have been. He told her he had discovered a plot by evil spirits to drive her insane and force her into a trance, at which point the father, believing she was dead, would bury her alive. But Laura's late mother Sarah reassured the daughter from the grave of her protection. The power of her love remained strong, Sarah said, although now shared with the inhabitants of Mars to whom the mother had grown attached.[62]

Laura was distressed to discover her own mediumistic powers. Judge Edmonds had been "persecuted, ridiculed, and lampooned" for his beliefs, and she had no wish to be mocked herself. But the spirits gave her a power to heal and to console. No decent person could refuse it. So, she began to work her wonders. She lost friends who considered her practices satanic but made new ones in their stead.[63]

The young woman was Edwin's neighbor, living a two-minute walk away. He found her home crammed with spirits, said a wit, with William Penn in the inkstand, Daniel Webster in the curtains, and Henry Clay in the flowerpot. Edwin was lucky Laura received him, given that her health was delicate and she had cut back on spiritualist work.[64]

Laura had every power Edwin needed. She was a clairvoyant, able to see and describe distant events as they happened. She was a telepath, able to communicate mentally with absent friends. And she was a medium, able to communicate between the physical and spiritual states of existence. Well-meaning and sincere, she welcomed all without regard to rank or fortune. She never took money from her callers. Not unexpectedly, the demands on her were many.

Edwin had four or five sittings with Laura. "My Father and [Mollie] have both been with me and have written and spoken through Miss E. in a curious manner," he told Badeau. "It *does* seem reasonable to me. I won't believe that her deep love for me is buried in her grave—and, living and loving still, why should she not seek me even yet? So, I shall dream on, believing she is near me."[65]

While Edwin was convinced of the immortality of the soul, Badeau was not. His believed everything human perished at death. There was a God, but He did not answer prayers. Grievously wounded on the battlefield, Badeau sent none skyward. "I don't want to believe in another life. I don't want to live again for life is not worth having without love," he said. "Why then wish to prolong a life whose greatest happiness is only a sort of misery?"

A séance shook his convictions. Badeau formed one of a circle. When he joined hands with Edwin, "I instantly felt a strong nervous influence pass from him into me, such as I never experienced before," he wrote his army friend Harry Wilson. "In a few minutes my right hand and arm were seized with an involuntary motion which I could not control and shaken more rapidly than any human being can shake his own arm. So rapidly that you could not see my hand." Then Badeau's arm was slammed up and down on the table so hard it hurt. Someone put a pencil in his hand and he began to write furiously. He was unable to stop. Badeau was confused and alarmed by what happened. Perhaps it was just nervous excitement, he speculated. If it were anything more, "my philosophy is all upset."[66]

Meanwhile, chaos ruled the streets. Protests against the military draft turned into riots throughout Manhattan. Arson, looting, and killings of African Americans were widespread. Mother Mary Ann, sister Rose, and Edwin's baby daughter Edwina were in the house, and Edwin feared the trouble might spread to the Booth neighborhood. John went out several times a day to assess the situation. Returning angry, "he spoke with detestation of the burning of houses, shooting Union officers, and murdering inoffensive Negroes," recalled Badeau. When it appeared that Randall, a Black servant who had accompanied Badeau from New Orleans, might be in danger, John suggested hiding him in the cellar. He said he would stand guard over Randall and protect the young man with his own life.[67]

Lincoln was angered and exasperated by the rioters. Urged to suspend the draft in New York in order to calm things, he replied that before he would give in to the mob, he would order the victors of Gettysburg into the streets. Fortunately, the violence spent itself in three days, making that unnecessary.[68]

The president considered asking Judge Edmonds, Laura's father, to conduct a formal inquiry into the riot's causes. The old judge's integrity as well as his thick skin made him the perfect choice for a task both thankless and dangerous. Badeau speculated there were 30,000 Southern émigrés in the city plus 50,000 antiwar Copperheads and an uncountable mass of working-class natives and immigrants who formed the bulk of the troublemakers. All opposed a reunification war based on conscription, high taxes, emancipation by bayonet, and enforced social equality with Blacks. Edmonds told James R. Gilmore, his daughter Laura's fiancé, "If I should undertake that [inquiry for Lincoln], my life wouldn't be worth a bad half-dollar. There's not a rough in New York who wouldn't shoot me on sight."

The judge was willing to serve, but, happily for him, Lincoln decided against an investigation.[69]

Gilmore, a journalist and self-anointed political operative, called at the White House. He discovered Lincoln in an anxious frame of mind. "He wore a fagged, dejected look and for a time indulged in none of his accustomed raillery and jocoseness." The battlefield news from Virginia was not good, and from the armies before Vicksburg and Port Hudson there was no news at all. "Nothing from Grant!" cried Lincoln. "Why don't we hear from Grant?" The words were almost a plea.

Hoping to encourage him, Gilmore read a letter he had received from New York. "I know you'll see Old Abe," a woman wrote. "Tell him that all good men and women everywhere are with him. That they pray for him, and bless him, for what he has done and will do yet. Bid him, 'Godspeed.'"

Lincoln was so affected by the words that Gilmore thought he saw the president's lip tremble. "Who is she?" he inquired of the writer.

Gilmore replied that it was Laura, the judge's daughter.

"Tell her that I thank her—that I hope God will bless her. Be sure to do this," he replied.[70]

With the president's knowledge (but not his blessing), Gilmore decided to undertake a personal peace mission to Richmond. Lincoln's terms were simple: "If they want peace, all they have to do is lay down their arms." Gilmore traveled to the rebel capital and ran into the same brick wall that had divided the country since the beginning. "You would deny to us what you exact for yourselves—the right of self-government," Confederate president Jefferson Davis told him. "Leave us alone, and peace will come at once." When Gilmore emerged in defeat from Davis's office, his Confederate escort, waiting in the hall, asked, "Well, what is the result?"

"Nothing but war," replied Gilmore gloomily. "War to the knife."[71]

A FEW WEEKS later Mary Lincoln had a serious accident. On the morning of July 2, 1863, she was traveling in Washington when the driver's seat of her carriage suddenly detached from the vehicle. The coachman fell to the ground and the horses bolted. Mary jumped or was thrown into the road, striking the back of her head on a rock. The cut bled freely and the wound became infected. Nurse Rebecca Pomroy was summoned to attend her, staying three weeks. Mary found her presence so comforting that she wanted the nurse to remain as a full-time companion. Pomroy, devoted to the care of her wounded and ill soldier-boys, declined. "One of the best women I ever knew," Lincoln said to Secretary of War Stanton.[72]

FOR ALL HIS faults, General Tim was right about one thing. There was never any need to assault Port Hudson. When Vicksburg surrendered on July 4, its fate was sealed. The beleaguered garrison ran down its flag on July 9 after learning the news from upriver.[73]

At midnight a week later, Pomroy was sitting with Mary when she heard a messenger hurrying up the White House stairs. Moments later the door to the sickroom burst open and Lincoln came in. Standing under the chandelier, he looked as radiant and happy as she had ever seen. "Good news! Good news!" he exclaimed. "Port Hudson is ours!"[74]

WHY WAKE ME?

Actor James Henry Hackett hit the jackpot when he sent President Lincoln a personally inscribed copy of his new book, *Notes, Criticisms, and Correspondence Upon Shakespeare's Plays and Actors.* Lincoln had recently seen Hackett play Falstaff and enjoyed his performance. The president laughed throughout the play and joined a standing ovation at curtain. "He has forgotten the war," wrote William Stoddard, who was present. "He has forgotten Congress. He is out of politics. He is living in Prince Hal's time." Hackett had achieved the actor's highest ambition—transporting the audience member to an imaginary place.[1]

Lincoln acknowledged the gift of Hackett's book by letter on August 17, 1863. He told the actor that the best compliment he could pay the comedian's Falstaff "is to say, as I truly can, I am very anxious to see it again." "For one of my age," Lincoln continued, "I have seen very little of the drama. Some of Shakespeare's plays I have never read, while others I have gone over perhaps as frequently as any unprofessional reader. I think nothing equals Macbeth. It is wonderful." Lincoln went on to give his opinion as to which of the seven soliloquies in *Hamlet* was the best.[2]

Hackett was ecstatic to receive Lincoln's letter. He had it printed for distribution among friends, then feigned shock when it appeared in newspapers nationwide. The president's opponents always looked for any little misstep Lincoln made, and they pounced. The *New York Herald* summed up their glee, rebuking him for his awkward writing style, poor grammar, and literary pretensions.

Embarrassed, Hackett wrote to apologize for the abuse. He found Lincoln unperturbed. "These comments constitute a fair specimen of what has occurred to me through life," the president replied. "I have endured a great deal of ridicule without much malice and have received a great deal of kindness, not quite free of ridicule. I am used to it." This time Lincoln took the precaution of marking his letter "Private." He underlined the word to make certain Hackett saw it.

The comedian called on Lincoln later in the year. He proved an entertaining guest, "as sparkling and full of life as an uncorked bottle of champagne." But Hackett quickly lost his fizz. Like so many others he had an agenda. Although he lacked any diplomatic experience, he wanted the post of American consul in London. Lincoln groaned, distressed "that it seemed impossible for him to have any close relations with people in Washington without finding that the acquaintance thus formed generally ended with an application for office."[3]

Hackett's was the first Shakespearian play Lincoln ever attended. The president quickly made up for lost time. In the remaining two years of his life, he attended sixteen more performances of the Bard. He also went to operas, tragedies, melodramas, and comedies, perhaps totaling sixty entertainment outings in all.

On such a diet it was inevitable Lincoln would see the Booths. June Booth, John and Edwin's older brother, had relocated from San Francisco to New York. He played in Washington for Lincoln as Shylock in *The Merchant of Venice*. John Sleeper Clarke, Asia's husband, came to town and entertained the president as a silly soldier, a befuddled husband, and a meddlesome busybody, in two nights of comedy. Both actors played at Ford's Theatre. They were favorably noticed by critics, although there is no record of what Lincoln thought of them.[4]

After a six-month hiatus following Mollie's death, Edwin resumed

Three Booth Brothers. *Posing in their costumes for* Julius Caesar, *John Wilkes, Edwin, and Junius Jr. (left to right) were photographed in November 1864. A second image was required as John Wilkes, his mustache shaved away for his role as Mark Antony, moved his outstretched hand, spoiling the shot.*

acting. Lincoln saw his Richard III at Grover's Theatre in Washington in early 1864. The president had definite ideas about the evil prince's famous line:

> Now is the winter of our discontent
> Made glorious summer by this son of York.

The text was usually presented as Richard's celebration over his family's improved fortunes. It should be spoken, Lincoln argued, with sarcasm. Richard was a man "burning with repressed hate and jealousy" over the success of his brother Edward, the new monarch.[5]

Lincoln returned a few nights later with Mary to see Edwin in the title role of the play *Brutus*. "Father Abraham visited Rome with me last eve," the actor boasted to Badeau the following day. "Tonight, he and [Secretary of State] Seward and their et ceteras will join [me again.] My trade is good." Six subsequent performances followed, including *The Merchant of Venice*, in which Lincoln thought Edwin did well but said he would rather have read it at home.[6]

The president's favorite among Edwin's plays was *Ruy Blas*, a play in which he saw himself. The title character was a Lincoln-like commoner with high ideals. Born low, he, too, rose high, loved problematically, fought rivals, and met a tragic end. Seward preferred *Richelieu*, a tale about a crafty French minister who out-plotted his adversaries to save the state. It was a role that suited Seward's own ambitions.

Looking like a wiry old scarecrow, Seward remained as intelligent, active, and social as ever. He held an elegant dinner in Edwin's honor at his home, a red-brick townhouse across from the White House. Frances, Seward's "et cetera," was present. This was unusual as she was a semi-invalid who remained mostly at their home in Albany, New York. That night, hosting duties devolved to daughter-in-law Anna, who was married to the Sewards' son Fred. The preternaturally self-confident Secretary Seward presumed to give Edwin acting tips—all graciously received—while Fred mused on how things changed with the North's improving military fortunes. Richmond, the battered Confederate capital, was threadbare. "But in Washington," Fred reflected, "people are inclined to eat, drink, and be merry." A year earlier his father was deemed unfeeling and unpatriotic because he gave dinners. "Now the only complaint is that he *don't* have dancing."[7]

Edwin rarely felt comfortable in such settings. He was affable and, like any good actor, he had a stock of sayings that made him seem intelligent, but his inferior education and his inclination to solitude made him ill at ease. "I observed how hard Edwin endeavored to overcome inborn reclusiveness—times when he literally forced himself to admit gentle, well-disposed familiarity," wrote an intimate friend. "He never regretted the society, companionship and adoration. How could he? They were so sincere, even if they did lay a hardship on him by trying to make the world believe he was vastly erudite and something of a sage." People like Tom and Lillian Aldrich, "who toiled diligently to disseminate the idea that Booth was richly cultured," did him no favor.[8]

Lincoln saw John Wilkes perform on several occasions, although only the night of November 9, 1863, is well documented. John Hay wrote in his diary that he and fellow White House secretary John Nicolay accompanied the president, Mary, Mary's friend Maria Hunter, and Simon Cameron, former secretary of war, to Ford's Theatre. They watched the actor portray the sculptor Raphael in *The Marble Heart*. Hay described the evening as "rather tame than otherwise." John generally chewed the scenery in his plays, so this was an odd observation, but *The Marble Heart* lacked the sword fights and other derring-do for which the star was famous. The play was a romantic melodrama in which John portrayed a hapless artist destroyed by an unwise love affair. Raphael's longing for the unobtainable appealed to the young and the young at heart.[9]

Ten-year-old Tad Lincoln saw John's Raphael earlier in the year at Grover's Theatre. It fascinated the boy. In John's journey to self-destruction as the ill-fated Raphael, his character shouted, cried, staggered, fell, leaped up, threw things, laughed crazily, left clothes on the floor, spoke to invisible people, wandered a darkened stage, and finally dropped dead. A child's delight. "I'd like to meet that actor," Tad said to his companion Gus Schurmann. "He makes you thrill."

Between acts the boys went backstage to the star's dressing room. John was applying his makeup. "He was a dark handsome man with brilliant black eyes," recalled Gus.

"This is President Lincoln's son," said the stage manager. John shook the boys' hands and talked pleasantly with them, asking which parts of the play they most enjoyed. When the third act was called, John rose to check himself in the mirror. Light brown trousers, silk waistcoat, black frock coat, small beard. The future murderer of Tad's father gave a rose to each child from a bouquet presented him over the footlights. Then, he smiled happily at them and returned to the stage.[10]

Tad loved Grover's Theatre and came to rehearsals when he could. "A jolly little fellow," said actor John T. Raymond. "Everybody liked him." Far too restless to watch, he met the stage attachés, and they gave him the run of the house. Tad joined in, helping the property men set the stage. Discovering the wardrobe chests, he and Grover's son Billy dressed as little red devils and set out up Pennsylvania Avenue to frighten people.

Tad was particularly delighted by the production of *The Seven Sisters*, with its fanciful costumes and bright scenery. On opening night, he inserted himself onstage at the end of a line of singing soldiers. Lincoln, sitting in the audience, was initially confused at the sight of his younger son—in misfit trousers, jacket, and cap—belting out "Rally 'Round the Flag" at the top of his voice and waving the American flag. "The President had a bad quarter minute of shock at the sight," recalled Grover, "but the humor of the situation quickly restored him, and he laughed immoderately." Raymond said, "The pleasure, the affection of the father was so intense, so spontaneous, it was glorious to see."[11]

Unlike his son, Lincoln was not interested in being on the stage or behind the curtain. "He used to say that to do so would spoil the illusion," wrote William E. Sinn, Grover's brother-in-law. The president did enjoy inviting stars to his box between acts and asked John to come out and be introduced. The passionate young Southerner refused. Mounting rebel defeats were agony to him, and he held the president as responsible for them as if Lincoln himself had fired every shot in every battle. Fellow actor Frank Mordaunt, knowing how much Lincoln admired John's acting, tried repeatedly to get him to go and greet the president. "Booth said that he would rather have the applause of a negro," wrote a contemporary.[12]

WHEN LINCOLN RODE the court circuit as a young lawyer, he carried a volume of Shakespeare in his saddlebags. At night in his lodgings, he lit a candle and pulled it out. Partner John T. Stuart noticed that he didn't just read it. He lay back and thought about it, too. Ninian Edwards, Mary's brother-in-law, observed that in the first years of the war he still read Shakespeare every evening. "Not the Bible," lamented Edwards.[13]

Lincoln felt that while the comedies were best enjoyed at the theater, the tragedies were best read at home.[14] That was because Shakespeare's works were secular scripture to him. Shakespeare was no preacher, of course, but his knowledge of human nature was profound and his plays and poems address timeless ethical, philosophical, and religious questions. Lincoln never saw a performance by the elder Booth, the leading dramatic light of the president's early years, but he shared the old man's opinion on the Bard's power. When criticized for holding a benefit performance of *Hamlet* for the poor of Philadelphia on a Sunday, Junius Booth snapped, "A good play is worth forty sermons."[15]

The conversation turned to Shakespeare one day as artist Francis Carpenter sketched Lincoln for a grand portrait to be titled *First Reading of the Emancipation Proclamation of President Lincoln*. Carpenter learned that the president planned to see Edwin's *Hamlet*. In fact, the performance had been arranged at his request. Surprisingly, Lincoln said, "It matters not to me whether Shakespeare be well or ill acted. With him, the thought suffices."[16]

The best part of the play, Lincoln continued, was not the well-known scenes in which Hamlet was visited by the ghost of his father nor when he struggled with the morality of revenge. It was the soliloquy of Claudius, Hamlet's uncle, who murdered the prince's father, married his mother, and usurped his place. For these crimes, Claudius realized he was damned. Fratricide put him beyond salvation.

O, my offence is rank, it smells to heaven.
It hath the primal eldest curse upon 't.
A brother's murder!

Lincoln recited all thirty-seven lines of the soliloquy from memory—300 words of rather dense text. It was clear to Carpenter that the president had studied Claudius's thoughts. Lincoln declared they were "one of the finest touches of nature in the world."[17]

David Bartlett, Washington correspondent for the *Springfield Republican*, found Lincoln and Tad at Grover's for *Macbeth* one rainy night. "The President has become quite a theater-goer," the journalist informed his readers. Knowing that this was Lincoln's favorite play, Bartlett watched closely to see how the passages about death might strike the commander in chief.

During the witches' scene a figure on crutches limped into Lincoln's box. It was Major General Daniel Sickles, invalided from the loss of his right leg at Gettysburg. Oddly, Tad's playmate Gus Schurmann was Sickles's bugler at the battle and had tied his handkerchief around the wounded man's leg, probably saving his life.

In act 4 Malcolm suggests to Macduff that they retire to some dark place and weep over the terrible state of affairs in Scotland, where a civil war for the throne rages. Macduff replies that swords, not tears, would save their homeland where

Each new morn
New widows howl, new orphans cry
New sorrows strike heaven on the face.

Bartlett saw Lincoln sink back into his chair, out of the glare of the auditorium's chandeliers. "For a long time [he] wore a sad, sober face as if suddenly his thoughts had wandered from the play-room far away to where his great armies contest with the rebellion [for] a vast empire."[18]

JOE JEFFERSON ARRIVED in Sydney, Australia, on January 7, 1862. While his prospects in an economy infused with its own California-style gold rush were good, no one knew him or would hire him, so he rented a theater, recruited a company, created some sets, and, within a month, raised the curtain. "We had a hog-killing time of it," boasted his son Charley. "Cash was abundant. My father had more money at the end of two weeks than all the Jeffersons put together ever had before."[19]

Joe had successfully gotten as far away as possible from Abraham Lincoln and Jefferson Davis. On the day in August 1862 when Richard Cary fell at Cedar Mountain, Joe was leading the laughs at the Royal Princess Theatre in Melbourne. There was more of the same at that city's Royal Haymarket when Adam Badeau was wounded in May 1863, and that July, when Port Hudson and Vicksburg surrendered, he wowed them at the Victoria Theatre in Adelaide. Atlanta was captured in September 1864, securing Lincoln's reelection two months later, as Joe dispensed comedy at the Prince of Wales Theatre in Sydney. His sympathies were Southern, but he stuck to his maxim that when heavyweights bloody the canvas, it's best to sit in the bleachers.

During his second year in Australia, Joe took a vacation on a sheep station in western Victoria. Alone on horseback, he wandered the Murray River country. As he watched a flock of white cockatoos with their yellow crests circle a forest of blue gum trees, a man and his dog emerged from the woods. Tall and gaunt, the man was poorly clad, barefoot, and wore a wide-brimmed straw hat. The vacant look of one devoid of human company showed him to be a shepherd, as did his busy companion, a large black collie named Jack.

The recluse was an English lawyer who had exiled himself to the bush as a cure for his alcoholism. He invited Joe to stay in his mud-and-stick hut. Worn out by travel, Joe accepted the offer, and they settled in for tea to watch the night come on. The silence of the wilderness was striking. One heard only tinkling sheep bells and the crackle of their campfire, whose plume of smoke went straight up in the still air.

"Do you think the spirits of those we loved in life can return and stand beside us?" the shepherd asked him. The man assured Joe that his dog Jack certainly did. "He'll start up and look around slowly as if his eyes were following something in the hut. At these times he will give a low, strange sort of moan."

The men went to bed. When Joe noticed the moon's light falling directly on the shepherd's face, he cautioned him. "People have been known to go mad for committing this indiscretion." The shepherd did not reply.

The oddity of his situation, together with the strong tea, kept Joe awake. After an hour or so he noticed the shepherd leave his pallet and crawl stealthily toward him. The man stopped at a chair where Joe had hung his coat and retrieved the actor's whiskey flask from a breast pocket. He held it, seemed bewildered, rose to his knees, struck a prayerful attitude, returned the flask, stretched out on the floor, and went to sleep. The episode, framed in moonlight, was unforgettably haunting to Joe.

"The old craving came over me. So strong," the shepherd explained the following morning. "Well, at that moment, there was a hand laid on my head. A calmness came over me that I had not felt for years. As God is my judge, I believe it was the angel hand of my dead wife."[20]

Joe knew all about this. His late wife Maggie often visited him in material form. She came, sat on his lap, and comforted him.

"[Jefferson] inclines his ear very strongly to the doctrines of spiritualism," wrote one of his friends. "It might be supposed that with stage illusions, ghost scenes, and the like, whose hollowness are known to those behind the scenes, [the so-called spirit world] would have less effect upon him, but it appears that is not the case." Henry Watterson, a Confederate editor who knew him well, worried these beliefs might cloud his mind, but Joe brushed off his anxiety with humor. "He knew he was credulous and joked about it but went on being credulous just the same. He could not help it. It was an attractive, beautiful part of the man's optimistic makeup," recalled Francis Wilson, a fellow actor who attempted to put the best face on it. "Like all such natures, he was strongly inclined to accept the inexplicable. He did not hide in dark places with his theories. His friends knew them. And he and they smiled at them."[21]

THE SEED ROOM, a division of Isaac Newton's Department of Agriculture, was located in a building several blocks east of the White House. At the behest of Mary Lincoln, Nettie Colburn was given a job there. The petite spiritualist joined several dozen people, mostly women with a few children as young as ten, who sewed cereal, vegetable, and flower seeds into small bags. These were distributed by the department throughout the country in an effort to increase the quality and variety of American agriculture. It was light work—only six hours a day—with lots of time to chat. "A mere pastime," Nettie called it. The easygoing Newton found a place not only for Nettie but also for her companion Parnie Hannum. Sir Isaac was so accommodating that the Seed Room had three times as many employees as it needed.[22]

Newton's tenure as commissioner of agriculture had gotten off to an awkward start. Proud with his appointment, he turned up for a regularly scheduled cabinet meeting. Pausing at the door, Newton considered whether to park himself by the stately Seward or the grim Secretary of War Stanton. Or perhaps by the hirsute Secretary of Navy Gideon Welles, whose wife Mary was a fellow spiritualist. He was informed that department heads did not attend cabinet discussions and was ushered into the hall.[23]

Barred from the inner circle, the commissioner lost none of his access and influence with the Lincolns. He remained a key facilitator for visiting spiritualists. And he mediated trouble between the government and his fellow Quakers, as Cyrus Pringle of Charlotte, Vermont, found out. Drafted in mid-war, Pringle was a member of an orthodox meeting of the Society of Friends. He refused to serve or to pay a commutation fine. Pringle was enlisted against his will and hauled to the front in Virginia. When he wouldn't serve, he had cords tied to his wrists and ankles. Then he was staked to the ground in the form of an X. When Pringle remained defiant, military officials, uncertain what to do with him next, sent him to Washington for the bureaucrats to deal with. Newton took up his case, appealing to Lincoln. The president told him to tell Stanton to parole the Quaker. The secretary of war refused, forcing Lincoln to go personally to the War Department to get the parole done. "It is through the influence of Isaac Newton," Pringle wrote in his diary, "that Friends have been able to approach the heads of Government in our behalf and to prevail with them to so great an extent."[24]

Sometimes with Newton or Pierpont—more often with Parnie—Nettie sat with the Lincolns at the White House. Her autobiography, published in

1891, reveals about a dozen séances over a two-year period. These were not dreary events in darkened rooms filled with candles and skulls. Some sittings were held on sunny afternoons, others in evenings lit by gaslight and fireplaces. They generally started with piano music, the singing of favorite songs, recitations of poetry, and chitchat.

Jerks and twitches announced a spirit moving over Nettie. Then "Pinkie" might appear. This control was "a little Indian maid" said to be an Aztec princess who lived in Mexico hundreds of years ago. "Pinkie's" youth, innocence, and purported mystical connections (as a Native American) with the primal spirits of the land gave her authenticity. "Dr. Bamford," another visitor, was the spirit of Amos Bamford, a patent-medicine maker and family friend who died in 1835. Lincoln enjoyed listening to the doctor's quaint New England accent and odd expressions. Nettie seemed like an actor taking on roles in these characterizations. Yet she was entirely sincere. Artist Francis Carpenter, himself a spiritualist, thought Nettie incapable of deliberate deception.[25]

The Spirit Cabinet. *Critics of spiritualism poke fun at Lincoln (far right) and his cabinet of ghostly advisers. Here, Nettie Colburn (seated, right) has summoned "Pinkie" (holding wand) and the president's favorite, "Old Dr. Bamford" (standing between Lincoln and Nettie).*

Her sittings were entertaining, never disturbing, and explain why Lincoln's friend Joshua F. Speed knew that a visit from her was a relief to the president, whose visitors generally sought favors. Nettie's spirits never counseled the Lincolns on the death of Willie—at least, she never mentioned it—or any other highly personal matter. They spoke on politics, army morale, and the condition of the freedmen. In other words, concerns on the mind of any public-spirited citizen. Once, "Dr. Bamford" informed Lincoln that he would be reelected to a second term in office. Lincoln gave a sad smile and replied, "It is hardly an honor to be coveted, save one could find it his duty to accept it." The ghostly guests always closed with words of encouragement, and Nettie was proud of the fact that the president left her séances with a lighter step than when he entered them.[26]

DRESSED IN TRAILING black crepe, Emilie Todd Helm rushed toward Mary. Her cheeks were pale, her eyes red and puffy, her lips tight and drawn, and when the half-sisters fell into each other's arms, both wept. Emilie's tears were for her late husband Ben. Mary's were at the shock of seeing the happy girl she knew transformed into a sad-faced shell, for the three brothers the women had lost in the war, for anxiety about her husband, for Willie.

"Kiss me, Emilie," said the First Lady, "and tell me that you love me."

In life's rich irony, Emilie was the widow of Ben Hardin Helm, a Confederate general killed recently at the Battle of Chickamauga in Georgia. Penniless, rudderless, and mourning, she turned to Mary, who willingly took in her Southern sister.

"You should not have that rebel in your house," exclaimed General Sickles, slapping on a table in disgust.

"My wife and I are in the habit of choosing our own guests," Lincoln snapped back.

As distraught as she was, Emilie realized that Mary was troubled, too. "Little Sister," Lincoln said privately to her, "you and Mary love each other. It is good for her to have you with her. I feel worried about Mary. Her nerves have gone to pieces. She cannot hide from me that [the] strain she has been under has been too much for her mental as well as her physical health." His tone was anxious. "What do you think?"

There was no denying the obvious. If a book fell to the floor, Mary grasped her chest as if she were having a heart attack. If a bell rang in the hall, she blanched in fear as if she were being attacked. "She seems very nervous and excitable," Emilie replied.

"Stay with her as long as you can," pleaded the president.[27]

Nurse Pomroy believed that "nothing is the matter with Mrs. Lincoln but deep sorrow, such as others have felt." In Pomroy's view Mary loved fashion too much, and Willie's death was meant to humble her before God. Whether prompted by the nurse or not, Mary said the same thing. Willie's death was, in some measure, her fault. "I had become so wrapped up in the world, so devoted to our own political advancement, that I thought of little else besides," she wrote two years later. "Our Heavenly Father sees fit, oftentimes, to visit us at such times for our worldliness."[28]

Mary grieved hard. She wore mourning for many months. Her letter stationery was similarly trimmed. She curtailed White House entertainments and dropped old friends who brought Willie to mind. She refused to look at photographs of the child. It was two years before she would visit the Library, the dead child's favorite room. When she entered it for the first time in 1864 with Commissioner French, her eyes filled with tears, he wrote in his diary, and it was painful to be with her. The bereaved mother never entered the Guest Room (in which Willie died) or the Green Room (in which he was embalmed). "There was something supernatural in her dread of these things," recalled Elizabeth Keckly, "something she could not explain."[29]

There was one comfort. Mary believed the veil separating her and her dead was slight. For that reason, she welcomed those who could pull it aside. Although she boasted that she read people better than her husband did, Mary's need was greater than her judgment in this matter, and a series of odd individuals trooped into the White House.[30]

One prominent visitor was the talented and dissolute medium John

Conklin of New York City. His spirit messages from Willie were written backward, his trademark style. Lucy Hamilton of Simsbury, Connecticut, also offered comfort. This eccentric was a clairvoyant doctor who provided medical diagnoses by mail (as long as the complaints came wrapped in two one-dollar bills). Always at hand was Georgetown's "Lady in Gray," as Belle Miller was known for her dress. She sat with Mary more than any other medium. A large woman with bright black eyes and a reddish complexion, Belle purportedly levitated pianos while entranced. She also drew charts in luxuriant floral patterns. When under the influence, "she had a far-off look and appeared like an enthusiast at a sacred shrine."[31]

Charles H. Foster was the most famous of Mary's mediums. He was a tall man with a full fleshy face, dark mustache, and black hair parted in the middle. A hard-drinking, cigar-chomping oracle, he was a master test medium, able to prove in this world that he was in touch with the next. As a spirit mailman, Foster answered inquiries about the dead by pressing visitors' questions in sealed pellets to his forehead and then, in a dreamy listless way, divining their content. He also performed skin writing, producing on his forearm, wrist, or back of hand the letters of a spirit's name or initials.[32]

When Foster went to London early in the war, he was closely followed by a letter from Judge Edmonds to William Wilkinson, editor of the influential *Spiritual Magazine*. Edmonds claimed that Foster was a fraud. The judge also added details of the medium's "sickening criminality" in a matter unrelated to spiritualism. What that meant was not spelled out, but, given Victorian wordage, it referred to sexual transgressions. Wilkinson printed the judge's charges.[33]

None of this hampered Foster's success. Touted by the *London Times*, he held sittings with the Duke of Wellington, Dickens, Browning, Tennyson, and Napoleon III. On his return to the United States the medium learned that Frances Conant, who held séances in Boston, had received a message from Willie urging his parents to contact Foster. Receiving his own message from the boy, Foster wrote it out and sent it to Mary. The door to the

Charles Foster. *A preeminent medium of the Civil War era, Foster held séances for
both Mary Lincoln and the Booths. He and an otherworldly friend are photographed
here by William Mumler, a "spirit photographer." Foster was later committed to the
State Lunatic Hospital in Danvers, Massachusetts.*

White House flew open, and in he went, explaining that he offered no
trances, darkened rooms, mysterious music, or trickery. "The spirits come
to him, and take possession of him, and communicate with him, and all
he can do is submit to their influences, to do as he is told, and to tell others
what they tell him," he explained. Multiple sittings followed. Lincoln found
him curious; Mary was bedazzled. "She went beyond all bounds," recalled
George C. Bartlett, Foster's business manager, "and seemed to think that
every trifling occurrence had some wonderful spiritual significance."[34]

One night Mary came to Emilie's bedroom. Her eyes were full of tears,
yet she was smiling. "I want to tell you," the First Lady said excitedly, "that
one may not be wholly without comfort when our loved ones leave us. Willie comes to me every night and stands at the foot of my bed with the same

sweet adorable smile he has always had. You cannot dream of the comfort this gives me."

Her voice trembled in excitement as she spoke. "Her eyes were wide and shining," Emilie wrote in her diary, "and I had a feeling of awe as if I were in the presence of the supernatural. It *is* unnatural and abnormal. It frightens me."

Bartlett wrote, "I think that an over-belief causes more discord and unhappiness in a family than an under-belief."[35]

It was fortunate for Mary and her husband that the public's awareness of visitors like Foster was limited. Those who knew of the séances viewed them as a harmless diversion of the president or just another quirk of his quirky First Lady. Negative publicity was entirely partisan. It presented the sittings as attempts by a failed administration to find any path to military victory. The *New York World*, a leading voice of Lincoln's Democratic critics, noticed them with a jab at Belle Miller. "The President is reported to have consulted again the Georgetown witch," wrote editor and publisher Manton Marble in 1864. "It is not generally believed he is an open convert to spiritualism, but he consents to be instructed by mediums as a military necessity."[36]

According to Ohio attorney David Quinn, a particularly bitter critic of the president, Lincoln had a secret space in the White House in which he hid a rapping table. No need for a constitution when it tapped, thumped, and banged out orders from Hannibal and Attila the Hun that were the new law of the land. The table directed the president's every move, claimed Quinn. "It gathers armies, presages events, equalizes whites and negroes, and converts paper into gold. The nation is virtually on fire, its property melting in the general conflagration, and the blood of its children flowing from its mountains to its oceans, while its executive councils gather in dark rooms and direct armies and a great nation's policy, as they themselves are directed by spirit rappings."[37]

Three decades later, in reaction to the publication of Nettie Colburn's autobiography, Lincoln's secretary John G. Nicolay told an interviewer that the allegation that the president was a spiritualist was too absurd to need comment. He then proceeded to do just that. "I have no doubt that Mr. Lincoln, like a great many other men, might have had some curiosity as to spiritualism, and he might have attended some of these séances solely out of curiosity. But he was the last man in the world to yield to any other judgment than that arrived at by his own mature deliberation."[38]

As his closest friends knew, Lincoln was born short in the faith department. His mind was practical. "He was not impulsive, fanciful or imaginative, but cold, calm, precise, and exact," said law partner Herndon. "In his mental view he crushed the unreal, the inexact, the hollow and the sham." "In order to believe," the friend continued, "he must see and feel and thrust his hand into the place. He must taste, smell and handle before he had faith or even belief." Once he reached a decision, no one could change his mind. A particular pressing of the lips meant the discussion was over.[39]

Lincoln listened patiently as Foster channeled the spirit of Andrew Jackson. It seemed the former president was passionately opposed to the Emancipation Proclamation. Thomas Jefferson, on the other hand, favored it. But Lincoln's view about what he heard was the same as that of Sickles, who also sat with the medium. This was entertainment.

The general attended a séance in the Red Room when someone—Nettie, he thought—delivered a message in a slow, methodical voice. Mary listened approvingly, then exclaimed to her husband, "There! Do you believe now? Are you convinced?"

"Pshaw!" replied Lincoln with a smile.

Then what about the Lady in Gray's ability to play the piano and make it dance to the music, she asked?

Lincoln slowly unfolded himself from his chair and walked over to the piano. "He couldn't play a note understandingly, but he sat down as though he had taught music for years," said Sickles. "He shoved his long, bony, strong legs under the instrument, stretched out his arms, and produced a series of utterly discordant sounds on the keys. At the same time the piano began to jump up and down. We were amazed."

Looking over his shoulder at Mary "with an expression of mingled fun, seriousness, and sadness on his face, Lincoln said, 'See, mother, our piano can dance, too!' He actually exerted enough strength with his legs to lift the piano from the floor."

"I was particularly hostile to spiritualism," Sickles said. "I cannot say positively that President Lincoln entertained the same views, but in tender consideration of his wife, did not ridicule her belief as openly or in such a gruff way as I did."[40]

Lincoln found comfort in the thought that he could communicate with Willie, as Foster and the others promised. But it was impossible. As he told an army officer with whom he shed tears over lost loved ones, it just wasn't real. Communications from the other world were delusions, he said.[41]

WHEN ADAM BADEAU entered the Booth home to convalesce from his Port Hudson wound, he was unable to stand. In short order he mastered his crutches, learning to hobble around and get downstairs on his right foot. The arch of his left foot was gone, however, and the wound, raw and sore, was too painful to cover with a blanket. Fortunately, no destructive infection developed, with its potential for loss of life. The dreadful-looking injury remained open for months—draining, tender, and throbbing—and it was clear Badeau could not rejoin the army anytime soon.[42]

Badeau had not seen James H. Wilson, the South Carolina friend whom he called Harry, since the previous year when he entered the service. Wilson was a square-shouldered young man in his mid-twenties with blue eyes, dark wavy hair, narrow appraising eyes, and tightly pressed lips hidden by a large mustache twisted to points at the ends. He took to soldiering and climbed rapidly through the ranks. Nominally a captain, Harry was assigned to duty as a lieutenant colonel on Grant's staff. A brigadier generalship was on the horizon.

The handsome officer enchanted Badeau. A brilliant conversationalist, Harry took a brotherly interest in Badeau, who was still grieving the loss of intimacy with Edwin. "Badeau's disgust of life, distrust of men, and disbelief in friendship" aroused Wilson's sympathy, and he offered his friendship. Harry had helped Badeau prepare for service, even giving him horseback riding lessons. Most wonderful of all, Wilson was cheerful, steady, and mature, unlike Edwin, "the most fitful, tantalizing, unreliable of human beings."[43]

The invalid wrote Harry regularly about army rumors ("Sickles intends to overthrow the government and make himself dictator," etc.), foreign affairs, and what Badeau considered Lincoln's drift toward radicalism. The letters also touched on personal matters, like Badeau's lack of religious faith and his frustrations with Edwin. Nevertheless, the actor remained his "Right Arm," as he put it. Wilson, "my darling friend," had become his "Left Arm." "Will you think me foolish and womanish if I tell you how much good every word in your letter does me?" he asked. "Your letters give me keen pleasure. They are full of *affection*. You are not afraid of the word any more than the thing."[44]

One evening in Washington in February 1864, the men finally caught up with each other, and Badeau discovered the limits of intimacy. Nothing is known of what transpired that night; plenty is known of its aftermath. "I'd give ten years of my life to annihilate one day and its consequences," he wrote Harry shortly afterward. Badeau's behavior was "the result of physical weakness and what you know never occurred before." He had failed morally in Harry's eyes, he knew, by committing "an error you thought unpardonable."

Badeau quickly regained his footing, however. He was comfortable with who he was—an identity never specifically spelled out in the sources—and he pushed back. "Do you think you have any right to be so intolerant, so arrogant in your judgment? Is it fair, is it generous, is it honest?" he asked Wilson. The friend "erred in repelling what is rare in this world." Perhaps it was just "the work of Fate, jealous that men should be so purely happy and so happily pure." Badeau insisted he was an honorable person, "and you must take me as I am—him who once loved you as no one will ever love you again.

"In regards to our relations, I agree with you it is better not to discuss them," he stated. "Tears many I shall hereafter shed, but will not call on you to witness them."[45]

Edwin, as usual, was too preoccupied with himself to offer sympathy. "Forgive me," he wrote Badeau, "I am so selfish that others' woes seem nothing to mine." Whenever he was idle, his mind filled with self-reproach over his neglect of Mollie. "Could I hate an enemy as I hate myself, there'd be more elbow-room in the streets someday," he continued. "Her little life was one long kiss of love wasted on a cruel wretch unworthy of her slightest thought." No need to explain further. "You know too well what that coldness is."[46]

Although he received messages from both Mollie and his father through Laura Edmonds, he was unsatisfied. "Find out for me when Foster will be here," he told artist Walter Brackett. "I want to see him. I *am* convinced— only I get so restless that my faith seems to need *rubbing up* occasionally, and Foster gives more than any medium in the way of physical proofs. Therefore, I wish to have him operate on me and the disease (doubt) will soon be radically cured."[47]

Meanwhile, at Badeau's suggestion, Edwin called on Maggie Fox, the original spiritualist pioneer, for a two-hour sitting. "The raps began very loud the moment she entered," he wrote Badeau. "'Cover your hand,' the message said. I did so. 'Sit close and feet back.' All of these instructions were obeyed, I having my left hand wrapped in my handkerchief on the table."

After a few minutes, he felt a slight tug at his right trouser leg. He asked that the spirit tug more strongly, and it touched his knee. "I said, 'Stronger still,' and a three-fingered something squeezed me *very tightly* on the knee. At the same time, I felt a strong current of electricity about the point touched. I was frightened, I confess.

"I'll take my oath no human being touched me, but was it a spirit? I want to believe it, and yet I fear to do so."

As he got ready to leave, Fox closed her eyes and began writing backward. The message? "Meet me here some evening, [signed Mollie]."

"Now, Ad," asked Edwin. "What is this?"[48]

On the first anniversary of his wife's death in 1864 Edwin called on Foster. Expectations were high. Foster's spirits were the ones who informed sculptor Thomas Gould that brother Joe Booth was in Australia. That night the otherworld was present in force, Foster assured him. Mollie was distinctly visible to him. Standing right there. Edwin saw nothing.[49]

This failure shook the actor's faith, but Foster reeled him back in at a second session in which the medium "astounded and overwhelmed him," Edwin wrote Richard Stoddard. "He told me all about Dick Cary—how he died and what I gave him before he went to war! Said again that Mary died of an internal fever. Showed me the initials in large red letters of Mary's and Cary's names on the back of his hand—which lay on the table untouched by him or anyone else. In a deep trace he almost smothered me with caresses (he afterward said 'twas as much as he could do to keep from kissing me all the time) and talked like Mary talked."[50]

Warned to be wary, Edwin replied, "Fraudulent mediums may fool me, but I can't fool myself."[51] "Mary, my Father and my friend Cary converse with me as truly and distinctly as though they were in the flesh. Incontestable proofs have been given to me day after day, night after night. All is clear—solid—true," he wrote Badeau.[52]

"As Coleridge or someone else says, 'If it's a dream, why wake me?'"[53]

8

❧

FATAL VISION

John Pierpont, the poet, was a venerable-looking man with long flowing white hair and beard. He had a lively manner, a rosy face, and merry eyes. Nearly eighty, Pierpont still climbed the tall stairway daily to his clerk's desk in the Treasury Department where he worked alongside men the age of his grandchildren.

One night a group of young government clerks gathered to form the Washington Lecture Association. They wanted to bring the nation's leading cultural and intellectual figures to the capital for a series of Friday evening programs. It would give them, said William Croffut, one of their members, an opportunity "to poke up the sluggards of this slaveholding city." Disturbed by a knock at the door, they found Pierpont. "Gentlemen, I saw an advertisement summoning young men to come here to consult tonight," he said. "Here I am!" The old man was invited in amid laughter and applause and immediately elected the group's president.

Pierpont was a happy choice. The best lecture room in Washington was in the Upper Main Hall of the Smithsonian building (the Castle). It had fine acoustics and good sightlines from pew-like benches accommodating 2,000 people. But Pierpont and Croffut, the association secretary, were disappointed to learn that Joseph Henry, the Smithsonian's boss, wouldn't let them use the space. Henry was a conservative whose Southern friends had always supported the institution. He feared for the

John Pierpont. *A poet and former minister, Pierpont was one of wartime Washington's foremost spiritualist figures. He was a friend of Mary Lincoln and counseled the First Family when Willie Lincoln died in 1862.*

Smithsonian's future if the men brought in liberal speakers to expound on controversial topics.

While Pierpont promised to be nonpartisan, the problem was he didn't know how. He filled his lineup with radical all-stars. They seemed normal to him. Of course, most were critical of the president's tardiness on emancipation and alleged lackluster prosecution of the war. The name of Horace Greeley, a prominent abolitionist and early patron of the Fox sisters, as a speaker only confirmed Henry's fears. Science was neutral on contemporary social issues, Henry insisted. It must be.

Pierpont countered that humanists addressed "the science of man." He would never drag a speaker into an anteroom to preview and censor his remarks. There the matter remained until congressional arm-twisting by Pierpont's friends—and a push from Lincoln—finally unlocked the doors.

Henry grudgingly acquiesced but insisted that Pierpont announce before each program that the proceedings were against his wishes and had nothing to do with the Smithsonian.[1]

Orestes A. Brownson, an important Catholic thinker, was the association's first speaker. Pierpont called the large meeting to order and introduced his guest. Then he added, "Ladies and Gentlemen, I am requested by Professor Henry to announce that the Smithsonian Institution is not in any way responsible for this course of lectures. I do so with pleasure, and desire to add that the Washington Lecture Association is in no way responsible for the Smithsonian Institution." Laughter greeted his remark.

Each week thereafter Pierpont would rise, grasp the lectern, stare out mischievously, assume a grave tone, and repeat the caution. The audience grew to expect it, and as soon as he said, "Ladies and Gentlemen . . . ," he was drowned out by a wave of cheers, laughter, and hooting.[2]

Francis Carpenter, the artist, called on Pierpont at his attic office in the Treasury Department shortly after Brownson's speech. He had nearly completed the portrait of Secretary Salmon Chase in his painting of Lincoln and the cabinet at the first reading of the Emancipation Proclamation. He wanted the opinion of those, like Pierpont, who knew the secretary well. The two men walked together to the White House.

The canvas rested against a wall in the State Banquet Room that served as Carpenter's workshop. Pierpont studied it and said he felt that the artist's Chase was more lifelike than his Lincoln. The First Lady joined them. She was satisfied with her husband's likeness but flashed her sharp wit when she suggested the painting of the contentious cabinet members be titled "The Happy Family."

"What puzzles me," Mary complained to Pierpont, "is what on earth we are ever going to do with it?" She had the notion that the large painting, which measured nine by fifteen feet, was coming home with her to Springfield when the family left the White House.[3]

Pierpont customarily took his lunch of rolls and coffee with William Croffut at a table in the lower west corridor of the Treasury Department. Other poets joined them, like Edmund Clarence Stedman, Edwin's friend

from the Stoddard salon in New York who clerked for Attorney General
Edwin Bates. Walt Whitman, who worked at Interior, often dropped by.

The group also gathered weekly to brush up on their French. Victor
Hugo sent them advance page proofs of *Les Misérables*, which they trans-
lated orally into English. Whitman was the only one proficient enough to
decipher the street jargon of Hugo's Parisian criminals.

One evening Whitman arrived late, explaining he had a run-in with
the police. He was walking along F Street when an officer grabbed him on
suspicion of criminal intent for wearing a mask. Whitman was hauled to a
police station where it was apparent he had no mask on. That was his face.
"You looked so queer—your long white hair and whiskers, sir," apologized
the arresting officer, "and your eyes set well back, and your pink face looking as if it was painted."

Whitman, initially angry, grew amused. When Pierpont expressed his
sympathy, the poet replied, "We all of us wear masks."[4]

BEFORE THE INCIDENT with Badeau, Harry Wilson had recommended him
to General Grant as a staff member.

"Oh, yes, I remember him," the general replied. "A little pale, blue-eyed
man who wore spectacles and looked like a bent fo'pence." Grant made the
assignment; Port Hudson came before it could be carried out. Intensely
ambitious, Badeau feared that the extended convalescence from his war
wound would cost him the job. Still on crutches with a steel boot to steady
his foot, he headed back to the front and joined Grant on February 12, 1864,
in Nashville, Tennessee. It was love at first sight. "His purity, his unselfish-
ness, his thorough patriotism, his devotion to his friends are moral traits
that I have never known more splendidly exhibited," Badeau wrote of his
chief. "He is a wonderful man."[5]

In March 1864, when Lincoln ordered Grant east to fight Lee in Virginia,
the general brought Badeau with him. Wilson cautioned him that Grant
would need "the courage of heroes, the purity of angels, and the omni-
science of the gods" to prevail against the South's best general. Badeau

replied with absolute confidence in his latest hero. "He deserves to be what I hope and believe he will—the Savior of his country."[6]

Grant found his new aide loyal, hardworking—and amusing. The general was leading his staff on horseback up a heavily wooded hill when the trees became too dense to continue forward. He turned off, followed by the others. The inattentive and nearsighted Badeau rode straight ahead into the thicket. As his horse squeezed between two trees, he and his saddle were pushed backward. "I say, I'm going off!" he cried. Saddle and rider were swept over the horse's rump and plopped onto the ground. "General Grant stopped, and, looking back at the ludicrous sight, fairly screamed with laughter," recalled Colonel Horace Porter, a fellow staffer. "Grant cracked jokes at his expense the rest of the ride and for two or three days afterwards."[7]

Badeau persevered. Since Grant never went to sleep early, the new aide stayed up with him at night after others went to bed. Sometimes he wrote the general's letters. Often he just kept him company. In these quiet hours the normally reserved Grant spoke more freely, and a bond developed between the pair. The general felt protective toward an individual so different, so needy, and so misplaced. Oddly, Badeau felt it was Grant who needed protection from rivals and politicians. The ambitious Badeau never forgot where the power lay, but he responded equally to Grant's decent nature.[8]

Politically, they were congenial. Both favored Lincoln's magnanimity toward the South. Grant had been a Democrat in the 1850s. Badeau had been, too, voting against Lincoln in 1860. He still disliked the abolitionists in the remake-the-world wing of the army and thought they were misleading the president. But time had taught Badeau something important. To have one country, not two, he told Harry Wilson, one couldn't distinguish between the war effort and the government waging it.[9]

Robert Lincoln showed up at Grant's headquarters in February 1865. His father told the general that the son "wishes to see something of the war before it ends," a phrasing so casual it could have been used if Robert intended to see a circus before it left town. The president wondered if

Adam Badeau with General Ulysses S. Grant. *Badeau (left) joined Grant's staff in February 1864 and became the general's admirer and sidekick. He was present with Grant at Appomattox and later served as American consul general in London while Grant was president.*

Grant could take him into his military family. Robert would have enlisted earlier if not for parental opposition, especially from his mother. It stung him to hear his father's critics accuse him of hiding out from the war at Harvard. Now, reborn as Captain Lincoln, he joined Grant's staff. "He is young, but I like him," Badeau wrote Wilson. "He is a nice fellow, bright, manly, gentlemanly."[10]

When Robert learned that Badeau was Edwin's close friend, he told him a story.

A few months earlier, on a trip from New York to Washington, Robert was at the railroad station in Jersey City, New Jersey. He waited in line near the cars to purchase a sleeping berth on the midnight train. Suddenly, the train moved, the crowd scrummed, "and I was screwed off my feet, which dropped into the slot between the car and the platform," he told his Aunt Emilie. "I was for a few seconds in a dangerous position from which I could not rescue myself." Then a hand reached out, grabbed Robert by the collar, and yanked him back up on the platform. "I was probably saved from a very bad injury if not something more."

Turning to his rescuer, he exclaimed, "That was a narrow escape, Mr. Booth." It was Edwin, well known on sight to Robert, who belonged to an amateur acting club at Harvard.[11]

Edwin had no idea whom he rescued until months later when he learned it from Badeau.[12]

EDWIN SAT ALONE in the Walnut Street Theatre's darkened parquet. In such moments he always felt the presence of his late wife Mollie. Crunched into his seat, he was lost to the world when fellow actor Edwin Adams disturbed him to introduce merchant William Bispham. Although the latter was a stranger, Edwin shared with Bispham his highly personal séance experiences. "Booth was a firm believer in the ability of the denizens of the world of spirits to communicate their thoughts and messages to friends in this world," the newcomer later told friends.[13]

Bispham realized that Edwin was unhappy, however. Spiritualism didn't relieve his grief; it prolonged it. "I feel the need—the absolute necessity—of something practical," he said. "Something to draw me out of myself." That was why he was in Philadelphia. He and his brother-in-law Clarke, Asia's husband, had purchased the theater. The cost was two hundred thousand dollars—more than four million dollars today. It was a huge gamble, with a heavy mortgage, but it focused his thoughts. "If buying theatres on time won't do me good, naught but a bullet will," he wrote.[14]

Although Edwin was superbly talented and made good money, he knew that John had more of the inborn acting genius of the Booths. The younger brother inherited their father's "divine spark" of talent, passion, and eccentricity, a combination that study, training, and experience could never produce. Theatrical impresario John T. Ford, who knew all there was to know about actors, told a reporter in 1885, "I have managed all the Booths that have ever been on the stage, and I regard Wilkes as the greatest of them all." William Seymour, who acted with both brothers, stated, "If John had lived and continued on the stage, he would have outstripped in fame, ability and popularity not only Edwin, but *all* the tragedians who were his contemporaries."[15]

"He might have been a great man," lamented comedian John T. Raymond, a friend.[16]

Unlike Raymond and his colleagues, however, John didn't live to act. He found being a star "the hardest work in the world." It was unreal, this life where one worked while others played. Indeed, one's work *was* others' play. The wear and tear of nightly performances (most involving sword fights), the constant travel, the lack of roots, and the temptations of the road exhausted him. Bronchitis and bouts of hoarseness came on in 1864, raising questions about his future as an actor.

When the season closed in May 1864, John quit the stage to speculate in Pennsylvania oil leases. His investments were a total loss. Joe Simonds, a partner in his oil ventures, feared the results. What would John do with no profession, no income, no reason to get up in the morning?[17]

Simonds was right to worry. It was only his mother Mary Ann's frantic pleas that kept John from enlisting in the Confederate army in 1861. He lived uneasily with the decision and acted, but, as the war turned against the South, he was filled with self-reproach. "I have lived a slave in the North," he wrote his mother in a letter placed among his papers for her to find, "not daring to express my thoughts and sentiments, even in my own home, constantly hearing every principle dear to my heart denounced as treasonable. I have cursed my willful idleness and begun to deem myself a coward, to despise my own existence. I cannot longer resist the inclination to go and share the sufferings of my brave countrymen.

"It seems that uncontrollable fate, moving me for its ends, takes me from you, dear Mother, to do what work I can." The old Romani woman's curse recurred to him—death at an early age, death as a soldier.[18]

John had no intention of putting on a rebel uniform. He would use what he boasted was a brain worth twenty men to aid the South in a remarkable scheme. During his lifetime (he was twenty-six when he shot Lincoln) no president ever had a second term. The fact that Lincoln sought one at a time when there were no term limits convinced John that the president wanted to be a dictator. He could prevent that by abducting Lincoln and taking him to Richmond. That would thwart what John believed were the president's kingly ambitions as well as give the South a bargaining chip with which to negotiate the release of Confederate prisoners of war.

He got his plot underway in August 1864 when he enlisted the services of two boyhood friends, both ex-Confederate soldiers. Over the next few months his team expanded to include a rebel agent, a blockade runner, a Confederate deserter, and others. There were also Southern sympathizers in the Maryland countryside near Washington who promised to help move the president, once abducted, over the Potomac River to Virginia.[19]

Three times in March 1865, John went after the president. He attempted to get near him on the day of the second inauguration, jumping into the official procession that escorted Lincoln to the speaker's platform. What he intended is unclear, as he was seized by Capitol police and thrown back into the crowd. Several weeks later he orchestrated an abduction effort at Ford's Theatre where Lincoln was expected to attend an opera, only to learn that the president was out of town. Each failure made him angrier and more volatile.[20]

John lived in Washington more or less full-time, absorbed with his plot against Lincoln. "It seemed to be his only thought by day and, from his conversation, his frequent dreams by night," recalled Sam Arnold, one of his conspiracy team. "Destroying in its onward march the better feelings of his nature, it absorbed every other thought of his mind." John's sister Asia later realized that in his manic preoccupation with the president he was self-immolating.[21]

Mary Ann had frightening dreams about him. She sent June to Washington to bring him to New York. John had lied to his brother about his financial situation—and God knows what else—and June confronted him. As they stood talking in the street, tears streamed from John's eyes as he spoke about the dying Confederacy. June had never seen him wound so tightly.

It was his father's legacy, friends later acknowledged "The mind that broods over its own thoughts, that lives in a world of its own creation, that pictures in its own imagination the ideal," wrote John Cooper Vail, Junius's contemporary and biographer, "reaches a point at which reason and madness began to mingle."[22]

On March 17, 1865, John received word that Lincoln would attend a theatrical event at Campbell Hospital, a military facility for sick and wounded soldiers near the northern boundary of Washington. Heavily armed, John and five of his men rode out to the hospital area and lurked nearby. To their surprise and disappointment, they learned that Lincoln was not present. He was downtown, making a speech. John hurried back to the city and joined an audience gathered to greet the president on Pennsylvania Avenue. Leaning against an ornate lamppost that was a local landmark, he stared up at the president, who spoke from a hotel balcony overlooking the street.

Thomas E. Richardson, a theatrical agent, was a friend of John's and came over to say hello. He was startled to realize that the actor couldn't hear those speaking to him. He seemed transfixed. "His face was the very embodiment of tragedy," recalled Richardson in a postwar interview, "every feature distorted into one of the most demonical expressions I have ever seen on or off stage."[23]

OF ALL THE spiritualists of this era, none was more talented or more trouble than Charles J. Colchester.

This medium was an energetic man with a ruddy complexion, sandy-colored mustache, brilliant blue-gray eyes, and a high forehead crowned with brown hair. He looked intelligent, or at least shrewd, and had "nothing of the long-haired, vegetarian, dreamy look which characterizes the mass of his followers," wrote journalist Joseph Warren. It was curious to Warren that Colchester, unlike most mediums, was lighthearted, "with a jolly appreciation of life somewhat inconsistent with what some people might call *his mission.*" He made a wonderful impression.[24]

Colchester was the professional name of Jackson Sealby, the son of Isaac Sealby and Sarah Jackson, a couple from Keswick, Cumberland, in England's Lake District. The child attended Croft House Academy in Brampton, one of the best schools in the north of England. When his mother and two infant siblings died, his father, an edge-tool maker, went bankrupt, remarried, and started a new family. Jackson moved on, immigrating to the United States in 1852 at the age of sixteen. Times were hard, and he was jailed for embezzling money from a pawn store in the Bowery where he worked (or so said spiritualist gossip many years later).[25]

Colchester commenced his career as a test medium in the bohemian environs of Manhattan's Amity Street shortly before the war. He was known for his ability to read sealed messages. Sitting in an armchair before a cloth-covered table, he invited visitors to sit opposite him and write on slips of paper the names of dead friends along with brief questions for the deceased to answer. The notes were wadded tightly together (to preclude his seeing the contents) and placed in a hat near the medium. Colchester then mixed them up so no one would know their order. Taking one, he would twist, sigh, grimace, roll his eyes, and finally give a message from the spirit without opening the paper to learn the decedent's name or question. This, someone said, was truly "the dead-letter office" in operation.

He also performed blood writing. Given the name of the deceased on a paper, he would crumple it up, throw it across the room, tap one arm with the other, and pull up his coat and shirt sleeve to reveal the name of that person on the skin of his left arm below the elbow. The name appeared in scarlet or blood-red letters on unbroken skin. A third manifestation involved tying an assistant with loops of twine to immobilize him, then placing a banjo on a table. Colchester doused the lights and joined hands

Charles J. Colchester. *Jackson Sealby, known professionally as Colchester, was an English medium whose career was marred by bouts of drunkenness and cheating. In the weeks before the Lincoln assassination, he was both medium to the First Family and close friend of John Wilkes Booth.*

with the circle of sitters. In the darkness the twang of the banjo could be heard circling above their heads.[26]

Elizabeth Keckly, Mary Lincoln's seamstress and confidante, encouraged the First Lady to see Colchester, whom she might have met as she grieved the loss of her son George at the Battle of Wilson's Creek in 1861.

The Lincolns had a cottage at the Soldiers' Home, a government facility for invalid soldiers three miles north of the city, that allowed them to escape the hubbub of the presidential mansion. Colchester visited there and, "playing on [Mary's] motherly sorrows," conjured up Willie by means of scratching noises on the walls, furniture, and wainscoting. The medium was a master at reading people—their moods, gestures, interactions, sidelong glances, even clothes. Armed with the information these provided, he was halfway home with a sitter as eager to believe as Mary.[27]

Predictably, the First Lady was wowed by her experience. She invited Colchester to the White House for private sittings. Lincoln attended several of these and found the medium's ability to summon noises from different parts of the room mystifying. He asked the wizard to submit to an examination by Joseph Henry at the Smithsonian. "He is one of the pleasantest men I have ever met," Lincoln said. Amiably, Colchester agreed.[28]

Unsurprisingly, the Castle proved to be a shark tank for the young Englishman. Henry was an expert on acoustics as well as an opponent of spiritualism. The secretary had discussed mediums with Pierpont, who told him how he had seen one rise and waft himself out a window. "You never saw that," replied Henry, "and, if you think you did, you are in a dangerous mental condition."

Henry's office was located near the lecture room on the north side of the building facing what is today the National Mall. The tests got quickly underway, and Colchester summoned noises from every direction. Henry turned his head left and right, cocking his ear up and down, in pursuit of the singularities. Then he said, "I do not know how you make the sounds, but this I perceive very clearly: they do not come from the room but from your person."

Chagrined, the secretary reported back to Lincoln that he had no immediate explanation for what he heard.[29]

WHY DID WILLIE have to die? Lincoln asked nurse Rebecca Pomroy. The loss of the boy with his innocence, exuberance, and affection was the hardest thing he ever endured, he told her. He repeated the question on the mind of every similarly suffering parent. "*Why?*"[30]

The president would have been less than human if he had not sought to find the highest possible purpose in the suffering in and around him. That interest deepened after Gettysburg. Lincoln read the Bible more frequently and attended New York Avenue Presbyterian Church with Mary. She became a member; he never did. He was not a traditional Christian, Mary told William Herndon, Lincoln's old law partner. The president explained: "The long, complicated statements of Christian doctrine which characterize their articles of belief and confessions of faith" made joining any church difficult. "A simple faith in God is good enough for me," he said.[31]

When Lincoln went to his knees, he told a friend, he did it because he had nowhere else to go. During the Battle of Gettysburg, he prayed for victory. "A sweet comfort crept into my soul that Almighty God had taken the whole business there into His own hands," he told General Sickles, "and we were bound to win." Realizing how odd this sounded, he added, "Of course, I don't want you to say anything about this—at least not now. People might laugh if it got out."[32]

The belief that God might answer prayers came slowly to Lincoln, raised in a religious tradition that held that whatever happened was ordained by God long ago. If God had already decided the course of events, there was no purpose in beseeching Him to change His mind.[33]

Now Lincoln prayed often and sought the prayers of others. Nearly half a century had passed, but he still recalled the prayers of his mother Nancy. "They have always followed me," he told nurse Pomroy. "They have clung to me all of my life." When Tad was ill, he told her he was grateful for her nightly supplications. "I hope you will pray for him," said the president, motioning to the boy, "and also for me, for I need the prayers of many."[34]

His youthful doubts had moderated. There had been no blinding moment of epiphany. Skepticism about biblical miracles and tall tales was too baked into his nature. But life had forced Lincoln to think anew about faith, with its sustaining power.

Joshua F. Speed—perhaps his most intimate friend—saw him reading the Bible near a window one day. "I'm glad to see you so profitably engaged," Speed said.

"Yes," Lincoln replied, "I am profitably engaged."

"Well," responded Speed, "if you have recovered from your skepticism, I am sorry to say that I have not."

Looking Speed in the face, he placed a hand on his shoulder and replied, "You are wrong, Speed. Take all of this book upon reason that you can and the balance on faith, and you will live and die a happier and better man."[35]

Lincoln at Prayer. *While Lincoln told people that he prayed, no one reported seeing him in any such melodramatic pose as shown in this 1917 engraving. The image suited the nation's sensibilities at the time, however.*

LEARNING THAT HER father Amasa was dangerously ill, Nettie Colburn called at the White House with her friend Parnie to tell the president that she needed to cancel an engagement with the Lincolns as her presence was required at home in Connecticut.

Lincoln was in a teasing mood. "Cannot our friends from *the upper country* tell you whether his illness is likely to prove fatal or not?" he asked.

Nettie replied that she had consulted the spirits and they assured her that his treatment was wrong. She was needed to straighten things out.

Turning to Parnie, Lincoln laughed, "I didn't catch her, did I?"

Nettie said she was sorry to miss the president's second inauguration the following week. But, she continued, the crowd would be so great and she was so short, she probably wouldn't have been able to see him anyway.

"You could not help it," Lincoln replied. "I shall be the tallest man there."[36]

It rained that morning—March 4, 1865—a leaden, windy, somber day. A dense crowd of spectators, the largest ever to witness an inauguration, waited at the east front of the Capitol. As Lincoln came out of the building and onto the ceremonial platform, "the sun burst from behind the clouds and covered him with its radiance," wrote Nathan Daniels, the spiritualist, in his diary, "an omen that was immediately accepted as auspicious." Lincoln, too, thought it was a happy sign.[37]

Reflecting the changes in his own beliefs, the president's address differed entirely from the one he had delivered four years earlier. That speech lacked a religious tone. This one, delivered in a clear, high-pitched voice, was practically a sermon. It mentioned God fourteen times, referenced biblical quotations or allusions seven, and prayer three. The key point was that, although the war's outcome wasn't as swift or as sure as most wanted, it was the playing out of God's will. "The Almighty has His own purposes." The conclusion pledged a lack of malice toward the rebels and promised charity to all. It was crowning evidence of Lincoln's humanity.[38]

He was proud of the effort. "Lots of wisdom in that document, I suspect," he later told friends as he filed the speech away in his desk.[39]

COLCHESTER LIVED AT the Washington House Hotel on Pennsylvania Avenue; John was three blocks down the street at the National. They met, and the actor liked the medium immediately. Colchester was a prophet, he had access to Lincoln, and he was fun. Since both were drinkers, they hit the town. John got excited when he drank. Colchester just got smashed. Asked out for a drink, Colchester would say that he must ask permission. He would slap his hand on a lamppost, commune with the spirits, obtain their consent, and start the party. He might be found at the end of the evening passed out in the street, his nose in the gutter.[40]

Colchester's behavior drew notice. "His associations were villainous. His haunts—gambling halls and houses of ill fame," wrote editor Enos Reed of the medium's visit to Cincinnati. "He looked upon himself as peculiarly *killing* among the fair sex while in truth a virtuous woman would read the man at a glance. While flourishing fine-quality kid gloves and jeweled opera glasses, "the graceless swindler" left his bills unpaid. Whatever Reed thought, the rank and file remained loyal, and Colchester flourished. He knew he was a rogue, but that was how he lived well. All was fair that advanced that goal.[41]

Judge Edmonds was among the first to denounce Colchester's deceptions at the séance table. When he cautioned people to stay clear of the young Englishman, the rest of the spiritualist establishment piled on. "Colchester is an imposter and a cheat whose practices are calculated to inspire distrust of spiritualism," wrote novelist John Hovey Robinson. "I went to see him to see new and strange phenomena, not to waste my time and pay my money for sleight-of-hand performances. Life has higher meanings and money better uses."[42]

A few weeks after the inauguration, John arranged for Colchester to take a part in a play at Ford's Theatre. He became Trueworth in *The Love Chase*, a romantic comedy. Having played this character as a young actor, John could help, and Colchester needed all the coaching he could get. The part was no walk-on. Trueworth had several hundred lines in four of the play's five acts in a role that required considerable comic timing. Since the medium was in debt, the effort was worth the money and John's help was appreciated. As his character in the play said, "Men sometimes find a friend's hand of avail / When useless proves their own."[43]

One of Colchester's biggest flaws was a love of talk. The gregarious medium revealed his trade secrets to three different business agents, and, when they fell out with him, all three ran to the newspapers. They told reporters that, when stirring a bowl of sealed pellets, Colchester retrieved one, deftly hiding it in the hollow of his left hand by the third and fourth fingers. Distracting sitters by asking them to write the names of deceased friends, he let the hand drop into his lap where, concealed by a tablecloth, he unfolded and read the message. That way, reading one pellet ahead, he appeared to know the contents of unopened packets as he retrieved them.

For blood writing, Colchester wore a coat with large heavy sleeves, underneath which was a woolen shirt split open from the wrist to the elbow. Using a red pencil of medium hardness, he wrote any name required on his left arm. A knitted brow, a spasmodic jerk, and an expression of pain preceded the big reveal as Colchester pulled up his sleeve. The sounds whose source the Smithsonian's Henry failed to discover at the institution were created by an apparatus fastened around Colchester's biceps that, when contracted, produced clicks by a motion not discernable to an observer. Floating instruments were held and played when hands tied by ropes slipped out of their knots. Raps were made by tapping boots on table legs. It was skillful work, nothing more.[44]

"CAN YOU NOT visit City Point for a day or two?" Grant telegraphed the president on March 20, 1865. "I would like very much to see you, and I think the rest would do you good." Lincoln needed no urging, and four days later he arrived with Mary and Tad at the general's large military base on the James River below Richmond.[45]

On the warm, clear morning of March 25 the Lincolns and Julia Grant, the general's wife, set out to visit the headquarters of General George Meade. After a brief train ride, the president proceeded on horseback while "the Presidentress" (as Mary was called) and Julia followed in a military ambulance, a sort of half-open carriage. Badeau was assigned as their escort, and he sat backward on the driver's seat, facing the women.

Passing the time, Badeau remarked casually that officers' wives had been ordered away from the front—a sure sign that the spring campaign was in the offing. All were leaving except Sallie Griffin, the elegant wife of General Charles Griffin. She had obtained special permission from the president to stay.

"What do you mean by that, sir?" Mary exclaimed. "Do you mean to say that she saw the President alone? Do you know that I never allow the President to see any woman alone?"

"She was fairly boiling over with rage," Badeau realized. "She was absolutely jealous of poor, ugly Abraham Lincoln." Shocked at what he had ignited, he faked a smile. It incensed her.

"Let me out of this carriage at once!" she shouted. When he hesitated, she reached past him and grabbed the driver. Julia convinced her to stay until they reached their destination, where Mary took General Meade's arm and marched away. "I saw them go off together and remained in fear and trembling for what might occur," wrote Badeau. When the First Lady returned, she told him that Meade informed her it was Secretary of War Stanton, not the president, who gave the permission. She said, "General Meade is a gentleman, sir," with a hard stare at Badeau that said he wasn't.

"Stuck-up, vulgar vixen!" Badeau thought to himself. That evening he and Julia talked over the incident, and she told him "the whole affair was so distressing and mortifying that neither of us must ever mention it." Badeau agreed, little realizing that worse was to come.

The following day he was ordered to go with the Lincolns and a large party to review soldiers of General Edward Ord's Army of the James near Malvern Hill. Once again, he would ride with Mary and Julia. Frightened of losing more tail feathers, he asked Grant to send Horace Porter, his tentmate, with him. Badeau had no desire to be the only officer in the carriage.

Lincoln, with Grant, Ord, their staff, and guests, rode off on horseback toward the parade field while Mary and Julia got into an ambulance to follow. There was no room for Mary Ord, the general's wife. So, this "remarkably handsome woman" (in the opinion of one of those present) turned her horse onto the road and disappeared with the men. She was an excellent rider.

The ambulance was a specially adapted vehicle from Grant's headquarters fitted with added springs and cross-seats for comfort. Unfortunately, the two-plus miles to the parade ground traversed a swamp. The road was partly corduroyed, with small tree trunks laid out like bricks in a sidewalk. Better than hub-deep mud, it was still rough traveling, and the improved spring design bobbed the passengers around like corks. The women's hats hit the top of the wagon repeatedly and sometimes their heads smacked it as well.

The military review was underway when the ambulance arrived on the field and the First Lady, exhausted and very put out, saw Mary Ord riding with the president and others. "As soon as Mrs. Lincoln discovered this," recalled Badeau, "her rage was beyond all bounds."

"What does the woman mean," she cried out, "by riding by the side of the President? And ahead of me? Does she suppose that *he* wants *her* by the side of *him*?" Was she trying to pass herself off as the First Lady?

Mary Ord noticed the ambulance's arrival. Reining out of the crowd, she galloped over to join the women.

When she rode up, "Mrs. Lincoln positively insulted her, called her vile names in the presence of a crowd of officers, and asked her what she meant by following up the President," wrote Badeau. "The poor woman burst into tears. Everyone was shocked and horrified."

"Oh, Mrs. Lincoln, what have I done?" pleaded Mrs. Ord. Mary turned on Captain John S. Barnes, the unfortunate woman's escort. He would be dismissed from the service, she declared. "We both backed out of hearing, absolutely dumb with astonishment," Barnes recalled. He knew that was the only thing to do when an unbalanced mind was at work.

At dinner that evening Mary continued her attack on Sallie Griffin and Mary Ord, urging that the latter's husband be removed from command. When Lincoln demurred, she went after him. "I never suffered greater humiliation and pain on account of one not a near personal friend than when I saw the Head of the State—a man who carried all the cares of the Nation at such a crisis—subject to this inexpressible public mortification," wrote Badeau. "He pleaded with eyes and tones, and endeavored to explain or palliate the offenses of others, till she turned on him like a tigress. Then he walked away, hiding that noble, ugly face that we might not catch the full expression of its misery."[46]

The rebel army abandoned Richmond one week later, fleeing west. When Badeau entered the Confederate capital with Ord, whose troops were the first to occupy the city, fires still smoldered. Around them destitute citizens and refugees from the countryside wandered the streets amid a litter of official papers from the dying government or wads of its now-worthless paper money. "This attempted empire, which held its front so high and cost such expense of life and labor to subdue," wrote Badeau, "was a wreck and a ruin, and the fragments were all about me like the blocks of a trembling temple in an earthquake." While it was all he had fought for, Badeau found it sad to see.[47]

Appomattox County, with its farms, pastures, and gentle hills, was a startling contrast to the devastated countryside around the Confederate capital where Badeau had spent the last eleven months. The area was untouched by large armies. Its pastures were green, fields plowed for planting, and fruit trees ready to blossom. Balmy and placid, it sparkled in the early spring weather.

By some miracle the South's Army of Northern Virginia had made it here—ninety miles from the Richmond-Petersburg defenses—before being trapped. Realizing that further fighting would lead to the slaughter of his men, General Lee sued for peace on April 9, 1865, and that Sunday afternoon he waited for Grant at the home of Wilmer and Virginia McLean near the county courthouse. Lee attended with a single aide. Grant arrived about thirty minutes after Lee. He entered the parlor, shook his opponent's hand, and brought in about twenty Union officers and staff who wanted to meet the man who had tormented them for so long. The group included Badeau, Ord, Porter, and Robert Lincoln.

A born storyteller, Badeau fixed an eye on the rebel chief and gathered observations for Harry. "Lee was tall, large in form, fair in person, handsome in feature, grave and dignified in bearing," he wrote the friend. "He behaved with great dignity and courtesy but no cordiality. He seemed depressed and talked but little."

Grant was Grant. His fatigue coat dusty and soiled, he was younger, shorter, and without the imperial presence of his adversary, but he remained simple, composed, and in charge. "He was perfect in his demeanor and spoke and acted as plainly as if he were transacting an ordinary matter of business," said Badeau. "No one would have suspected he was about to receive the surrender of an army, or that one of the most terrible wars of modern times had been brought to a triumphant close."[48]

Grant couldn't fathom Lee's state of mind, "but my own feelings were sad and depressed," he wrote in his memoirs. "I felt like anything rather than rejoicing at the downfall of a foe who had fought so long and valiantly, and had suffered so much for a cause, though that cause was, I believe, one of the worst for which a people ever fought, and one for which there was the least excuse. I do not question, however, the sincerity of the great mass of those who were opposed to us."[49]

Grant wrote the surrender document without notes or prior thought on a delicate-looking Elizabethan-style table. Lee took out his glasses and read the paper with a resigned air. He signed it without debate.

Badeau sat with three other officers on a long couch in the room. In his own mind he was elsewhere. He later commissioned an engraving of himself standing alone, his elbow resting on the fireplace mantel. Sword at hand, he looked dashing in his double-breasted frock coat and heavy cavalry boots. The silver oak leaf on his shoulder straps framed with gold announced his rank as lieutenant colonel. A step or two away from both commanding generals, he placed himself poised as if ready to advise them.

When Lee left after the ninety-minute conference, Badeau was the first person to Grant's side and told him that what had just happened would live in history. "I am sure from the expression of his face that the idea had not occurred to him before," said the aide. Grant was thinking about disarming the soldiers, getting them home, and other practical matters. "He had not thought of himself or his own fame. He was so simple, so unambitious, so unstudied, so apparently unconscious of self, so utterly unlike what I supposed a great man to be," said Badeau.

The following day Grant received several high-ranking Confederate officers at the McLean house. "General, we have come to congratulate you for having wound us up," one of them said.

"I hope it will be for the good of us all," replied Grant.[50]

ON THE DARK and chilly evening of April 11, Lincoln spoke to a large crowd gathered on the north lawn of the White House. The mansion was illuminated and the president framed by light streaming from the second-floor window where he stood.

Mary listened from an adjoining window with her young friend Clara Harris, the daughter of a New York senator. Clara noticed John Wilkes in the crowd. He was prominent enough to draw notice.[51]

Lincoln's listeners, celebrating the news from Appomattox, expected a victory speech. He gave them instead a think-piece on the political situation in Louisiana. The remarks were better suited for a cabinet discussion, but Lincoln was concerned about the future. The audience listened patiently as raindrops drummed on their umbrellas. They were content, sharing a historic moment with the man who—more than anyone else—had made it possible.

On the controversial issue of Black voting, Lincoln did not equivocate. He realized it would be wrong to deny the vote to African American soldiers and supporters of the Union. "I would myself prefer that it were now conferred on the very intelligent and on those who serve our cause as soldiers," he said.

"That means nigger citizenship," muttered John, who stood in the audience with David Herold, one of his men. "Now, by God! I'll put him through." Herold later told his attorney that from this moment, John was determined to kill the president. "That is the last speech he will ever make," growled the actor.[52]

Colchester was not a member of John's conspiracy team; at least, those

The Dark Circle. *Séances conducted in the dark featured overhead apparitions and floating instruments. In this illustration, William and Ira Davenport, two of John Wilkes Booth's favorite mediums, remove their boots to lessen the noise of their movements.*

who were never mentioned him. Yet he was more than a friend. G. W. Bunker, the desk clerk at John's hotel, saw the medium go in and out of the actor's room so frequently that he felt the two were up to something.

Like other intimates of the star, Colchester was struck by John's threats against Lincoln. The spiritualist had his faults, but at the end of the day he was a man of misdemeanor, not felony, and this type of hatred was over his head. Frightened, he gave Lincoln vague but repeated warnings to take care. When someone else also advised the president to be cautious, Lincoln replied, "Colchester has been telling me that for months."[53]

Meanwhile, the medium—broke again—made a very poor decision. He told Mary that if she didn't provide him with a pass to travel free to New York, he would talk publicly about her. Unscrupulous individuals had a field day with the personal information shared at séances by people like Mary. As she now came to realize, it was a common way to blackmail someone.[54]

Panic-stricken, Mary turned to Noah Brooks, a close family friend.

Brooks knew Colchester, as he had attended one of the medium's séances at a private home. It was a "dark circle" with a drum, a banjo, and bells on a table. When the lights were extinguished and all held hands, the noise of these instruments sounded above the sitters' heads.

Pulling his hands free, Brooks grasped in the direction of the drumbeats, fastened onto something, and yelled, "Strike a light!" The next instant something whacked him on the head. When the gas was relit, Brooks was standing with a forehead covered with blood and a hand in possession of Colchester, who held the drum and bells. Chaos followed, and the medium fled the room, muttering that he had been insulted.

Brooks and Mary hatched a plan. She invited Colchester to the White House. When he arrived, she left the room and Brooks confronted him. "Do you recognize this?" he asked, lifting the hair from the wound on his forehead.

As Colchester sputtered a reply, Brooks continued. "You know that I know you are a swindler and a humbug. Get out of this house and out of this city at once. If you are in Washington tomorrow afternoon at this time, you will be in old Capitol prison."

Brooks was a journalist. He had no power to put anyone anywhere. But Colchester realized he knew those who did. "The little scamp pulled himself together and sneaked out of the house, and, so far as I know, out of Washington," continued Brooks. "I never saw or heard of him afterward."[55]

WHEN THE BUSINESS partner of John's friend Richard M. Johnson was murdered in 1864, John drove with him to the undertaker to make arrangements for shipping the body home. To Johnson's surprise, the actor wouldn't come inside. "My God, man, no, no," said John. "I cannot look upon the dead. It is a terrible sight to me. The sight of human blood is terrible to me. I cannot look upon it." As John said this, he shrank back into the corner of their carriage. His face grew dark. His features worked violently.

He trembled. He put his hands up as if warding off an invisible blow. "It is terrible for a man to shed the blood of another," John said.[56]

Suffering from both hemophobia and necrophobia (irrational fears of blood and of dead bodies), John was an unlikely assassin. Friends knew he was impulsive and bullheaded, of course, but he seemed essentially harmless. They admired him as a loving family member. They envied him as a popular actor. They appreciated him as a generous companion. If John was hard-charging by nature, they didn't think of him as violent; if opinionated, not obnoxious; if unsettled, not unhinged.

But the fear of abolitionists that marked his teenage years deepened into a white-hot hatred as he matured, and Lincoln, who ended slavery in the rebel states with the Emancipation Proclamation, personified all he abhorred. With Appomattox, this turmoil grew to a frenzy and overwhelmed his limited store of common sense. Both to punish the North for its aggression and to incapacitate its war machine, the time had come to act. John found legitimacy in the examples of William Tell and Brutus, heroes of resistance to autocratic rule. He felt sure people would appreciate what he did. After all, audiences had applauded both characters on the stage. He heard it.[57]

Our American Cousin, a comedy staple, was in its third act when John climbed the stairs to the Dress Circle, the second floor of seats at Ford's Theatre. It was ten past ten in the evening of April 14, 1865, and the house was well attended. Several of the actor's friends stood along the walls. They nodded to him as he passed, but John ignored them. His attention was on the State Box, a private suite of seats projecting over the stage where Lincoln, Mary, and two guests sat. He walked steadily toward it.

The president was essentially unguarded. John Parker, a plainclothes policeman, escorted the Lincoln party to the theater. Depositing them, he left the building for a drink. Mary's friend Clara Harris was present in the box along with Major Henry Rathbone, her fiancé. An unarmed guest in civilian clothes, Rathbone was a pencil pusher whose health precluded field service. Charles Forbes, sitting outside the box's outer door, was a presidential messenger and valet.

Neither Rathbone nor Forbes—nor Parker, if he could be found—feared for Lincoln's safety. Why should they? Lincoln had visited Richmond without incident shortly after its capture. Now he was home, seated among hundreds of friends and admirers, many of them soldiers and sailors. The mood was celebratory, the evening festive. The nightmare of the brothers' war was over.

On reaching Forbes, John took out a small pack of visiting cards, studied one, and handed it to the valet. It was rumored that the card bore the name of a distinguished senator. Knowing how warmly Lincoln welcomed visits by actors, it might have been one of John's own, however. Either way, mystery attaches to this card. It vanished, and for some strange reason Forbes—the man with the awful responsibility of having waved John into the president's presence—was never called upon to explain himself.

The actor entered a small antechamber leading to the State Box. He wedged a wooden brace between a previously prepared mortise in the wall and the door. This prevented anyone from entering after him.

Two small doors led off the entryway to the State Box. Neither had working locks, and one was actually ajar. A quick look by John revealed Rathbone and Harris seated to the right at the far end of the box. Opposite them sat Mary and her husband, the latter bundled up in a rocker. The president was the closest of the box's occupants to John. He was only four feet away.

Scene 2 played in the background. John knew it like a familiar tune. He had performed in *Our American Cousin*, once nine nights in a row. He was aware that Harry Hawk, as the folksy American Asa Trenchard, had a soliloquy to deliver. Hawk would be alone on a stage unencumbered by props or furniture. The musicians' seats, located near the stage in a pit, were empty. There was no one and nothing on the stage or near it to impede his escape in that direction.

"He knew just what he was going to do, and how much time he had," said Harry Ford, the theater's treasurer.

Hawk's speech was six lines of cornpone, rebuking a fortune-hunting English matron who just stormed off the stage. It would take him about thirty seconds to deliver it.

"Don't know the manners of good society, eh?" began Hawk. "Well, I guess I know enough to turn you inside out, old gal—you sockdologizing old man-trap."

John stepped behind the president. He held a derringer pistol that fired a bullet about the size of a small grape. It was a compact weapon with low muzzle velocity, but, at point-blank range, it delivered a fearsome blow. Pointing the pistol at a spot behind Lincoln's left ear, he cried, "Freedom!" and fired.

The bullet slammed into the president's head. His right arm jumped reflexively, and he sank forward in his chair, his head falling onto his chest. There was no cry of pain, not even a sigh. His eyes closed. It appeared as if he had fallen asleep. He never knew what hit him.

The sharp crack of the shot rang throughout the auditorium, lobby, and backstage. It startled those in the theater and stunned those in the State Box.

John's pistol was a single-shot weapon—a one-and-done. Since he had no time to reload it, it was useless now, and he threw it on the floor. Pulling out a large knife, he rushed past Mary, brushing the shawl from her lap as he passed to the front of the box overlooking the stage.[58]

Rathbone, sitting four steps from Lincoln, was facing away from the president when the shot was fired. Turning, he saw a cloud of whitish gun smoke filling the box. Suddenly, John emerged from it like a ghost. Realizing something was very wrong, the officer leaped up. Wrapping his arms around the assassin from behind, Rathbone pulled him back from the box's railing.

Rathbone had fight, but he was badly mismatched. He lacked the assassin's remarkable strength and feral intensity. John twisted around in his grasp. "I might as well have tried to hold a machine of iron," recalled Rathbone. "He seemed endowed with sinews of steel." When the men drew chin-to-chin, the sight of John's face horrified the officer. "His countenance was like that of a demon."

"Let go of me, or I will kill you!" John gasped.

"No, I will not!" shouted Rathbone, seizing him by the throat.

John's knife was in his right hand. Freeing this arm, he plunged the blade down at Rathbone. As the officer raised his left arm to parry the blow, the knife struck it, slicing deeply from the elbow toward the shoulder. Rathbone fell away.[59]

John returned to the balustrade. There was an eleven-foot-plus drop from it to the stage. The distance was substantial, but he had made jumps of similar height in his acting career. He knew he could do it.

Straightening himself up, he faced the audience and cried in a loud clear voice, "Sic semper tyrannis!"

As John scrambled over the railing, Rathbone reappeared and grabbed for the assassin. He got only a handful of coat. John pulled away, but the action threw the assassin off-balance, and, as he swung over the railing, the rowel of the spur on his right heel became entangled in a flag used to decorate the front of the box.

John fell toward the stage floor, a part-jump, part-fall. Ripping into the silk banner and bringing a strip of it with him, he crash-landed onto the green stage carpet. His impact sounded nearly as loudly as the shot.

The fibula in John's left leg above the ankle snapped when he hit. The smaller of the two lower leg bones, it broke as cleanly as a stick of candy breaks. A blinding pain shot through him, followed by lightheadedness and nausea. "I felt that I was going to swoon upon the stage, and I would have been captured right there," he later told a friend.[60]

Gathering himself, he shook off the haze, stood up, and looked around. Hawk, the only actor onstage, was astonished to see him. Realizing that John holding a bloodstained knife could not possibly be good news, he turned and ran for the stairs. John let him go, of course. It was center stage he wanted. His injury—serious but not disabling—allowed him to move. Fired by adrenaline, John stepped to the footlights, dragging a piece of flag on his spur.

There was a commotion behind him in the box where Rathbone staggered about, but in the house an unaccustomed attentiveness reigned. A single cough could have been heard. Sixteen hundred people watched

Assassination of Lincoln. *In this contemporary illustration, Mary Lincoln reaches for her mortally wounded husband as John Wilkes Booth declaims his deed onstage. The audience was uncertain of what was happening, however, and did not react immediately as shown here.*

expectantly as John came forward. Some thought this was part of the play. Others, recognizing John, were sure of it. Almost no one realized what was happening.

Approaching the footlights, John paused. His pale face, set with black hair and dark eyes, was wild with excitement. Drawing himself up with professional composure, he flung his dagger above his head. The weapon glittered like a diamond in the gaslight. In a deliberately theatrical tone, he exclaimed, "The South is avenged!" A more dramatic moment was unimaginable, but, due to ignorance of what had happened in the State Box, its drama was apparent only in hindsight.

"Stop that man!" Rathbone cried. "Stop him!"

Turning, John fled to the first entrance stage right, where Laura Keene and William Ferguson stood at the prompter's desk. He was gasping for breath as he passed between them.

The assassin turned into a wing space that connected the dressing rooms and backstage to a door that exited the theater into an alley. The space was narrow—three feet at places—and always kept clear for the passage of the actors, but there stood William Withers, the orchestra leader. He blockaded the way as he chatted with Jeannie Gourley, a prospective girlfriend.[61]

"Let me pass! Let me pass!" cried John.

Turning to see what the fuss was about, Withers was shocked and confused. "I did not know what was the matter and stood completely paralyzed," he said. "I could not get out of his way."

John collided with the music man, spinning him around. The assassin swung his knife twice at Withers to back him up, cutting his coat at the shoulder and giving him a nick on the neck. Withers got the message, dropping to the floor.[62]

John scrambled over him and rushed out the exit.

Attorney Joseph B. Stewart, sitting with his family near the orchestra pit, was the first person in the theater to react to what happened. John was still onstage when Stewart mounted the orchestra railing, preparing to leap after him. Slipping, he fell among the musicians' chairs. He got onto the stage with a second effort and followed the path John took to the wings. The lawyer was only steps behind him.[63]

When Stewart finally opened the exit door, John was completing his mount of a horse he had left in the alley. The lawyer was the last person John wanted to see. Stewart was an athletic six-feet-four-inches tall with the body and fortitude of a giant.

"I have never had any desire to take the life of any human being," said Stewart, "but, if the opportunity had then been presented, it would have been a struggle to the death, and I would have been the survivor."[64]

John was unfamiliar with his horse. He had rented her that afternoon when his favorite sorrel was unavailable, and she proved spirited and uneasy. The excitement in the alley spooked her further and, under John's awkward mount, she circled hard to the left.

Stewart hoped to grab her reins, but the mare stamped and turned. Her hooves struck fire on the alley's paving stones as John struggled to control the animal.

As Stewart approached her flanks, the assassin finally headed the horse up and spurred her. The bay lunged forward with John crouched over the saddle.

Flinging dirt from her hooves at Stewart, she darted off.

In an instant horse and rider disappeared down the moonlit passage.[65]

ARE WE SO
SOON FORGOT?

"**B**ring him in here!" shouted Henry Safford from the steps of a townhouse across 10th Street. He held a candle and beckoned to the soldiers carrying Lincoln as they stood uncertainly at the curb before the theater. The doctors who came to the president's assistance in the box said that placing Lincoln upright for a carriage ride to the White House would kill him. So, what to do?

"Bring him in here!" repeated Safford, a boarder in the home of merchant tailor William Petersen. The body bearers moved slowly across the street to the residence, maneuvering the president up its red sandstone steps and through the door. Safford directed them to a bedroom at the end of a hallway. Mary followed, crying, "Where is my dear husband? Where is he?" Behind her came the excited crowd from the street.[1]

The room was small and drab. Its furnishings were simple, its carpet worn, and its brownish wallpaper adorned with cheap engravings. The single bed in the room was too short for Lincoln, so he was laid diagonally across it. Bizarrely, John had napped on the bed a few weeks earlier when the room was rented by his friend, the actor John Mathews.[2]

Charles A. Leale, the first doctor to enter the box, had been in charge of the president since the start, and he asked Mary to leave the room so that he and two colleagues could make an examination of the president's entire body. She complied, and the physicians removed all of Lincoln's clothes. No injuries were found except the head wound. That was more than enough. Leale had realized at the theater that Lincoln was a dead man. "The history of surgery fails to record a recovery from such a fearful wound," he later wrote, "and I have never seen or heard of any other person with such a wound and injury to the sinus of the brain itself who lived even for an hour."[3]

The bullet had traversed Lincoln's head, coming to rest near the front of the skull over his right eye. The best that Leale and his colleagues could do for the president was remove the clots of blood that had formed at the wound's entrance point. Better to have a slight oozing of blood and brain tissue than let a coagulum form, compressing the brain and threatening breath and heartbeat.[4]

Leale held Lincoln's right hand throughout the ordeal. He was certain the president couldn't see him, "but I acted on the belief, if his sense of hearing and feeling remained, to let him in his blindness know, if possible, that he was in touch with humanity—and had a friend."

Anguished and inconsolable, Mary stretched out on a sofa in the front parlor. "All through that dreadful night," Clara Harris wrote, "she would look at me with horror and scream, 'Oh, my husband's blood, my dear husband's blood.'" Clara couldn't convince her that it was Rathbone's blood on her dress, not the president's. The officer had bled so freely that he collapsed after their arrival at the Petersen house.[5]

Mary visited her husband three or four times during the night. The doctors covered the bed's bloodstained pillows with clean napkins before she came in, but they could not hide from her the changes in Lincoln's face. The orbits of his eyes became greatly discolored from effused blood; the right eye protruded. Mary struggled with the horror, sometimes urging her husband to speak, sometimes sobbing and swooning. Her cries rang through the house.[6]

There were at least two dozen other people in the room. Crowded into a space that could barely accommodate a modern midsize car were nine military officers, nine cabinet members and government functionaries, six doctors, and one minister. Robert was at the bedside along with two female friends of his mother, stand-ins for the First Lady when she wasn't there.[7]

About 5:30 in the morning, as a gray rainy day looked in through the room's two windows, the discharge from the wound ceased. Respiration became more labored and the pulse almost imperceptible. There might be a minute between breaths. Bystanders looked at their watches to note the time of death only to have a fluttering breath draw their eyes back to the president. As the end neared, the gloom in the room increased. Most of those present had deeply personal connections with Lincoln. This was the end of the most memorable association of their lives.

At twenty-one minutes, fifty-five seconds after seven, Lincoln took his last breath. His heart ceased to beat fifteen seconds later.

Surgeon General of the Army Joseph Barnes, who had his finger on the president's neck to monitor the carotid artery, leaned back. "He is gone," whispered Barnes.[8]

DESPITE HIS PROFESSIONAL and personal successes, John always believed he was unlucky. True to form, he tripped at the theater, breaking his leg in his moment of glory.[9]

There were two bits of good news, however. John escaped the city without a hitch and was joined by David Herold, one of the conspirators, as he fled south into Maryland. Herold was a born outdoorsman with no interest in politics. He signed up with John solely for the comradeship and adventure. With his freckled face, dark hair, and blue-black eyes, he was "a seedy, frowzy, monkey-faced boy," wrote an acquaintance. But Herold was also clever and dependable, and he knew the roads they must travel to flee south.[10]

The break in John's fibula was essentially a high ankle break. It was very painful and almost impossible to walk on. His back hurt, too. After two hours of galloping on his horse, the assassin's discomfort was so great he was forced to seek a doctor. He turned to Samuel A. Mudd, a physician involved in John's earlier abduction plot. During most of April 15, the day after the shooting, he rested at Mudd's home thirty miles from Washington. He was there when Lincoln died.

Pursuing soldiers rode past him while he was at Mudd's, leaving him *behind* them. The fact that he had not outrun the search parties was troubling. Fortunately for him, pursuers were initially uncertain which way he went. They were off to every point of the compass. They even searched his childhood home in Harford County. He had a secret cave there (just like his father) and had told a friend the previous year that "a man could live well there and conceal himself for a long time."[11]

Rebel sympathizers lined John's escape route, but they understood something he didn't. The murder of Lincoln did them no good. In fact, the retribution sure to come would be worse for them than Appomattox. They passed him off like a hot potato, praying that their assistance would not be discovered.

Samuel Cox, a leading rebel figure in Charles County, hid John and Herold in a pine forest near his home. Thomas Jones, Cox's foster brother, was asked to attend to the men and get them across the Potomac River to Virginia as quickly as possible.

"Take care how you approach them, Tom," cautioned Cox. "They are fully armed and might shoot you through mistake."[12]

A prearranged signal of whistles got Jones safely into their presence. He found the pair camped on the ground in a dense thicket.

The shabbily dressed Jones was a simple fisherman who knew the Potomac well and over the years had become a shrewd Southern agent. His ability to get mail, goods, and people safely over the river was legendary in rebel circles.

Jones did not know John, but when he saw the assassin's pain-wracked face, he was won over. "No sooner had I seen him in his helpless and suffering condition than I gave my whole mind to the problem of how to get him across the river. Murderer though I knew him to be, his condition so enlisted my sympathy in his behalf that I felt it my bounden duty to do all I could to aid him—be the consequences to me what they might. I told him so. He held out his hand and thanked me."

Over the next three days Jones brought ham, bread, coffee, and whiskey to John and Herold. The assassin asked for newspapers, too, anxious to learn what good had resulted from the assassination. They came bundled in a small roll. What John read when he flattened them out astonished him.

After a few hours of confusion, the government had righted itself. Vice President Andrew Johnson was sworn in uneventfully as Lincoln's successor, and things went on just as before. There were no revolutions, no riots, no collapse of the Northern armies, no revival of the Southern ones.

There *were* near-universal expressions in the North of shock, horror, and rage. John was labeled a coward and a monster. For an individual who prized his manliness, these charges shocked him.

The hardest thing for him was to read how fellow Confederates disavowed his act as a hellish crime. Said one: "Lee's surrender was nothing to it." Particularly hurtful were the words of colleagues like John T. Ford, who denounced him. Even Edwin rebuked John, writing in a public letter that Lincoln was "a good man and a most justly honored and patriotic ruler."[13] The older brother had supported the North during the war, voting for Lincoln in the 1864 presidential election, and he meant every word of his rebuke.

Determined to vindicate himself, John turned to the small pocket notebook he carried. "I struck boldly and not as the papers say. I walked with a firm step through a thousand of his friends, was stopped, but pushed on," he wrote in a diary note. "In jumping, broke my leg. I passed all his pickets, rode sixty miles that night, with the bone of my leg tearing the flesh at every jump.

"Our country owed all her troubles to him, and God simply made me the instrument of his punishment. I do not wish to shed a drop of blood, but *I must fight the course.* Tis all that's left to me."[14]

Jones got John and Herold on the river in his lead-colored skiff on the night of April 20. The weather was thick and foggy—good crossing weather—but due to more bad luck it was the morning of the 23rd before they landed in Virginia. Increasingly beleaguered and rebuffed by those he thought would acclaim him, John spent the night of April 25 in the barn of farmer Richard Garrett near the Rappahannock River.

About 2:30 in the morning John heard barking dogs and shouting voices. Twenty-seven soldiers of the 16th New York Cavalry Regiment and two detectives were at the Garrett house. Informed by one of the family that two strangers were in the barn, the troopers surrounded it. "You men had better come out of there," shouted Luther Baker, one of the detectives. "We know who you are."[15]

There was a moment of silence, and then John answered. "Who are you?" His voice was clear and composed.

A parley of questions, demands, and threats ensued. The upshot was that John swore he would never surrender, and Baker replied that in that case he would burn the barn down with the assassin in it.

Herold, realizing he was somewhere he didn't want to be, decided to give up. Initially angry at him, John regained his composure and said, "Go out, my boy. Save your life if you can."

Now alone, John remained defiant. "Well, my brave boys, prepare a stretcher for me!" he cried. "Make quick work of it! Shoot me through the heart!" These words made it clear there would be no peaceful resolution of the standoff.

"If there was anything in the assassin's career which prompted admiration, it was his courage," wrote Everton Conger, the senior detective on the scene. "I was twice wounded in the war, was under fire at many of the most disastrous battles, led my command right through the teeth of almost certain annihilation, and yet this exhibition of sublime courage—with death lurking at every corner—was a lesson to me."

The barn was a square building with a wooden floor. It was slat-built, having gaps between the boards to air tobacco. Inside were farm implements, furniture, and hay.[16]

Conger went to the rear of the barn and lit a twist of straw. Thrust between the planks, it fell onto a pile of dry stubble. Flaming up, a blaze spread quickly to nearby piles of fodder and corn shucks. In seconds the barn's interior lit up like a stage at night, and soldiers, peering through the gaps in the slats, got a look at their prey.

John was leaning against a haymow. When he noticed the flames, he struggled to his feet and tried to stamp them out. Then he overturned a table onto the blaze.

No luck. The barn was filled with combustibles, and the fire spread. Smoke poured from the floorboards. Flames crept up the walls, searching for the rafters.

Coughing heavily, John moved to the center of the barn. His face was wild with excitement. He ran the fingers of his right hand through his hair as if to compose himself. "One more stain on the old banner!" he shouted. Throwing down his crutch, the assassin took a stagger-step toward the barn door with a pistol in one hand and a carbine in the other.

This was too much for Boston Corbett. The ranking noncommissioned officer present, the little sergeant had asked permission from Conger to enter the barn and confront John one-on-one. When Conger refused, Corbett turned to a higher authority. "I heard the voice of God calling on me to fire." One way or the other he intended to be John's executioner. "It was time the man was shot," he said.[17]

The assassin was extremely dangerous, but the danger was mostly to himself. With a wall of fire behind him and a locked barn door in front, he was trapped. John vowed to take his own life in such a situation. He had no intention of being chained, paraded, tried, gawked at, and hanged like John Brown.

Before he faced that moment, Corbett acted. Without order or excuse, the sergeant laid his Colt revolver on his arm, aimed, and fired.[18]

The shot hit John in the neck. It tore straight through, fracturing two cervical vertebrae and cutting the spinal cord. The assassin fell headlong to the floor with a scream.

Soldiers rushed into the barn and pounced on him. He was paralyzed and couldn't resist. The barn was turning into a furnace, so the men carried him outside to the grass. His eyes closed, his head drooping, he

Death of John Wilkes Booth. *Twelve days after murdering Lincoln, Booth was cornered in a Virginia barn and shot fatally. Union soldiers dragged him from the burning building while David Herold (right), who fled with him, was taken alive and later hanged.*

seemed dead. The muscles of his mouth moved, however, and someone shouted, "The damned rebel is still living!"

John was trying to speak, so Conger pressed his ear close to the assassin's lips. The words he heard were unmistakable. "Tell my mother I die for my country."

The barn was now an inferno, forcing the soldiers to haul John farther off to the Garrett house porch.

He gasped, struggling for breath. Since his respiratory muscles were affected, he felt as if he were choking. Repositioning and stimulants didn't help. A doctor arrived; he pronounced the wound mortal. All knew it, and one of those present said he had never seen a harder death.

John held on for four agonizing hours. The night faded, the dawn came and then the sunrise, its rays falling directly on the deathwatch. Slowly, John asphyxiated. A gasp, a quiver, and he was finished.[19]

The assassin's body was taken immediately to Washington. On the afternoon of the following day, April 27, 1865, it was formally identified and autopsied. Workmen dug a pit under the brick floor of a storeroom of the old Washington Penitentiary building. When it was dark and the facility was deserted for the night, a party of soldiers placed John's body in an arms case and lowered it into the excavation. Then they covered the site with bricks.[20]

Two years later demolition work on the building required John's remains to be moved. A fifteen-foot-long trench in another storeroom became his new home. He was joined by Herold and three other associates executed for their roles in his plot.

In February 1869, President Andrew Johnson released John's body to the Booth family. It was exhumed again and taken to a funeral home that shared the alley behind Ford's Theatre. Since John had escaped down this alley, the thought could not be avoided—the murderer had returned to the scene of the crime.[21]

The Booth remains were transferred to John H. Weaver's "Undertaking Parlor" in Baltimore on February 15. Two days later Mary Ann, Rose, and Joe arrived from New York to claim the body. They were shown into a darkened room, lighted feebly by two flickering gas jets. Still dressed in the clothes in which he died, John was a pile of blackened bones. Mary Ann would not approach him, but Joe came forward with John T. Ford and Weaver.

The younger brother said John could be identified by a peculiarly shaped gold filling in a molar near his right eyetooth. Weaver and Ford found the filling as described, and Joe confirmed the identity of the remains. Of course it's him, said Ford. That firm lower jaw belonged to no other person.

After the family left, Weaver transferred John's body to a receiving vault at Green Mount Cemetery in northern Baltimore. It remained there until June of that year, when the Booth family came together for his burial.

The day was hot and cloudless—a real summer scorcher. Edwin, Mary

Ann, June, and Rose arrived at the cemetery in a closed carriage. A party of fifty-or-so people awaited them. Also present was an Episcopal priest in gown and surplice. He conducted a brief service.

John was then lowered into a brick-lined grave. Frederick, Elizabeth, and little Mary Ann, the children who had died before his birth and had been buried at the farm, had been exhumed and brought to the cemetery. Their traces were placed in a box that was set on top of his coffin. Then the grave was filled.[22]

Edwin ordered that no marker be put on John's grave. It remains unmarked to this day. The brother knew such a stone would become a flash point of anger for some and of pride for others. He wasn't trying to hide the gravesite, nor could he, as the burial was widely reported.

One Sunday afternoon in the summer of 1870, the following year, the families of rebel soldiers buried at Green Mount met to garland the graves of their dead. At the end of the day no grave in the cemetery bore more decorations than John's. One report claimed that friends and strangers left a pyramid of blossoms an astonishing twenty feet tall over his remains while robed clergymen offered memorial prayers.

When Northerners read about this, they were dumbfounded at the spirit of hostility shown to Lincoln in Maryland, a state that never even joined the Confederacy. "If the richness and profusion of the emblems is to be taken as a measure of affection in which the deceased soldier is held, John Wilkes Booth is the greatest hero of them all," wrote a reporter for the *Baltimore American*.[23]

Even today, flowers are occasionally left at the site. Some are for John and some are for the Booth family (as his parents, sisters Asia and Rose, and brother Joe are buried there as well).

One is more likely to find dozens of Lincoln pennies scattered about. Since John has no individual marker to target, the pennies are placed on the Booth obelisk, gravestones, and footstones of his family members.

The tradition of leaving tokens of remembrance on graves is ancient. Coins go back at least to the Greeks' "Charon's obol," a coin left with the dead to ensure their safe passage over the River Styx.

Leaving coins has become increasingly prevalent, particularly in military cemeteries. They are placed as a shout-out from an old comrade or as a sign of respect from a stranger.[24]

A different feeling motivates visitors to Green Mount. Coins left with the president's face up convey an unmistakable message—John lost the battle of history.

GRIEF-STRICKEN, MARY LINCOLN took to her bed. She did not attend her husband's funeral in the East Room nor accompany his body on its trip to Springfield. As the days went by, Robert apologized to President Andrew Johnson, her husband's successor, for his mother's delay in turning over the White House. Mary couldn't accept the thought of leaving the mansion poorer than when she arrived by the loss of an indulgent husband, an exceptional child, a king's salary, and a queen's perks.[25]

"Time seemed blotted out," she later told Mrs. B. S. Edwards, an old friend who had attended her wedding in 1842. "I must have been living all those weeks in a state of unconsciousness, for I remember nothing." Then she added, "The awakening was terrible."[26]

She did not depart empty-handed, preparing a caravan of wagons loaded with boxes and trunks to go with her. The woman who so brilliantly furnished the mansion when she entered it left it unfurnished with equal skill. Unsupervised servants, souvenir-hungry visitors, and Mary's sense of entitlement did a number on the place. "All I know is what was left when the house came into President Johnson's possession, so far as bed and bedding and table linen and the necessary housekeeping utensils are concerned," Commissioner French wrote in his diary, "there was absolutely nothing left."[27]

Belle Miller got to the White House the morning Lincoln died almost as fast as Mary had. The Lady in Gray was the second person to see her. Other spiritualists followed. "They poured into her ears pretended messages from her dead husband," recalled William Crook, a White House guard. "These women nearly crazed her," and Robert ordered them off the premises.[28]

In later years Miller wore a gold medal around her neck that she claimed the Lincolns presented her for her wartime services—if such there were. An estranged husband said Belle's medal was as phony as she was.[29]

Isaac Newton remained welcome. He had been the first person to bring the news of Ford's Theatre to the White House. "O, my God, they've shot the President!" the old man exclaimed to Tom Pendel, the doorkeeper. Pendel ran upstairs to tell Robert what had happened while Newton quivered, slumped against the door, and cried. Sir Isaac advised Mary on floral arrangements for the funeral, and she gave him a monogrammed linen handkerchief that she said her husband carried on the night of his assassination.[30]

"WITH THE DEEPEST sorrow and great agitation, I thank you for relieving me from my engagement," Edwin wrote Henry Jarrett, manager of the Boston Theatre, on the day Lincoln died. "Mourning in common with all other loyal hearts the death of the President, I am oppressed by a private woe not to be expressed in words. But whatever calamity may befall me or mine, my country—one and indivisible—has my warmest devotion."[31]

A few days later, a tall, hooked-nose detective called on him. The man told Edwin his presence was required in Washington.

"I would rather die than go," Edwin said.

Not an option, replied the detective with the implausible name of Ivory Blood. Edwin could shed light on John's movements and opinions. If the actor came peacefully, Blood would dispense with the handcuffs.

"I cannot understand why my brother did the terrible deed," exclaimed Edwin, trembling from head to foot. "It is an awful thing."[32]

Edwin had little to fear. He was sent home after an interview with Joseph Holt, the judge advocate general. Older brother June and brother-in-law Clarke were locked up with the rats and roaches in an annex of the Old Capitol Prison (now the site of the U.S. Supreme Court building). No evidence was found against either. Clarke was released after four weeks, June after eight, from what the latter termed the "United States Bastille."[33]

Friends like Badeau vouched for Edwin's loyalty, making known he voted for Lincoln in 1864. While that put the actor's person out of danger, his career was another matter. Would the public welcome him back or would it blame him for the actions of his brother? He knew only one thing. He had to work. Besides his daughter Edwina, he was responsible for his mother Mary Ann, sister Rose, brother Joe (recently returned from California), his late wife's sister Catherine and her husband Harry, three servants, and three mortgages.

With a deep breath, Clarke ventured back onstage in Philadelphia on August 26, 1865. Edwin watched in anxiety from a private box. To his delight the comedian got a rousing reception. "The audience scarcely found sound enough to express their feelings," wrote a theatrical editor, who predicted a similar reaction for Edwin in New York. "That city is not in the habit of punishing the innocent for the guilty, and a still more enthusiastic welcome awaits his return to the stage."[34]

Filled with shame, Edwin never would have acted again if he could have avoided it. It pained him to realize that the only way he had to make money was to show himself in front of hundreds of strangers nightly. But, with the courage of necessity, he announced *Hamlet* for January 3, 1866, at the Winter Garden.

"The public must be surprised to learn that a Booth is to appear on the New York stage this coming week," wrote James Gordon Bennett of the *New York Herald*, the most widely circulated newspaper in the nation. "[This is] in shocking bad taste. *Will he appear as the assassin of Caesar?* The blood of our martyred President is not yet dry, and the very name of the assassin is appalling to the public mind."[35]

Broadway was blocked with ticketholders and their carriages on the night of the performance. A cordon of police arrived to ensure order and deter troublemakers. There had been threats to shoot Edwin if he showed himself, but the crowd was uniformly friendly.[36] Buzzing expectantly, they surged through the lobby and found their places. When the curtain rose, every seat was occupied, every inch of standing room filled. "Seldom has any New York theater been thus crowded," wrote journalist William Winter, "and never by an audience of a more intelligent class."[37]

Edwin did not make an entrance from the wings. He was discovered onstage when the lights went up for the second scene of the first act. The audience saw him and roared with approval and encouragement for five minutes. "The men stamped, clapped their hands, and hurrahed continuously; the ladies rose in their seats and waved a thousand handkerchiefs. Surely, such a scene was never before witnessed in a theater."[38]

Edwin was overcome. As bouquets fell in a shower on the stage, he dropped his head on his breast as his body shook with tears and emotion.[39]

He was not his brother's keeper, after all.

JOSEPH JEFFERSON LEFT Australia for England in March 1865. After two months at sea his ship stopped at Callao, Peru, where he asked caulkers who were in a rowboat for the latest war news from America.

"The war is over," shouted one. "Richmond has fallen, and Lee has surrendered."

Joe heaved an audible sigh of disappointment.

"And Lincoln has been assassinated," the man continued.

"That's a great pity," replied Joe.

"Wilkes Booth shot him."

The words sent Joe backward like a punch. "I believe he would have fallen had not the captain and I caught him," recalled his son Charley. "He was as white as a sheet and trembled like an aspen. I can't recall the time I ever saw father so moved. He was depressed for days, and as taciturn as I ever saw him."[40]

In London, Joe found that the managers wouldn't book him unless he had something new. Still believing in *Rip Van Winkle*, he hired actor-dramatist Dion Boucicault to rewrite it. The result became theatrical history. Joe had played the title character as a middle-aged man. Boucicault proposed having a young and an old Rip. The young Rip was "a thoughtless, gay curly-headed fellow as all the village girls would love and the children and dogs run after." This contrasted nicely with the old Rip, who awakens after his twenty-year sleep, is unrecognized in his own village, and wonders, "Are we so soon forgot?" When Rip recovers his family and fortune, he blesses everyone with the play's final words, "Live long and prosper," later made famous as Spock's Vulcan salute in *Star Trek*.[41]

Joe produced the play at the New Theatre Royal, Adelphi, on September 4, 1865. It was a sensation, running for 170 nights. "From that time forward, he was Rip, and Rip was he," wrote friend Francis Wilson. "It was never necessary for Jefferson to play anything else. It was his whole existence." Joe earned a fortune and became the most beloved actor of his generation.[42]

Joseph Jefferson as Rip Van Winkle. *Joe fled to Australia rather than take sides in the Civil War. When he returned to the United States in 1866, he made a fortune playing Rip Van Winkle, the idle villager who encountered ghosts, drank their magic brew, and slept for twenty years.*

WHEN LINCOLN AWOKE in the upper world, he was bewildered, spiritualists said. He wasn't aware he had been shot or was dead. Because of his experiences with Nettie, he adjusted quickly, however, realizing that he was in a place filled with loving people. Lincoln enjoyed talking with them, particularly historical figures like the Founding Fathers. On visits to earth he discussed Reconstruction with Judge Edmonds. He helped Nettie recall incidents for a book she wished to write. And he dropped in on Isaac Newton. "Friend Newton, there is a great deal better place up there than down here," the president told him. As the commissioner maneuvered around behind him to see where John's bullet hit, Lincoln pointed to the White House and said (in Newton's fractured grammar), "Things is as wrong as they kin be. I must go up there tomorrow and try to fix 'em right." The sociable commissioner invited Lincoln to spend the night, only to realize the president was too long for the bed.[43]

Lincoln's relationship with John was complicated.

When the president descended to meet him, the assassin wanted to fight. Waves of anguish and despair tormented the young man. "When I first entered the new life, I experienced a baptism of fire," John's spirit said at an 1872 séance. "It consumed the dross of my being until the scales fell from my eyes, and I was enabled to see my surroundings clearly and to understand my duty toward the world, myself, and my God."

In time John met his father, and they spoke. His spirit calmed. He came to realize the enormity of his crime and he regretted it. He confessed his sorrow to the president. "Lincoln tenderly brushed away his tears of remorse with the hand of forgiveness." They became friends. Sometimes they took walks together in fields of lovely summer flowers. The hereafter really was a beautiful place.[44]

Meanwhile, back on earth, Colchester had not disappeared, as Noah Brooks thought. In fact, the medium became even more famous.

On June 24, 1865, the young Englishman was indicted for carrying on the trade of a juggler practicing carnival-style legerdemain without the occupational license required by the Internal Revenue Act of 1864. The law, passed to raise money for the war effort, provided for a hefty fine. It also carried a potential two-year jail term for each offense (although the government did not threaten prison in this case). The medium was indignant at his arrest. "According to the Constitution, the Bible, and all known authorities, no man can be compelled to take out a license to worship God as he pleases," he declared.[45]

Perhaps sincerely—probably not—Colchester raised a vital point. Was spiritualism a religion, protected by the First Amendment? Or was it a scam, practiced by con artists who preyed on the troubled and the brokenhearted?

Due to the constitutional issue involved and the strong interest in spiritualism, a large crowd gathered in the courtroom of the U.S. District Court for the Northern District of New York in Buffalo on August 18, 1865. General Grant, who had attended a Colchester séance, was subpoenaed as a defense witness; to no one's surprise he failed to appear. Judge Edmonds, whom Colchester asked to help with the defense, was also absent, having joined the enemy. "Colchester sells the truth—sells it like cattle in the market," said the judge in a public rebuke, "and is tempted to fabricate the manifestations when they will not come of their own accord."[46]

The trial was highly entertaining. Jurors were chronically late, dog fights erupted in the courtroom, and spectators were spectacular themselves. "Old men and old women, youths and maidens gay, the brethren of the mystic tie, and the sisters, too, necromancers, jugglers, sorcerers, magicians, and prestidigitators" gathered in knots and whispered to each other. Some protested the persecution of their favorite apostle; others complained that if Colchester were so gifted, why didn't he tell the government where John was hiding during the assassin's escape and collect the reward money?[47]

Defense lawyers, having few cards to play, grabbed at what they could. Once they argued ingeniously that if Colchester produced table raps with his foot, as a witness alleged, that was not the sleight-of-*hand* with which he was charged. The indictment was defective. He should have been charged with sleight-of-*foot*.

After hearing twenty witnesses over four days the jury returned in ten minutes with a guilty verdict. Judge Nathan K. Hall confirmed it. "Our reason, as well as our instinct, tells us that if our departed parents and children and friends can communicate with us, and give us information and advice for our benefit," he wrote in his opinion, "then they would not refuse to exercise this power because we decline to fill the pocket of a strolling performer."[48]

Colchester was ordered to obtain a twenty-dollar license. There was also a bill for one thousand dollars in court costs and legal fees. He shrugged in defeat. "There is no use trying to make the United States believe in spirits," the medium told the press.[49]

Having few friends left in the East, Colchester headed to the heartland. He held séances in homes, hotel rooms, and theaters in Indiana, Illinois, and Kentucky. At times he showed flashes of his old ability, then followed it with a boozy display of cheating. Increasingly eccentric, he painted his face white and red and wore affectatious rows of buttons on his trousers. If he wasn't serious, why should others be? Visitors teased him by asking the spirits questions like, "Is it right to frighten two small boys with an opossum?" or "Who stole Aunt Hattie's ham?"[50]

In St. Louis Colchester met comedian Ben DeBar. He was the brother of Harriet DeBar, June Booth's first wife. Due to the couple's domestic troubles, Ben raised their daughter Blanche, John and Edwin's favorite niece.

An actor-manager, Ben ran a rattrap of a theater in bad repute with actors for its inferior accommodations. He allowed Colchester to take the star role of Claude Melnotte in *The Lady of Lyons*, a piece John had played there. The performance was unreviewed by the press.

Colchester's spirit manifestations were not so fortunate. On the evening of March 5, 1867, the medium took the stage after a play. A reporter for a local newspaper wrote that he brought two audience members up to watch him and ensure things were on the up-and-up. Then he wrote spirit messages at a table. That failed when the witnesses couldn't read them. One man didn't have his glasses, the other couldn't decipher Colchester's handwriting. Blood writing fared no better. Colchester excused himself and went behind the scenes for a minute. When he returned, he had the spirit message already written on his arm. The medium was tipsy—filled with spirits he couldn't summon, it was joked. Grumbling, the audience headed for the exits.[51]

In late April, Colchester arrived in Keokuk, Iowa, on the Mississippi River. A number of clairvoyants offered its citizens mysticism by mail, but Keokuk had no resident wonder-worker, so Colchester's prospects were good. He went to work at the Deming House, a newly refurbished hotel just off the main street.

Unfortunately, he fell ill on May 1 with a severe "congestive chill," probably pernicious malarial fever. This was marked by soaring fever, bloodshot eyes, diarrhea, and hot and dry skin. He weakened steadily. On May 4, as a violent storm pounded the Deming House, he grew delirious. The gloomy day went on. Hail the size of marbles pelted the building and thunder rattled the windowpanes of Colchester's room as he passed away at ten that night.[52]

Colchester was buried the next afternoon in the Keokuk cemetery. No gravestone marked the place. Being an indigent stranger, he may never have had one. Local lore speculates that Colchester, having no family connections in the area, was up for grabs. Students of the College of Physicians and Surgeons of Keokuk, the medical department of the state university, may have dug him up for study. If true, it was not the afterlife of which he had spoken.[53]

Colchester's friends Isaac Newton and John Pierpont died within months of each other shortly after the war. Newton suffered sunstroke while at work at his department's experimental farm. It was the final and fatal addition to a series of illnesses. "Whatever opinions may have been entertained of his capacity," said a friend, "he was earnest and faithful in his private life and without a reproach as a Christian." Pierpont died of heart disease in his sleep while on a holiday. He, too, was fondly remembered. "Pierpont went to the angels," wrote spiritualist Nathan Daniels in his diary, "crowned with the laurels of a perfect earth existence, and ripe with knowledge, experience and love."[54]

Nettie Colburn retired from spiritualist work. Confined to her bed for many years by rheumatoid arthritis, she dictated an autobiography that detailed her encounters with the Lincolns and lived to see it published before her death in 1892.[55]

Charles Foster died of "brain fever" in 1885 after a stay at the State Lunatic Hospital in Danvers, Massachusetts. He told a friend he had lost his appetite for alcohol, cigars, séances, and life. "I am so tired," he said, "so tired."[56] His critic, Judge Edmonds, died in 1874, still a believer, but daughter Laura withdrew from the spiritualist movement after a mental collapse in the late 1860s. A Paulist Brother exorcised her "obsessing devils," and she recovered to denounce trance mediumship. No spirit, living or dead, had the right to control another person, she declared.[57]

ADAM BADEAU ASSUMED charge of food relief in Richmond after Lee's surrender at Appomattox. One-third of the citizens of Virginia's capital city couldn't feed themselves, so he distributed ration tickets for army food. These were given out by the thousands without regard to race or political opinion. Many went "to persons formerly in good circumstances and not a few who were considered absolutely wealthy," he wrote Lieutenant Colonel Edward Smith, assistant adjutant general of the Army of the James. Ironically, continued Badeau, these people had "the alternative of starvation or acceptance of the charity of the very government they had striven to overthrow."[58]

Badeau called on General Lee, who had returned to his home in the city. Asked if he needed assistance, "Lee replied through an aide-de-camp that he was greatly obliged and did not know what he should have done had the offer not been made for he found nothing in his house to eat," Badeau later claimed.[59]

Exciting news came from Georgia, where Harry Wilson was now a major general. His cavalry command caught Jefferson Davis, the Confederate president, who had been on the run since the fall of Richmond. "The rebellion is finally ended by the capture of the arch rebel himself," Wilson reported proudly to Badeau, "captured by my command by my own order." He interviewed his prisoner on May 2, 1865. "Mr. Davis seemed quite cheerful and talkative," continued Wilson. "He seemed to regret that Mr. Lincoln had been killed. He remarked with a smile that he thought the U.S. would find graver charges against him than the murder of Mr. L. He asked no favors."[60]

When Grant became president in 1869, a new chapter in Badeau's improbable life began. He moved into the White House with the general. Apparently, Grant needed somebody to hold his cigars, Joe Booth joked to Edwin.[61]

Slow to form attachments, the new president was unshakable in his trust and affection once given, and he regarded Badeau as a sort of odd younger brother. Grant appointed him as secretary of the American legation in London for a few months until the choice job of consul general opened up. Badeau served in the latter post for the next eleven-plus years. For the society-obsessed aide it was a dream job in the capital city of the world. With an annual income that rivaled that of the president, he lived well, wrote, and hobnobbed.[62]

Badeau repaid Grant with an adulatory *Military History of Ulysses S. Grant* (1867, 1881). A three-volume "court history," the series was well researched and authoritative. It earned both money and some resentment from former officers for its blunt judgments, known to bear Grant's fingerprints.

After he left the White House in 1877, Grant, his wife Julia, and a small entourage left the United States on a round-the-world tour. Badeau came along part of the way as one of the family.

Since Grant traveled as a private citizen, Badeau was concerned that he be properly appreciated by the kings, khans, and lordlings of the Old World. He commissioned a gold medal studded with sapphires and other precious stones. It was inscribed with Grant's titles and the dates of his victories. Worn around the neck on a large ribbon collar, the medal was twice the size of a silver dollar. Delighted with the decoration, Badeau rushed to show it to the boss.

The down-home general took a look at the thing, puffed his cigar, and said, "I wouldn't have it around my neck if I were paid one thousand dollars a minute."[63]

On June 26, 1877, the travelers visited Windsor Castle. The Grants were given the apartment assigned to Alexander II, the emperor of Russia, who had made a state visit to Britain three years earlier. Badeau was sent with the Grants' teenage son Jesse to a room near the attic. Snubs continued when Jesse was invited to join his parents at a banquet held by Queen Victoria while Badeau was sent to eat with the household staff. Miffed, Badeau didn't make a scene at the time but took his revenge in the newspapers. "This might be royal etiquette, but it was not good breeding," he lectured the queen. When he was finally presented to her, "she was extremely gracious throughout and from anybody's point of view (but mine) she was amiable. I suffered for others, which is, of course, very much to my credit."[64]

Badeau's diplomatic career came to an end in the spring of 1884 when he resigned as consul general at Havana. Inconceivably, after years of top-paying government jobs, he was broke.[65]

A few months after Badeau returned home from Cuba, Grant invited him for a carriage ride. He wanted the younger man alone when he broke the news. The general informed Badeau that, despite promises to the contrary, he intended to write a book about his military experiences. Having never written anything longer than articles and reports, he wanted Badeau's help. Grant would give him ten thousand dollars from royalties for his assistance in getting the text into shape.

Badeau was stunned. The intimate quality of such a memoir would completely eclipse Badeau's formal history of the war, which they had agreed would be the general's final word on the subject. But what could Badeau say? Grant had lost his fortune in a banking scandal. He lived on borrowed money. This was his only way out.[66]

With the determination that marked every crisis in his life, Grant grimaced and set to work. Comfortably dressed in slippers, vest, trousers, and dressing gown, he began writing about nine in the morning at an ordinary card table in his bedroom. On his nose was a large, old-fashioned pair of hard-rubber glasses. The fireplace was to his right, with the big bay window overlooking East 66th Street behind him. Books and papers were piled handily nearby. He wrote until around noon and broke for lunch. After a carriage ride in Central Park, he headed back to the house for more work in the late afternoon.[67]

Badeau spent the winter months of 1884–85 with him. Often seated together at the same table, he and Grant worked over the pages as the general produced them. In the evening Badeau took the material to his room for rehashing.

What the aide did to the manuscript became the subject of a bitter dispute.

Badeau claimed to have been its animating force, refreshing Grant's memory, soliciting his thoughts, and inspiring his judgments. When Grant got confused—he mixed up his meetings with Lincoln, for example—Badeau straightened him out. Then he edited the result, removing entire pages at times. He provided his own maps for the general's use and came up with the title. "I suggested much," he said, and the general invariably approved the changes. While he strove to retain Grant's simplicity and directness of language, "the book could not have been made what it is without me. I constructed the work."[68]

As they labored away, a terrible backstory unfolded. The gnawing pain Grant felt in his throat was cancer. The illness was terminal.[69]

Realizing the gravity of his condition, Grant redoubled his efforts, working as hard as his energies permitted. He dictated until his voice failed, then wrote on a pad on his knee.

This was his greatest battle, wrote his contemporary Frank G. Carpenter, a journalist. "It was not fought during the bloody years between 1861 and 1865. It was not waged during his stormy administration in the White House, but it came during the last few months of his life. Bankrupted and penniless, wracked with pain and enfeebled by disease, he shook his fist in the face of death and wrote."[70]

By the spring of 1885, it became obvious that the book would be an enormous success. Grant's illness was national news, and sympathy for the ill man was widespread. The book came to be seen as his deathbed salute to

the nation. If it was Grant's obligation to write it under such brutal condi-
tions, it was the public's obligation to buy it.

When Badeau understood this, he wrote Grant an extraordinarily foolish letter. He told the general that a soldier like himself lacked "the habits
of mind" to complete the project alone. Grant produced only "disjointed
fragments." Badeau had to hammer them into the "simple story" that
would result. This was drudge work for a literary man like himself, and it
took time away from his own books and projects. Yet, if he didn't help, the
book would fail. Grant must pay Badeau more properly for his contribution. He wanted a better deal—say, one thousand dollars per month and a
percent of the profits.[71]

All Badeau had received to this point was a small monthly stipend and
the hospitality of Grant's home. Since the book had not yet been published,
it had earned no money. Badeau had seen no thousands. But to insult
Grant, who had one foot in the grave, makes one wonder if Badeau was
drunk when he wrote the letter. Did he think he could belittle Grant, then
ask for a raise?

Drunk or sober, Badeau knew what he had said. He proved it when he
handed Grant the letter and left the house before the general could read it.

Loyalty to his friends was a bedrock of Grant's personality, and he felt
blindsided by one he had patronized and protected for decades. "The letter
came upon him as a crushing sorrow and gave many a bitter moment to
his dying hour," said the *New York Herald*.[72]

"Read this and tell me what you think of it," said Grant, handing the letter to his son Fred. "Despicable!" the younger Grant exclaimed on reading
it. Fred felt that if there were anyone who should walk barefoot through the
snow to help his father, it was Badeau. Grant remained calm, however. He
was on an unaccustomed battlefield, but he faced this reversal as always—
assess misfortune and move on.[73]

Taking out a pencil and a pad of lined yellow paper, he composed a reply.
The initial sentences were firm, but, as he went on, the hand became trem-
ulous and irregular, betraying the wandering scrawl of its pain-wracked
writer.[74]

Grant informed Badeau that if he looked at himself in a mirror, he would see a petulant, irritable, overbearing, and mentally distempered person. As this person doubted Grant's ability, their collaboration ended now. The truculent aide was off the project. But Grant always had difficulty saying goodbye to problem people, and he showed it once again. He actually cared for the little misfit. He wanted Badeau to know they remained friends. The old comrade would always be welcome in Grant's home.[75]

If he could get past the door, that is. The family was incensed and unforgiving, and when Badeau came to the house several days later, Fred wouldn't let him anywhere near the general. The son gave him the father's dismissal letter and ran him off in a stormy scene.[76]

Grant struggled on with help from Fred and stenographer N. E. Dawson in a race against death. At times his pain was intolerable, at times he choked. His mind clouded with drugs. Awakening after a dose of morphia, he thought he was back home in Illinois. He saw the family barn very clearly, he said. He thought an old friend who lived three thousand miles away would be popping in for dinner. He needed to get dressed.[77]

His voice grew steadily weaker. The swelling of his neck interfered with his clearness of speech, forcing the tall, slender Dawson to double over and put his ear close to Grant's lips in order to catch his words.

As Grant struggled, he referred constantly to the difficulty with Badeau. "The memory of Gen. Badeau's letter made his mental anguish greater than that of the body," thought Fred. His last dictation was on June 22, 1885. Drugged, diseased, tortured, and voiceless, he completed the final chapter a week before he died on July 23.[78] He did not live to see the book published.

"If these chickens should really hatch according to my account," wrote Samuel Clemens, who owned the publishing rights to the memoirs, "General Grant's royalties will amount to $420,000, and will make the largest single check ever paid an author in the world's history. If I pay the General in silver coin at $12 per pound, it will weigh seventeen tons." The final payday exceeded even Clemens's expectations. He handed Julia Grant a check for $200,000 in February 1886. Another $250,000 followed.[79]

Months went by and Badeau received no money. When pressed, the Grants told him they would pay him a clerk's customary wages. Badeau was infuriated at the remark. He was no dime-a-dozen copyist. He wanted acknowledgment of his contribution and the ten thousand dollars the general had promised (less $250 advanced earlier). Surely, the Grants could find so small a sum in so large a pile.[80]

General Sickles offered to arbitrate between the parties. Badeau was amenable, but the Grants rejected the offer. In March 1888, Badeau sued Julia, as executor of the Grant estate. The Grants fought back, hiring Clarence A. Seward, the talented nephew of the late secretary of state William Seward, as their attorney.[81]

Rumors had swirled for a year about trouble between Badeau and the Grants, and the lawsuit made public the details of their dispute. The take away for most people was that Badeau extorted his dying patron, then turned on the man's grieving widow. Infuriated, editors nationwide sliced and diced. Cincinnati, Ohio: "Badeau is a vain and presumptuous and irritating person, with a false sense of importance and a foolish way of showing it." Louisville, Kentucky: "Ingrate! Filthy manners, callous selfishness, offensive conceit, and general disagreeability." Albany, New York: "A parasite, a money-grabber." Brooklyn, New York: "Badeau is a hog." St. Louis, Missouri: "A large and shining ass."[82]

Army friends were equally disappointed in him. Harry Wilson wrote in his autobiography: "Badeau proved to have weaknesses which none of his military friends and I, least of all, had ever suspected. He was essentially a vain and weak man, who owed everything to his chief and forgot some of it in the hour of adversity which finally overtook them both."[83]

No surprise, felt General Benjamin Butler, one of Grant's top subordinates. After all, the name *Badeau* is French for "dirty water."[84]

Humorists jumped in, mocking Badeau's pretensions of indispensability to the general. One told the story of the first day of the great Battle of the Wilderness in Virginia. The enemy armies squared off. The air was breathless in anticipation of carnage. The fate of two nations hung in the balance. "With that calm, imperturbable manner which always distinguished Gen. Grant in a great crisis, he turned to one of his aides and said, 'Is Historian Badeau present?' 'He is, General,' was the reply. 'Then,' said the great warrior, 'let the battle proceed!' "[85]

Spiritualists had their laughs, too. An anxious visitor asked a Chicago medium, "Do you sometimes have access to the spirit of General Grant?" "Quite often," replied the medium. The florid-faced seeker excitedly produced an invoice and cried, "My name is Badeau. Here is a claim I wish you would show him."[86]

Badeau's suit against Julia was settled on October 30, 1888, three days before it was scheduled to go to trial. He got his ten thousand dollars plus interest—get-lost money from the Grants.

Badeau told the press, "I never claimed the authorship or joint authorship of Gen. Grant's book." It should be remembered, he said, that he did suggest, revise, fact-check, guide, and superintend it.

"I appreciate all the honor and happiness that my relations with Gen. Grant brought into my life."[87]

DEATH CAME
AS A FRIEND

W hen Mary Lincoln and her two sons left the White House on the afternoon of May 23, 1865, few people gathered to wish them well. "I can never forget that day," wrote Elizabeth Keckly, her confidante. "She passed down the public stairway and entered her carriage. The wife of the president was leaving the White House and there was scarcely a friend to tell her goodbye. The silence was almost painful."[1]

Mary didn't return to Springfield. She couldn't live amid scenes of her former happiness with old enemies clustered on every street corner. Her other options were limited, however. While Lincoln's estate was sizable, Mary had access to the interest income only. That wouldn't pay for a new place. Estranged from her sisters, she couldn't stay with one of them. Friends did not come forward.

She moved to Chicago, living in boardinghouses or rented rooms. A self-described vagrant, Mary watched as others got plenty. She was intensely jealous of Grant. His admirers gave him four homes. Her husband made Grant *Grant* and then died at the hands of their enemy. Where was her free house?[2]

The melancholy ex–First Lady was difficult to be around. Traumatized by the murder of her husband, she suffered from depression, intermittent migraines, chills, dizziness, and exhaustion. Seclusion was proper for a widow in her circumstances, she believed, but that meant loneliness for the most sociable person on earth. She came alive only when worried about her sons or her husband's reputation or her finances. Life was burdensome. "If it were not for dear little Taddie, I would pray to die, I am so miserable," she wrote in the summer of 1865.[3]

Mary's financial situation was precarious. While she had no prospect of starving, it was unclear how she could get the money to enjoy a lifestyle befitting her expectations and her status as a president's widow. She had no way to earn an income and pay the thousands—maybe twenty thousand—she owed to Eastern merchants and bankers. When she wrote to Keckly, "I am very poor now," she felt it was as honest a statement as any she had ever made.[4]

Increasingly obsessed with money woes, she sent letters to those she had known in better days. While she deserved a hearing, her scheming and begging did little good. Acquaintances proved less helpful than she hoped. Friends proved less friendly. With Lincoln dead, her problems were no longer theirs. They had moved on.

She finally got one year of her husband's salary, a net of about $22,000. She wanted all four years of salary from his unfinished second term and declared one year a pittance. When her claim for an annual pension went before the public, she was chastised as a greedy termagant who insisted on forcing her vulgar self on the public.[5]

Determined to do something, she turned to her own resources. She sold her carriage, her horses, and much of her furniture.[6] Then she opened the treasure trunks brought from Washington. There were her shawls, rings, furs, boas, capes, lace handkerchiefs, dress patterns—years of sophisticated accumulation. All that fluffery, once so important, meant nothing now. She decided to sell the lot.

By the fall of 1867 she and the wardrobe were in New York. She consigned the finery to two commission merchants. They worked hard but sold little. The men then proposed touring her wardrobe for a fee. Any bloodstained garment worn on the night of the assassination would make an eye-catching centerpiece.

Mary was horrified at the idea, but, when the "Old Clothes Scandal" erupted in the press, everything ground to a halt. Was the oddball widow of the great president really hustling used clothes down in Manhattan's theater district? The debacle produced furiously hostile reactions and humiliating personal rebukes. "She has not been entirely in her right mind for several years," said a gossip in Springfield with pseudo-sympathy.[7]

"If I had committed murder in every city of this blessed union, I could not be more traduced," she wrote Keckly.[8]

Lincoln's estate was settled in November 1867. Mary got about $36,000 in cash and securities. Her sons got like amounts. The money was still not enough to purchase a house appropriate to her position, but it improved things. Congress added a three-thousand-dollar annual pension. President Grant signed the bill into law on July 14, 1870.[9]

With her finances enhanced, she traveled to Europe, hoping "to place the waters between myself and unkindness."[10] For two years she lived principally in Germany.

The fabled European spas and physicians did little to improve her health, but the change of scenery was beneficial. A woman with inborn aristocratic instincts, she reveled in following in the footsteps of long-dead monarchs and visiting their palaces, parks, and playgrounds. At Düsseldorf Castle attendants told her they frequently saw the headless ghost of the "White Lady of the Tower," the Princess Jakobea, who was found dead under mysterious circumstances in 1597. "The Germans are very superstitious," she wrote her friend Eliza Slataper, "and, from the King of Prussia down to his humblest subject, believe in her frequent appearance."[11]

During this period of time word reached Badeau at the London consulate that Mary "was doing strange things and carrying the honored name of Abraham Lincoln into strange and sometimes unfit company." When she arrived in England, she invited him to a get-together in her rented apartment off Russell Square near the British Museum. Although he gossiped freely about her at dinner parties, Mary didn't know this. Since she never forgave an insult, her invitation indicated she was unaware of his feelings toward her.

The consul general found Mary living like a middle-class tourist in a second-class part of town. He turned on the charm, and "she seemed touched by my attention," he recalled. "She wrote me a note of thanks, betraying how rare such courtesies had become to her."[12]

She and Tad returned to the United States on May 10, 1871. When their steamship *Russia* pulled into New York Harbor, a miracle happened. The band on Governors Island struck up the familiar old refrain of "Hail to the Chief." The guns of the revenue cutter *Bronx* fired a salute. Nearby vessels dipped their colors. Cheers sounded and handkerchiefs fluttered from the shore. It was a happy, heartwarming welcome home—for General Phil Sheridan, a fellow passenger returning from Europe after a tour as a military observer during the Franco-Prussian War. Mary was now but a footnote.[13]

Tad, too, was changed. No longer the bumptious and carefree child of Civil War days, he was a tall, well-mannered young man who spoke English with a slight German accent. Mary told a friend that he was like "some old woman" in his attention to her. It was a revealing remark. The death of his kindly father and life with his gloomy mother had taken the joie de vivre out of him. Only his affectionate nature was unchanged.[14]

The wet and chilly London winter cost him as well. Tad lacked his brother Robert's stamina. He had weak lungs, and when he got a cold, it lingered. Ill in New York, he did not improve in Chicago. Finally, he developed a severe cold that filled the pleural sacs around his lungs with fluid. He struggled to breathe. When he lay down, he felt as though he was suffocating. On the morning of July 15, 1871, he died of "dropsy of the chest"— perhaps pleurisy—at the age of eighteen.[15]

One husband, three children. It was enough to stagger the best-adjusted person. For the unsteady Mary the load was too much. Tad's death shattered her. He had been her kind and constant companion, seldom out of her sight. She said that this was the most grievous loss of all—"my idolized and devoted son, torn from me, when he had bloomed into such a noble promising youth." In a better world she would have gone with him. Only her own death could soften this blow, she said.[16]

"Time has at length taught and convinced me that the loved and idol-ized being comes no more," she wrote her friend Mary Jane Welles several months after her husband's murder. "I must patiently wait the hour when 'God's love' shall place me by his side again—where there are no more partings and no more tears shed." Having repudiated spiritualism, she now renewed her visits to mediums. "She hardly thinks of anything else," her only surviving son Robert wrote to David Davis, a father figure who had been Lincoln's campaign manager during the 1860 presidential elec-tion. "Almost her only companions are spiritualists."[17]

Mary traveled to Boston in February 1872. Dressed in mourning black, a bonnet covered with black silk flowers, and a crepe veil, she called on William Mumler in the city's South End. He was the nation's most famous spirit photographer. Professing not to know who she was, Mumler seated her, prepared a plate, and exposed an image.

Mumler had a controversial past, having had his own Colchester-style trial for fraud in New York City in 1869. Critics said his spirit photos were nothing more than double or combination printings of two photographic plates. Experts came up with nine methods by which Mumler's "shadows" could be produced without supernatural help. Undaunted, the photog-rapher moved to Boston and flourished, visited by Joseph Jefferson and Charles Foster, among others.

Mary picked up her photo several days later from Mumler's wife Han-nah, a clairvoyant. The photograph showed a puffy-faced Mary, seated in her widow's weeds. Behind her was a clearly recognizable Lincoln, his hands on his wife's shoulders. The small white blob to his right was a boy, asserted Hannah. Tad? The mist behind them must be a third person. Willie?

Mary studied the image closely. When Hannah asked her if she recog-nized the likenesses, she hesitated.

Hannah was instantly entranced. Turning to Mary, she said, "Mother, if you cannot recognize father, show the picture to Robert. He will recog-nize it."

"Yes—yes, dear," replied Mary. "I do recognize it. But who is now speak-ing?" The control replied that he was Tad.

Mary Todd Lincoln's Spirit Photograph. *Mary posed for this photograph of a
ghostly Lincoln, taken by William Mumler in Boston in 1872. Hannah Mumler, the
photographer's wife, claimed to be entranced by Mary's late son Tad, and the dead boy
confirmed the likeness's authenticity for his mother.*

Lincoln then took over Hannah and spoke to Mary for some time.

"When my wife resumed her normal condition," Mumler said, "she
found Mrs. L. weeping tears of joy that she had again found her loved ones,
and apparently anxious to learn, if possible, how long before she could join
them in their spirit home."[18]

The restless widow traveled on, avoiding family and friends and anyone
else who might tell her no. Her mind grew increasingly disturbed over
the winter of 1874–75. Telling nurse Mary Fitzgerald (mother of comedian
Eddie Foy) that gas was an invention of the Devil, she lit her room with
candles and hid behind drawn shades in their yellow half-light. She was

DEATH CAME AS A FRIEND

certain someone was in her head. An Indian removed bones from her face and pulled wires out of her eyes. In addition, a Jew talked to her through the wall of her room. Somehow he took her pocketbook.[19]

Robert believed his mother had not been in her right mind since her carriage accident in 1863. The assassination made her much worse. She was particularly irrational on money matters. Mary carried $57,000 in government securities—the bulk of her personal wealth—sewn into pockets in her petticoats. They were safe only if those around her were honest.[20]

Mary's financial irresponsibility was distressing, but it was her increasingly erratic behavior and hallucinations that triggered a crisis. Feeling her condition dire, Robert called in the doctors. On May 18, 1875, Dr. Ralph Isham examined her. He certified that she was insane and needed to be confined for treatment. Five other physicians concurred.

The son wasted no time. He and his mother lived in Chicago, and he applied to a city court on the morning of May 19 for a hearing on her competency. Judge Marion R. M. Wallace issued an immediate order for Mary's apprehension.[21]

Plainly dressed in black, she was brought into court that very afternoon. Her appearance was neat, but her look was pallid and her eyes watery and excited. Robert followed. He could be nowhere else, yet his distress at being his mother's adversary was obvious. An intensely private person, Robert loathed the idea of washing this laundry in public.

Behind mother and son came the doctors and witnesses in the case. "The persons entering the courtroom had more the appearance of a funeral procession than anything else," observed a reporter.

This was to be no secret proceeding behind closed doors held at the behest of a greedy relative. Mary's rights were better protected by law in Chicago than almost any other place in the United States. She had a jury trial in open court and an attorney. One of the jury members had to be a physician.[22]

The first witness was Dr. Willis Danforth, a homeopathic physician who had treated Mary for several years. He did not mention spiritualism but left no doubt it played a role in her disorder. Danforth said that Mary told him that her husband recently warned her that she would die within a few days. "She heard raps on a table conveying the time of her death." She sat at the table and confirmed the news. When Danforth said he heard no rapping noises, she put a paper containing the question of her mortality in a glass goblet on the table. The goblet was found to be cracked. "That circumstance she regarded as corroboration of the raps."

Other witnesses included doctors and hotel staff, the latter testifying to her paranoia and shopping mania.

Pale-faced and spent, Robert finally took the stand. His mother had always been exceedingly kind to him, he said. She was a good person. But they had reached a point where she needed more help than he could give her. He was obviously agonized, and he broke down twice while speaking. Knowing who mother and son were and the torturous path they had taken to reach this point in their lives, spectators found the scene painful to watch.

Mary listened attentively through three long hours of testimony. She knew exactly what was happening. Although clearly distressed, she did not interrupt the proceedings.

Her attorney, Isaac N. Arnold, had been one of her late husband's staunchest congressional allies in the fight against slavery. Because he agreed that Mary needed to be institutionalized, he mounted only a limited effort on her behalf. If lines of defense were suggested by the haste of the proceedings or the possibility of mental disturbance caused by Mary's frequent migraines or her unwise history of mixing medicines, he did not raise them.

When the jurors retired, Robert went over to his mother and offered his hand. She took it fondly and said, "Robert, I did not think you would do this."

The jury deliberated about as long as it took to fill out the verdict form. Its decision was that Mary was "a fit person to be sent to a state hospital for the insane."[23]

Mary was taken to Bellevue Place in Batavia, Illinois. Her new home was an asylum but not a dystopian madhouse. It was an exclusive sanitarium "for lady patients." While the bedrooms had barred windows and at night locked doors, it had a homelike atmosphere in which rest, diet, baths, fresh air, exercise, and as little medicine as possible were the order of the day. Mary's money, status, and nonviolent behavior meant that she got top-tier treatment.[24]

After a few months of care, doctors paroled her into the custody of her sister Elizabeth, whom she regarded as a sort of mother. Mary completed a year of supervision in the home on the hill in Springfield in which she and her husband were married in 1842. "I propose to act in a more *civilized* manner in the future," she promised her great-nephew Edward L. Baker Jr.[25]

A second jury decided on June 15, 1876, that she had been "restored to reason" and reinstated her rights (with power of attorney over her money held by a friend). She emerged boiling mad at Robert for locking her up. She wrote him a brutally formal letter, demanding the return of the paintings, diamonds, silver, and silks that she had given him or he had stored. Robert and his wife Mary were thieves, she declared. Young in years, old in sin. God would punish them.[26]

"Robert says I'm crazy, but he is crazy, too. He was bit by a mad dog when he was a boy," Mary told Elizabeth. Apparently, the madstone didn't work so well after all.[27]

It was back to Europe for four more years of vagabondage. Increasingly poor health and isolation made this trip less enjoyable than the first.

One morning on her voyage home in 1880, she took an early morning walk on the deck of her ship. The day was cold and the sea gloomy, colorless, and calm. As Mary approached a stairway, a sudden swell caused the ship to lurch wildly. She flew forward. Someone behind her grasped her skirt and stopped her from falling headfirst down the steps. The hand belonged to Sarah Bernhardt.

"You might have been killed, Madame!" exclaimed the famous French actor.

"Yes," Mary replied with a sigh of regret, "but it was not God's will."

When Bernhardt introduced herself, Mary stepped back, drew herself up, knitted her brow, and said mournfully, "I am the widow of President Lincoln."

Another actor had saved another Lincoln. Edwin had saved Robert, and now Bernhardt had saved Mary. But was this time really a favor? "I had just done this unhappy woman the only service that I ought not to have done her—I had saved her from death, from joining her beloved husband," Bernhardt wrote in her autobiography.[28]

"I am indeed a broken-hearted, bereaved woman, but God in his 'Own Time' will restore me to my loved ones," Mary wrote Baker. That gift came at her sister's home on the night of July 15, 1882. She was sixty-four years old.[29]

MARY McVICKER WAS a lively nineteen-year-old whose father ran a theater in Chicago. A petite and small-featured actor with long dark hair and bright gray eyes, she was a ball of nervous energy. Neither graceful nor buoyant, "she was no delicate geranium, rising from a Sèvres vase, but a strong, practical Western woman," wrote a critic in the New York Herald. Edwin, nearly twice her age and seemingly older than that, was captivated by her vivaciousness and sense of humor. She was fun and she was smart. He felt cheerful around her.[30]

There had been speculation that if Edwin remarried, he might choose Laura Edmonds. But it was Mary McVicker after all. Strange, thought Edwin's sister Asia. Her brother liked peace and quiet at home. Marriage to such an excitable person didn't make sense. But Asia knew she couldn't tell him anything. "He has only himself to please, and no one cares to oppose him."[31]

Edwin took higher counsel than that of his sister. The spirits of Mollie and of his old friend Richard Cary, killed at Cedar Mountain during the war, approved his choice. He didn't love Mary as deeply as her predecessor. But Edwina, aged seven, needed a mother, and he needed a companion. The couple married on June 7, 1869, at the home of Mary's maternal grandfather in Long Branch, New Jersey.[32]

The world lost little when the new bride, a middling talent, quit the stage to set up their new home and raise Edwina. Edwin, content to read and smoke, wanted the conventional life that had eluded him in his childhood, and he was happy to let the domineering young woman take charge of nearly every aspect of his life. Mary dictated his diet, laid out his wardrobe, and mothered his daughter. She made his costumes, applied his makeup, and watched his rivals. She monitored his box office, took his pay, and wrote his checks. Believing Edwin lazy, she pushed him. Then she pulled him. She even gave him a bedtime. When the clock struck the stated hour, she called his name. Off he went without protest.[33]

As Asia suspected, they were too different to be happy. Edwin was middle-aged and battle-scarred, a widower whose life was shadowed by the most notorious crime in American history. Mary, although hardworking and sincere, was too young to appreciate what Edwin had experienced, and he made little effort to explain it to her. Aware of the gulf between them, she attacked the problem by fixing on him with a jealous intensity. "She hated everybody who occupied any part of his time or attention," thought Junius Henri Browne, a Manhattan journalist.[34]

Calling on Laura Edmonds, Mary astounded the former spiritualist by telling her that she intended for Edwin to drop all his old friends. "She said *she meant to have it*," Laura wrote to Edwin. Laura replied that that was a bad idea. "Her plan would bring down misery all around—and most upon herself. You had noble friends and needed them, and they would be a help, not a hindrance, to her happiness." Laura herself was then dropped by Mary.[35]

Doubting his heart, Mary lapsed into what Edwin called "the tim-tams, the jim-jams, or the dim-dams and hell's bells." Her behavior was more serious than these playful terms indicate. Mary's mother, Harriet McVicker, who disliked Edwin intensely, convinced her daughter that he didn't really love her. "My crazy wife," he wrote, urged on by "her wicked mother," believed he married her for her family's money. Having gotten it, he neglected her. Edwina joined in the fun, Mary alleged, by pinching,

The Booth Family. *Edwin Booth and Mary McVicker, his second wife, shown with his daughter Edwina (standing), his child with his first wife, Mary Devlin. Mary two was unable to secure her husband's love as Mary one had done, and she grew to hate him.*

rough handling, and frightening her, then daring the wife to tell her father about it and see whom he would believe.[36]

"Misfortunes came," Edwin told actor Katherine Goodale.[37]

A son named Edgar was born on July 3, 1870. He arrived one month after Mary's due date. The delivery was protracted and torturous, and the baby was delivered with forceps, crushing his skull. He lived four hours. Three years later she miscarried. The couple couldn't get established.[38]

Edwin realized the ambition of his professional life in 1869 when he built and opened a magnificent theater on the corner of 23rd Street and Sixth Avenue in New York. It was the fulfillment of the dream he had shared with Cary before the war. Recognized as the finest theater in America, it was a "temple of the arts," devoted to the plays of Shakespeare. Plagued by mismanagement, untrustworthy advisers, and hard times, Edwin lost a fortune in the enterprise and declared bankruptcy in 1874. "He gave up all he had in the world, his personal and private property, his theatre, his library and theatrical wardrobe, and many treasures of his profession," wrote Badeau. The building later became a department store.[39]

To recoup financially, he toured. The travel, diet, inferior accommodations, and drafty theaters took a toll. He suffered frequent gastrointestinal problems and colds. The wear and tear of acting larger-than-life characters also exhausted him. He could hardly play madmen like Hamlet and Lear at night and be normal the next day. While the applause was generous and the dollars plentiful, he was often frustrated with himself and his career. He never encouraged anyone to enter the acting profession. "It is a life of wearisome drudgery and requires years of toil and bitter disappointments to achieve a position worth having," he warned one youngster.[40]

On April 23, 1879, while Edwin acted at his father-in-law's theater in Chicago, a man named Mark Gray fired two shots at him from a box seat to the actor's left. Both shots missed. The would-be assassin was arrested, and the show went on, as shows must. Gray, a clerk from St. Louis, claimed Booth was his father and had frustrated his own stage ambitions. He was hauled off to the Northern Illinois Hospital and Asylum for the Insane in Elgin.[41]

The Booths traveled to England in the summer of 1880 and spent a year there while Edwin acted. Although Mary had an undiagnosed respiratory issue that caused her to cough constantly, she had herself carried to the theater to attend Edwin as he dressed. Resting on a couch in the wings, she watched him act. Mary looked near death (and once went into convulsions). Doctors marveled that she kept going. Her willpower was astonishing.[42]

Sir William Jenner, the distinguished court physician to Queen Victoria, finally came for a consultation. He diagnosed Mary's condition as tubercular—"consumption of the throat and left lung." It was incurable.

"Mary is dying—slowly but surely," Edwin wrote his friend Dave Anderson in the summer of 1881. "Throat and lung consumption. She was utterly insane for two months. Poor Mary was never right. Her brain too great for her fragile body, and both are now wearing out. The end is near."[43]

When the couple returned to New York in June 1881, Edwin discovered that Mary's mother had been busy. The word was out in the city that the actor was "a drunkard, a profligate, a mercenary wretch, a cruel brutal husband, a monster of baseness and vice." While in London, he was said to have forced his gravely ill wife to perform "certain onerous offices" in his dressing room every night at the theater. Then, sending her home after the play, he crawled the pubs and clubs. Back stateside, he was said to sport about in a natty jockey suit with a slim walking stick, presenting a bachelor look inappropriate for a man of his age and station.[44]

"Having been absent from the city for two months," wrote journalist Bowne, "I was astounded to hear the atrocious stories circulating as to Booth's treatment of his wife, and inexpressibly pained to find that many of them actually credited, as infamous as they were."[45]

Edwin's thoughts wandered to happier times. Visiting the old house in Dorchester, Massachusetts, where he and his first wife lived, he stood in the room in which she died and watched the morning sun fall on Boston Harbor as it had that fateful morning. He called at the New York home of Reverend Osgood, where he had been married, and asked to see once more "the room where he secured his greatest happiness."[46]

The McVickers took Mary to a hotel, completing the couple's estrangement. When Edwin visited her, she turned on him like a lioness, screaming that she hated him and ordering him out. He left, banned from her presence. When Mary died on November 13, 1881, her parents, not Edwin, took charge of her remains and carried her to Chicago for burial.[47]

"Now, what next discomfort?" Edwin asked William Bispham. "What more sorrow claims acquaintance at my hand which I know not. *It will come.*"[48]

When it did, it hit close to home and in bunches. Brother June died in 1883. Mother Mary Ann followed in 1885, with sisters Asia in 1888 and Rose in 1889. While their deaths weren't entirely unexpected, each shrank the circle of those whose bonds were irreplaceable. Only brother Joe remained, and he, too, had his sorrows. Margaret, Joe's wife, died in childbirth along with a stillborn infant in 1884. Edwin's daughter Edwina married Ignatius Grossmann, a naturalized immigrant from Hungary, in 1885. Edwin despised the man. "My son—(of a b . . . h)—in law does nothing but spend money, smile, and live on his wife's father," he wrote critic William Winter. "A jolly old home is mine—Would you not rather have your child in Heaven? I would, particularly if I knew that her husband was in *Hell*, where he belongs!"[49]

Financially, Edwin never fared better. Between 1886 and 1891 he made five tours to dozens of cities coast-to-coast. Four seasons were with costars, one solo. These were "a perfect cyclone of success." He earned the phenomenal sum of $772,166.[50]

The final performance of his career was a matinee of *Hamlet* on April 4, 1891, at Brooklyn's Academy of Music. His health was precarious. He had had several small strokes and, with the death of his tour partner Lawrence Barrett the previous month, he canceled his performances for the following season. The public believed *this was it*, and they rushed to witness history. Three thousand people packed the large auditorium. Every available foot of standing room was occupied, and, to the consternation of the fire marshal, so were the stairs. "Brooklyn turned out such an audience as has never before been seen in the city in day time and one which has probably never been exceeded at night," wrote a critic.

His performance was melancholy to watch, like seeing a single lamp burning at night in a long-abandoned temple. Something was there, but what? Edwin showed little of his old fire or inspiration. His voice was husky and inaudible beyond the first few rows. His strength waned at key spots. Sometimes he spoke lengthy and unintelligible passages with his back to the audience. Nevertheless, patrons watched with an indulgent interest.

Called before the curtain at the play's end, he expressed thanks to the audience for its kindness. Perhaps he just needed rest. If things worked out, he might see them again. That was his hope. So, he would not say goodbye to them. "Au revoir," he said, "but not adieu."[51]

TO EVERYONE'S SURPRISE, Badeau got married. The bride was Marie Elise Niles, the daughter of a wealthy American diplomat. She was an unusual woman with a large nose, hazel eyes, high forehead, and dark brown hair. He was forty-three. She was thirty-two, thirty-eight, thirty-nine, or forty-three, depending upon the occasion.[52]

Their wedding took place in the parlor of New York's Gramercy Park Hotel on April 29, 1875. The windows beside the room's great mirror looked down on Gramercy Park. Beyond the park was a magnificent townhouse. Edwin would pass his final years in the house, and his statue would occupy the center spot in the park. Both townhouse and statue remain today.

Marie Elise was accustomed to the best, and her wedding reflected it. The elegant affair featured a virtual greenhouse of flower decorations in baskets, pots, and clusters. An archway for the bridal party was hung with vines and blossoms. An orchestra, silk ribbons, and champagne completed the festive atmosphere.

The bride's dress was made of white satin trimmed with antique point lace. A magnificent veil was fastened with a tiara of pearls and diamonds given to her by her fiancé. The diamonds that draped her neck were once owned by Empress Josephine, Napoleon's first wife. The groom wore black pantaloons, a dark Prince Albert coat, a white vest, a blue necktie, a turned-down collar, and gold-rimmed glasses.

Cardinal John McCloskey, attired in his scarlet mozzetta and cassock, with white linen rochet, led the wedding party toward a large floral marriage bell. He had just been consecrated as the first American cardinal, receiving the red biretta two days earlier, and his presence was considered quite an honor.

Stooped with age, McCloskey still towered over Marie Elise, who was four feet eleven inches, and Badeau, who was five feet six inches. He conducted a brief ceremony with no nuptial mass. After raising the biretta from his head, McCloskey shook hands with the couple. The instant he released Badeau, the groom turned to Marie Elise and gave her a kiss that sounded throughout the room.[53]

In June, Badeau and Marie Elise sailed to England, where he resumed his consular duties. She settled into Little Boston House, their London residence.[54]

The wife's late father owned a large amount of real estate in Manhattan that Marie Elise and her twin sister Amelia Rose inherited. Egged on by Badeau, who had a litigious streak, they sued the estate's executor, a cousin, claiming that he had neglected his duties and impoverished them. How could they receive only $125 a month from an estate worth one million dollars?[55]

The problem, replied an estate attorney, was Badeau and Amedee Wilbaux, Amelia Rose's husband. They spent too much money. "They are good enough fellows, both of them," he said, "but they cost too much."[56]

Badeau confided to a friend that something else was going on. Marie Elise was mentally ill. She was comfortable only when around her sister who, Badeau felt, was an unwholesome influence. Husband and wife fought constantly. After one blistering bout, Marie Elise and Amelia Rose sailed for New York. Her marriage with Badeau was over in all but name. She left behind huge debts, accrued without the husband's knowledge. "I am obliged to retrench in every way, and even then, I shall hardly avoid bankruptcy at the end of my term of office," he wrote.[57]

With the departure of Marie Elise and her fortune, Badeau entered the most challenging period of his life. He resigned his diplomatic post in Cuba amid a corruption controversy. Lawsuits followed, alleging that he illegally retained consular fees in both London and Havana. He lost a claim, taken to the U.S. Supreme Court, for army pay while on diplomatic service, known unflatteringly as "Badeau's double-salary scheme." He also owed thousands to Edwin. Attempting to recoup something somewhere, Badeau sued Charles L. Webster for reneging on a book deal when the

publisher insisted that Julia Grant vet his new manuscript on her late husband's life. Badeau felt certain this was payback for his role in the memoirs
controversy. With each controversy, friends fell away.[58]

His drinking didn't help. Historian Henry Adams, who lived at Badeau's
Washington boardinghouse in 1869, labeled his fellow lodger's habits
"regularly irregular." Badeau drank to buck himself up, Adams thought,
only to become irritable as a result. William B. Moore, who served with
Badeau during the war, saw his old comrade stumbling drunkenly near
the White House. Badeau actually made two or three circles before he
could right himself and head off in the direction he wanted to go.[59]

Grant had been aware of his aide's foibles—if they should not more
properly be termed his failings. Years earlier, when Badeau was consul
in London, Grant learned that the aide, sent to Spain with important dis-
patches, got drunk on the way. "He switched off by the wayside and did
not turn up in Madrid for some days," Grant was informed. Given his own
problems with alcohol, the president had been too charitable to cast stones,
and he let the matter pass.[60]

To earn a living, Badeau went to his pen, writing a feverish stream of
memoir, fiction, children's literature, and syndicated articles. His wide circle of acquaintances, unusual experiences, and anecdotal style made his
work enjoyable to read. Editor L. D. McCord liked the pieces but not the
author: "He seems to have been on hugging terms with all the lords and
lordesses of England in particular, and he has never mentioned a big man
in either hemisphere without giving some incident in which 'I' figured in
closest intimacy with him," wrote McCord. "Adam is the bloatedest toady
of forty centuries."[61]

As Badeau's world shrank, he turned to the friendship of George
Corsa and Catherine Chillman. He called these two his adopted children,
although he was more likely their guardian or sponsor. Corsa, whose parents ran a bakery in Queens, New York, acted as his secretary. Chillman
was an English child whose father may have been Badeau's butler at Little
Boston House. By age ten Chillman was traveling internationally in an

odd arrangement with Badeau and Corsa, a man who was fifteen years her senior.[62]

Edwin and Badeau saw each other infrequently in postwar years. Both were busy people, often traveling. When their paths crossed, it was just like old times. Badeau attended a public breakfast at Delmonico's held in Edwin's honor prior to the actor's departure for England in 1880. "After the breakfast, I went to his rooms, and he put his arms around me and begged that we should be to each other all we had ever been," recalled Badeau. "Each promised, and each kept his word."

Badeau spent the night of Mary McVicker's funeral in Edwin's room. But the actor's tours separated them again.

He read with pride of Edwin's mind-blowing financial success, "the results of which surpassed any known in the history of the stage." His friend was now the head of the American theater. Badeau wrote, "Booth's acting was ripened and chastened by study and long experience, by the development of his own powers, and by the opportunities he had enjoyed of comparison with his greatest foreign rivals." The diamond in the rough Badeau had found that Sunday afternoon thirty-five years ago had been polished into all he hoped. "He was accepted as the peer and companion of whatever was best in American society."

The person Edwin became was equally impressive. "I was very much struck with the dignity and composure which years of recognition had given to his bearing. The glowing beauty of youth was gone, his features bore traces of his own sorrows and experiences. Years, however, had enhanced his innate nobility."[63]

Edwin purchased the townhouse on Gramercy Park in 1888. Noted architect Stanford White redesigned and remodeled it. Edwin reserved a space as a residence for himself on the upper floor. He turned the rest of the building into a social club in which actors mingled "with minds that influence the world"—writers, artists, journalists, clergymen, and public figures. The Players, a name suggested by Hamlet's instruction to "see the players well-bestowed," was incorporated by Booth, Lawrence Barrett,

Joe Jefferson, Samuel Clemens, General William T. Sherman, and eleven others in 1888.[64]

Badeau moved to New Jersey after the Grant debacle but came into Manhattan regularly on business. Dressed in a dark sack coat and matching trousers, he looked like a prosperous farmer come to town for the day. Short and stout, "with almost as much paunch as height, he is certainly not a handsome man," thought an observer. Perhaps it was his square head and large face with its peevish-looking jaw and mouth. He still wore glasses for nearsightedness yet even with them couldn't recognize a close friend at any distance. Walking briskly, he seemed recovered from his war wound.[65]

His physical contrast with Edwin was striking. When he and Edwin took a walk, the actor needed assistance getting out the door of The Players. Reaching the street, Edwin took Badeau's arm and leaned heavily on it as they walked. The old friend stumbled frequently in the half hour it took him to circle the block. Then Edwin said he was tired and wanted to go back inside.

"There was something inexpressibly painful in the spectacle of him, whose physical faculties had been so bound up with the intellectual, whose bodily gift had been the incarnation of passion and romance and poetry, to see him decay," wrote Badeau, "his powers crumble, and waste away, to see him decrepit, weary, worn, who had been alive with expression, captivating in bearing, majestic, terrible, tender by turns. Only his eyes retained their marvelous beauty."[66]

Edwin died in the early morning hours of June 7, 1893. There were no last words or farewell look. Eyes closed, he just stopped breathing. Edwina held him and sobbed. Dr. St. Clair Smith went to a window in the dead man's room and waved a handkerchief to signal the news to reporters below.

"He simply fell into a profound sleep," the doctor told them moments later. "It was absolutely painless."[67]

On the morning of June 9, a funeral procession gathered at The Players. There were two carriages with pallbearers, followed by the hearse and then additional carriages with Edwina, her children, her uncle Joe, and her cousins, the children of June and Asia. Catherine McGonigle, Mollie Devlin's sister, was present, but no McVickers. About one hundred members of The Players followed the carriages on foot. They came in double-file, each wearing a rosette of purple and white.

The cortege made its way through the streets to the Church of the Transfiguration on East 29th Street. "The Little Church Around the Corner," as it was popularly known, had been associated with actors since an incident in 1870. Comedian George Holland died that year. His family attended the nearby Church of the Atonement on Madison Avenue, so Joe Jefferson, Holland's colleague, called on its church's minister, the Reverend William T. Sabine, to make funeral arrangements.

Abraham Lincoln was a great man, Sabine told Joe. But look where he died. A theater! "Unfortunate beyond expression," the minister declared, "an extremely distressing [place] for the dark angel to find his victim." Sabine said he would never read the burial service for an actor. "There's a little church around the corner where they do such things," the minister advised Jefferson. Its pastor, G. H. Houghton, had a reputation for working with marginal people.

Incensed, Jefferson replied, "Then, I say to you, Sir, God bless 'the little church around the corner.' "[68]

Arriving at Houghton's church shortly after ten, the funeral party found a mass of spectators lining both sides of the street. Two dozen policemen kept order, ensuring that only those with black-bordered tickets of admission were allowed past the churchyard gate.

Reporters elbowed in to note who was who. The distinct-looking Jefferson was instantly recognizable. With him came artists Augustus Saint-Gaudens and Eastman Johnson; E. C. Stedman and Tom Aldrich, alumni of the old Stoddard salon; and Badeau with Horace Porter, his colleague on Grant's wartime staff.

"After yourselves," Badeau told Edwina and her children, "no one can grieve more profoundly than I."[69]

John Mathews and W. J. Ferguson drew special notice. They were actors in the play at Ford's Theatre on the night of April 14, 1865. Mathews, one of John's most intimate friends, had lived in the Lincoln death room at the Petersen house shortly before the assassination. Ferguson was the callboy and novice actor whom John encountered in the wings as he fled the stage.

"Actors, artists, men of letters, men whose names are known as foremost in their professions on both sides of the Atlantic. Men of millions, men whom the great crowd pushed and squeezed and craned their necks to see," said an observer. "It was not only a profoundly impressive scene. It was an absolutely unique one."[70]

Across 23rd Street one group of spectators, wearing crepe in their buttonholes, stood out by their persistence in staying in front of the crowd. Some were old men, some were boys. Turned away for lacking cards, they held their hats and waited "with the look of men moved by a personal and deep interest in the occasion. Their names will not appear among the distinguished attendants at the service," noted the New York Sun. "They were the unknown men who work on or about the stages of New York's theatres, the men and boys who are never part of the shows they do so much to provide, but who were always remembered by Edwin Booth."

When the service was over and the mourners had left, these stagehands and roustabouts entered the church to search for a petal or piece of fern as a memento.[71]

One floral decoration seemed sacrilegious to touch, however. It was a star, eight feet from tip to tip, and composed of lilies and American Beauty roses. It carried an inscription in violets: "Good Night, Sweet Prince."[72]

AS EDWIN'S FUNERAL procession to the church passed in front of the Scribner Building, a newly constructed Beaux-Arts masterpiece on Fifth Avenue, a disaster took place some two hundred and thirty miles away. Three floors occupied by government clerks located in the old Ford's Theatre building in Washington collapsed.[73]

There were no warning sounds, cracking of timbers, or tremors. The workers in the front half of the third floor (the section fronting the street)

Ford's Theatre Disaster. *At the moment of Edwin Booth's funeral in New York in 1893, a portion of Washington's Ford's Theatre, remodeled into office space, collapsed internally. Twenty people died at the scene and many more were injured.*

simply found themselves dropping. Their floor slammed onto the second floor, which fell onto the first, and all cascaded into the basement, like a house of cards collapsing. Desks, chairs, document cases, and people were crushed in a pile of twisted iron, splintered timbers, and pulverized plaster. A dense cloud of dust billowed up from the hole, followed by the heart-rending screams of the injured.

Ford's Theatre was the former site of the First Baptist Church of Washington. When impresario John T. Ford purchased the building from the church in 1862, one board member predicted a dire fate for anyone who turned a house of worship into a theater. Some felt the site itself was cursed,

as a tornado once tore the roof off the structure. Ford went ahead with construction, only to have the building gutted by fire before the year was out.[74]

Ford hired James J. Gifford as architect and superintendent for a ground-
up reconstruction. Oddly, Gifford had built Tudor Hall, the Booth family
home, a decade earlier. Ford's opened again with a new (and now familiar) look in 1863, only to be shut down by the assassination. Remodeled
again after the government purchased the building from Ford, its interior
became an office space with three large open floors supported by iron pil-
lars. Surrounded by tons of books and records, many clerks who worked
there felt unsafe. Sure enough, excavations in the building's basement
for an electrical lighting plant compromised the integrity of the building. Twenty people were killed outright in the collapse. Scores more were
injured.[75]

"There is something gruesome and uncanny in the Ford's Theatre
disaster, no matter how you look at it," wrote Maurice Minton, a New York
journalist. "We may say that no other such tragic interest hangs about any
other building that can be thought of in this country. Through what mysterious combination of threads and events was brought about the melancholy
association of the Booths and the Lincolns?"[76]

EPILOGUE

Terence Mullen and Jack Hughes were Irish immigrants who lived in Chicago. They made a living passing counterfeit bills. Determined to move up in the world, the two decided to steal the body of Abraham Lincoln from Oak Ridge Cemetery in Springfield. They would return the bones for $200,000 and the release of their associate Ben Boyd, a master engraver, from prison.

Mullen thought November 7, 1876, would make "a damned elegant time to do it." Grant's term was ending, and it was the day of the next presidential election. The excitement would draw people into Springfield. As they milled about, waiting for the election results, a wagon carrying the thieves would pass unnoticed in the crowd.

Posing as a tourist, Hughes went to the cemetery that afternoon to reconnoiter. Just as he thought, the graveyard, located two miles out from town, was relatively deserted. It would certainly be so that evening, when no watchman was on duty.

Hughes paid his twenty-five cents admission fee, signed the visitor's register (under a false name), and asked John Carroll Power, the custodian, for a tour. Power didn't care for Hughes's appearance. He was "a very hard looking case," thought the official. But Power knew that all sorts of people visited Lincoln's grave. He readily answered Hughes's questions about the body in the catacomb.

The day was gray and chilly. Heavy clouds hung overhead. It was so dark by nighttime that a person wishing to check a watch would have been unable to tell the time.

At nine o'clock Hughes and Mullen swung into action. They jumped the cemetery fence and crossed to the large monument that contained Lincoln's remains. The two men carried a "bull's eye" or dark lantern that could focus its light forward like a modern flashlight. It illuminated a heavy steel door at the rear of the monument. Hughes had learned from Power that this opened into a small room where Lincoln's coffin lay within a white marble sarcophagus. The door was secured with a simple padlock. The men cut it off, entered the room, and pried open the tomb.

Now their troubles started. The body was in a double-layered lead-and-wood coffin. Estimates of its weight vary between 400 and 600 pounds. At any figure, it was too heavy for Mullen and Hughes to remove.

As the would-be ghouls pondered this fact, a pistol shot rang out. The body snatchers had been betrayed by a comrade who was supposed to bring up a wagon. Detectives were concealed nearby, and one of them accidentally fired his pistol as he crept up on the burglars.

Mullen fled as fast as his bowed legs could carry him. Hughes was on his heels. They reached the safety of a nearby grove of trees in seconds. Meanwhile, the detectives, confused in the darkness, began shooting at each other. It took some time to restore order, ending a potentially deadly confusion.

Mullen and Hughes made it safely back to Chicago. Their identity was known to authorities, however, and they were promptly arrested. The hapless pair was tried the following year. Curiously, the judge, the prosecutor, and one of the defense counsels were former law partners of William Herndon. It was like having the ghost of Lincoln himself present at the trial. The miscreants were found guilty and sentenced to one year in the state penitentiary at Joliet.

Reaction to the crime was predictable. "Horrible!" read a headline in the *Chicago Daily Tribune*. "Thieves Trying to Steal the Bones of the Martyr President. One of the Most Infamous Outrages Which the Mind of Man

Can Conceive." Veteran police officials declared that they had "never met, in their experience, anyone whom they thought low and mean and devilish enough to imagine such a thing [or] a mind so debased as to propose the robbery, let alone execute it."

If an attempt had actually been made. "There are men who affected to believe that the whole affair was a sham and a pretense," wrote custodian Power. No theft had been attempted, the argument went. Others believed one had, but thought it a scheme by government agents to boost their careers by conning two morons into mischief. Still others felt former rebels were behind it, hoping to scatter the fragments of the late president to the four corners of Hell. Or maybe it was a plot by partisans of Grant to garner votes for the Republicans.

Mary was in Pau, France, on the second of her two European exiles, at the time. She didn't leave any reaction to the episode that has survived. Robert lived in Chicago. Apprised of the plot in advance by detectives, he helped set the trap for the thieves and watched it unfold with understandable anxiety. Consistent with his private nature, he made no public comment on the attempted grave robbing once the affair was over.

Robert was concerned, however, that nothing like this ever repeat itself. In 1887 a vault was dug in the catacomb chamber. Abraham and Mary were placed in it, and their coffins covered with cement.

Then, in 1901, the couple were exhumed. Mary was placed in a crypt beside her dead children. Lincoln was reburied in a deep vault at the site of the attempted theft in 1876. His coffin was entirely enclosed in a cage of steel bars. Two tons of cement fixed it in place. It would have taken days for a team of well-equipped excavators to pry the dead man's bones loose from this tomb.

On both occasions Lincoln's coffin was opened before reburial. Spectators viewed the remains and attested to the fact that the late president's body was really there. Fleetwood Lindley, a thirteen-year-old boy, was present with his father in 1901. Lindley died in 1963, at the age of seventy-two—the last person who could say he saw the face of Abraham Lincoln.[1]

Badeau was overseas at the time of the attempted body snatching and wrote nothing about it. He was intrigued, however, with Mary's institutionalization the year before, and couldn't resist giving an opinion on the affair.

If the former First Lady was mad, not bad, that was in an odd way good news. She wasn't responsible for the incidents like those that frightened and angered him in 1865. "It relieved Mrs. Lincoln of the charge of heartlessness, of mercenary behavior, of indifference to her husband's happiness." Badeau was particularly pleased that it vindicated Robert, his old comrade on Grant's staff, as a good son. As for the martyred president: "who that reveres and loves his memory will not respect his character more profoundly and feel that he has another and a tenderer claim upon our sympathy?"[2]

It was sad to think about the fivesome in the box at Ford's Theatre, Badeau continued. Lincoln murdered, Mary crazy, John killed.

Clara Harris and Henry Rathbone, the young couple with the Lincolns at the theater that night, were cursed, too. They were step-siblings who lived in the same home. As such, it was wrong for them to marry, Badeau believed. Nevertheless, "the awful occurrence which they witnessed brought them into a singular sympathy," and they wed in 1867. While on diplomatic service in Germany in 1883, Rathbone shot and stabbed his wife to death. He thus reprised with pistol and knife John's act of April 14, 1865.[3]

Badeau's final days were spent at a hotel in Ridgewood, New Jersey. He had been in declining health following a series of cataract operations. Each procedure left him in worse shape, and a stroke finished him off on March 19, 1895, at the age of sixty-three.[4]

His funeral service was held at a Catholic church in Ridgewood on the morning of March 22. Badeau had prepared his own memorial arrangements with nationally known pallbearers. These included Senator William Chandler, who—strange to say—was married to Lucy Hale, John Wilkes Booth's fiancée at the time of the Lincoln assassination. Chandler was a no-show, as were the other high-profile designees. Local politicians filled in while Badeau's brother Charles, his two adopted children, and a few neighbors composed the mourners.[5]

They did him proud. He was dressed in his general's uniform and placed in a handsome red cedar coffin. A black cloth covered the box, and the sword he carried during the war lay on top of it.[6]

After the service, Badeau's remains were taken immediately to Tarry-town, New York, for burial in the family plot at the Old Dutch Churchyard. His grave may be found today ingloriously adjacent to a maintenance shed off the cemetery's Lincoln Avenue. Buried nearby is Washington Irving, whose character of Rip Van Winkle made Joe Jefferson's fortune.

In 1901, Badeau's literary possessions were auctioned at John Anderson Galleries in New York. Included in the collection were his library, corre-spondence, scrapbooks, photograph albums, and notebooks. The assort-ment was so large that the sale took two evenings to complete.

Among the lots were 300 Civil War letters from his friend Harry Wil-son. They formed an exceptional history of the war as Wilson experienced it—from the moment the two men met in 1862 through Lincoln's murder and the capture of Jefferson Davis ("whose flight is even more ignoble than I told it," the officer wrote). Many of these letters were forty or fifty pages long, indicating that, if there was never romance between the men, there was profound friendship.

Professional and personal papers from Grant in the sale included the most eagerly awaited message of the entire war. It was the original of Grant's telegram from Appomattox to Secretary of War Edwin Stanton. "General Lee surrendered the Army of Northern Va. this afternoon on terms proposed by myself . . . ," read the penciled note in Grant's hand. Dated April 9, 1865, the message was contained in Badeau's own field orderly book.

Dozens of letters from Edwin to Badeau were sold. Early in the war the actor playfully addressed his friend as "Capt. Bobo" and signed his letters "Boots." Later missives, written after the death of Edwin's first wife Mary in 1863, seem written by a different man. They revealed his depressed state of mind and described his séance experiences. The auction house's cataloguer characterized their tone as "pathetic" (in the old-fashioned sense of touchingly sad).

An 1867 letter from Edwin to Grant, begging for John's body, had wound up in Badeau's possession. It was included in the auction. So was artist Walter Brackett's 1858 portrait of Edwin that was one of Badeau's prized possessions. An 1893 card of admission to the actor's funeral service at the Little Church Around the Corner was hawked away along with an illustrated Shakespeare edition. "All men are bad, and in their badness reign," Edwin wrote in the book, underscoring the lines heavily.[7]

Edwin's effects were sold at the Fifth Avenue Auction Rooms in Manhattan in 1908. Under the hammer were 250 pieces of theatrical wardrobe. These included the actor's Hamlet wig, Brutus sword, Lear beard, and Shylock knife. The Richard III costume used by both himself and his father Junius went out the door along with furniture, paintings, and prints.

Reporters sat through the auction with mixed feelings. One wrote that the event's commercialism reminded him of when Roman soldiers at the crucifixion threw dice for Jesus' tunic. Another felt that this was only the way of the world. It had been two decades since Edwin was a force on the stage. A theatrical generation had passed. Many people scarcely knew who he was. Those who did remembered only four things: "the sudden death of his first wife, the shame cast upon his name by the assassin of Lincoln, the unfortunate character of his second marriage, and the failure of his effort to establish a splendid playhouse."[8]

Upon Joseph Jefferson's retirement from the stage in 1904, the *New York Dramatic Mirror* estimated that he had made five million dollars playing Rip. If that sum was exaggerated, it wasn't stretched by much. The actual figure was certainly a king's ransom. Now time meant more than money to the veteran actor, and he announced that henceforth he would fish, paint, write, and tend his garden. "All old people should have a garden," Jefferson said. "It's so full of hope."[9]

After years of struggle, he was at peace. He told former president Grover Cleveland, a fishing partner, he was "very grateful for having more than his share of the joys of life, and [was] prepared to meet, at any moment, the common fate of us all."[10]

Jefferson remained a spiritualist. He longed for his lost loved ones and had retained his childlike wonder at things. When someone began telling Cleveland tales of the supernatural, the ex-president waved his hand to cut off the speaker. Pointing to Joe, he said, "Tell it to Jefferson. He'll believe anything."[11]

The great comedian left the world at age seventy-five at his seaside home in Palm Beach, Florida, on April 23, 1905. His family were able to grant his wish to see the ocean. "Beautiful color out there," he said. "See those hazy clouds hanging low on the horizon?"[12]

Surrounded by family and servants, Jefferson's life ended at a villa he named The Reefs. The home was filled "with evidence of his love for the beautiful"—artwork, statues, fine books, and other mementos of an extraordinary life. There was a comfort and stability here unimaginable by the "Little Joe" and his hand-to-mouth parents who—despite Lincoln's best efforts—struggled for their next meal in Springfield, Illinois, seven decades earlier.[13]

SINCE 1991, THE two wars with Iraq and the Afghanistan intervention have taken over 7,100 American lives on the battlefield. As a percentage of the population of today's United States, the Civil War death toll, by contrast, would exceed six million people. If the dead numbered 700,000 (a recent estimate) and were the median height for soldiers of five feet eight inches, a disturbing image can be composed. Laid head to toe in a straight line, they would form a chain of bodies reaching from Atlanta to New York City.[14]

Almost all of these individuals were young men in the morning of their lives—the pride and hope of their families. No statistic does justice to the emotional weight of this loss to the bereaved nor the deaths of children and adults at home who perished by the thousands in an age of fevers, infections, and hard living.

Enter spiritualism. It was asserted that in 1860, the year of Lincoln's first election to the presidency, there were 1,600,000 followers of the movement in the United States. This number is a guess, but probably a good one. If one adds in the number of casual or curious inquirers, the figure would probably triple.[15]

Spiritualism offered them a unique hope. As Judge John W. Edmonds wrote in a book he sent Lincoln during the war, the dead were not obliterated from existence, as atheists taught. They lived on as the same people they had always been, just in a better way. The deceased consoled their mourners, then greeted them in the "upper world" upon their own deaths. Heaven, said the poet John Pierpont, might best be understood as the moment when the deceased experienced the joy of that reunion.

Interest in spiritualism would wane in the postwar years. The phenomenon was too individualistic. It had no formal creed, no paid clergy, and no luck establishing a viable national organization to announce and enforce its beliefs. Simply said, no one was in charge. Everyone was, and it often seemed that anything went. That hurt the faith as did the antics of people like Charles Colchester who undermined public confidence in the practice. By the 1880s many adherents drifted off to newer movements like Christian Science, theosophy, or radical social and political causes.[16]

Those who, in later years, thought back on the golden age of spiritualism often wondered what it was they had experienced. They asked the same questions asked today by those who seek the dead.

Was it real? Was it delusional? Or did that even matter? As Asia Booth, the sister of Edwin and John, said, "No one is the worse for having loved and believed."[17]

ACKNOWLEDGMENTS

It is a pleasure to acknowledge the following friends and colleagues for their contributions to this book. Each individual shared with me his or her extraordinary knowledge of my story's time period. Their insights improved the book immensely. I am deeply grateful for their assistance— and for them.

Michael Burlingame, Sidney Blumenthal, Angela Smythe, and Sean Wilentz (for their encouragement).

Ian Wilson (for three years of research, cheerfully provided).

Beth Carroll-Horrocks, Tom Horrocks, Ted Bennicoff, Katherine Anderson, Frank Gorman, Lawrence Lee Hewitt, James Capobianco, Dale E. Reddick, Lew C. Schon, Andrew Dick, Don Olson, Sarah Kiefer, Joe Suplicki, and Hannah D. Cox (for understanding of the nineteenth century).

Tom Bogar, John F. Andrews, Arthur Bloom, Dan Watermeier, Abbie Weinberg, and Heather Wolfe (for knowledge of the American theater).

Nelson Lankford, Paul Sherry, Bob Lesman, Nancy Alford, and Bruce Leggat (for reading and criticism of the book in manuscript).

John Buescher and Michelle Hamilton (for studies of American spiritualism).

Jason Emerson, Allen C. Guelzo, Rodney Ross, Gordon Leidner, Doug Wilson, Jasmine Leung, and Stacy Pratt McDermott (for knowledge of the Lincolns).

Ed Steers, Tom Turner, Tom Fink, Richard and Kellie Gutman, and Amelia Bathke (for interest in the Booths).

Jon White, Jim Holmberg, Roger Hunt, Michael Musick, Angela Gates, and Justin Martin (for love of American history).

David W. Rickman, Jeanne Solensky, Brianne Barrett, Nol Putnam, and Oscar Fitzgerald (for helping me understand the art and fashion of the book's time period).

Michelle Krowl, Joan Cashin, Jan Wade, Emily Forland, and Lisa Samia (for faithful friendship).

Dan Gerstle, Bob Weil, Peter Miller, Nick Curly, and Zeba Arora (for making this book a reality).

And to Carey, Jane, David, Migo, Suzanne, and Jeanette (for dogs, for cats, for walks, for mulch, and forever).

NOTES

ABBREVIATIONS

AB   Adam Badeau

ABL   Letters of Adam Badeau to Henry Wilson, AM 15793, Mudd Manuscript Library,
        Princeton University, Princeton, NJ

HI   Douglas L. Wilson and Rodney O. Davis, eds., *Herndon's Informants: Letters, Inter-
        views, and Statements about Abraham Lincoln* (Urbana, Chicago, and Springfield:
        University of Illinois Press, 1998)

FF   Terry Alford, *Fortune's Fool: The Life of John Wilkes Booth* (New York and London:
        Oxford University Press, 2015)

EB   Edwin Booth

EBG   Edwina Booth Grossmann, *Edwin Booth: Recollections by His Daughter and Letters
        to Her and to His Friends* (New York: Century, 1894)

HBTL   Hampden-Booth Theatre Library, New York, NY

Memoir Asia Booth Clarke, *John Wilkes Booth: A Sister's Memoir*, ed. Terry Alford (Jackson:
        University Press of Mississippi, 1996)

MB-AL   Michael Burlingame, *Abraham Lincoln: A Life*, 2 vols. (Baltimore: Johns Hopkins
        University Press, 2008)

MTL   Justin G. Turner and Linda Levitt Turner, eds., *Mary Todd Lincoln: Her Life and
        Letters* (New York: Alfred A. Knopf, 1972)

CHAPTER I: IF THE FATES ALLOW

1 "Monomania," *The Boston Pearl and Literary Gazette* 4 (Dec. 13, 1834): 114; Noah
   M. Ludlow, *Dramatic Life as I Found It* (St. Louis: G. I. Jones, 1880), 416–17; James

Freeman Clarke, *Memorial and Biographical Sketches* (Boston: Houghton, Osgood, 1878), 263–79.

2   "Meet Mary Ann," *Surratt Courier* 26 (April 2001): 4–5.

3   Asia Booth Clarke, *The Elder and the Younger Booth* (Boston: James R. Osgood, 1882), 53.

4   [John Cooper Vail], *The Actor; or, A Peep Behind the Curtain* (New York: W. H. Graham, 1846), 178; *New York Tribune*, Aug. 19, 1890.

5   Clarke, *The Elder and the Younger Booth*, 66–68.

6   *FF*, 13, 17.

7   Arthur W. Bloom, *Edwin Booth: A Biography and Performance History* (Jefferson, NC, and London: McFarland, 2013), 298.

8   *Providence Literary Subaltern*, Jan. 29, 1830.

9   *London Morning Post*, Jan. 12, 1830.

10 Clipping, n.d., Booth File, Harvard Theatre Collection [HTC], Houghton Library, Cambridge, MA.

11 Clarke, *The Elder and the Younger Booth*, 68.

12 "Massa": Asia B. Clarke, galley pages mounted into a copy of *The Elder and the Younger Booth*, opposite page 92, courtesy of Steve Archer; Hamblin: Thomas A. Bogar, *Thomas Hamblin and the Bowery Theatre* (New York: Palgrave Macmillan, 2018), 111; Clarke, *The Elder and the Younger Booth*, 92.

13 Clarke, galley page in *The Elder and the Younger Booth*, opposite page 92; Rogers to W. Stump Forward, Baltimore, Aug. 10, 1886, Misc. Mss. Collection, Manuscript Division, Library of Congress [LOC].

14 Clarke, *The Elder and the Younger Booth*, 71; "Ignoring": Ella V. Mahoney and Helen C. Milius, "The House That Booth Built. The House That Fell with Lincoln," ms. (ca. 1940–42), 46, Historical Society of Harford County [HSHC], Bel Air, MD.

15 W. Stump Forward, "Junius Brutus Booth," ms. (1887), Maryland Historical Society [MdHS], 198.

16 Adam Badeau, "Boyhood of Booth," *Portland Oregonian*, Jan. 29, 1893.

17 *Life and Times of Frederick Douglass* (Boston: DeWolfe and Fiske, 1892), 127.

18 *Washington Evening Star*, Jan. 13, 1919.

19 Thomas R. Forbes, "The Social History of the Caul," *Yale Journal of Biology and Medicine* 25 (June 1953): 495–508.

20 Dinah Faber, "Joseph and Ann Hall: Behind the Scenes at Tudor Hall," *Harford Historical Bulletin*, no. 104 (Fall 2006); *New York Mercury*, Sept. 17, 1887; *Memoir*, 60; Asia Booth Clarke, *Booth Memorials. Passages, Incidents, and Anecdotes in the Life of Junius*

Brutus Booth (the Elder) (New York: Carleton, 1866), 107, 141; seven faces: Mahoney and Milius, "The House That Booth Built," 46.

21 Forward, "Booth," 113–14; Stephen M. Archer, *Junius Brutus Booth, Theatrical Prometheus* (Carbondale and Edwardsville: Southern Illinois University Press, 1992), 136.

22 Edgefield, SC, *Advertiser*, March 22, 1838.

23 [Vail], *The Actor*, 2, 102.

24 *FF*, 11.

25 Cora L. Daniels and C. M. Stevans, eds., *Encyclopedia of Superstition, Folklore, and Occult Sciences of the World* (Chicago and Milwaukee: J. H. Yewdale & Sons, 1903), vol. 1, 261.

26 *Memoir*, 33–34.

27 *Memoir*, 5.

28 Asia Booth Clarke, *Personal Recollections of the Elder Booth* (London: printed but not published, 1880?), 36–37.

29 [Vail], *The Actor*, 4, 57.

30 *Chicago Evening Journal*, April 19, 1865; *Cincinnati Daily Commercial*, April 18, 1865.

31 Izola Forrester, *This One Mad Act* (Boston: Hale, Cushman, Flint, 1937), 99; Stuart Thayer, "Herr Driesbach, Lord of the Brute Creation," *Bandwagon* 30 (Jan.–Feb. 1986): 29–31.

32 Bloom, *Edwin Booth*, 8.

33 *Memoir*, 35.

34 Stuart Robson, "Memories of Fifty Years. Chapter 1," *Everybody's Magazine* 3 (July 1900): 87; George Alfred Townsend, *The Life, Crime, and Capture of John Wilkes Booth* (New York: Dick and Fitzgerald, 1865), 21.

35 "A thief": Clarke, *The Elder and the Younger Booth*, 89; flies: Clarke, "Personal Recollections," 41.

36 *Memoir*, 55.

37 Robson, "Memories," 86.

38 Interview with H. Stearnes Smiley in Ernest C. Miller, *John Wilkes Booth in the Pennsylvania Oil Region* (Meadville, PA: Crawford County Historical Society, 1987), 63.

39 *Memoir*, 36–38.

40 Clarke, *Booth Memorials*, 119–20.

41 Clarke, *Personal Recollections*, 51–52.

42 Clarke, *The Elder and the Younger Booth*, 115.

43 Cave: Statement of Thomas A. Hall, April 24, 1865, William C. Edwards and Edward Steers Jr., eds., *The Lincoln Assassination: The Evidence* (Urbana and Chicago:

University of Illinois Press, 2009), 630; Harwood: Mahoney and Milius, "House," 21–22; eyes/ax: Clarke, *The Elder and the Younger Booth*, 75, 87.

44 Clarke, *Personal Recollections*, 13.

45 Elizabeth Rogers to W. Stump Forward, Baltimore, Aug. 16, 1886, LOC.

46 "Saw the air"/"man-o'-war": William Winter, *Vagrant Memories* (New York: George H. Doran, 1915), 162.

47 *New York Times*, Aug. 1, 1856; Charles Dickens, *American Notes* (New York: John W. Lovell, 1883), 748.

48 *New York Tribune*, Aug. 16, 1885.

49 [Vail], *The Actor*, 179–80.

CHAPTER 2: HIS IMPERFECT SELF

1 Joseph Jefferson, *The Autobiography of Joseph Jefferson* (New York: Century Co., 1890), 24–30, 56–57, 64.

2 *FF*, 54–55.

3 Springfield *Illinois Weekly State Journal*, April 14, 1838.

4 *HI* (Robert Wilson), 201–2; *HI* (Joshua Speed), 588.

5 Benjamin McArthur, "Joseph Jefferson's Lincoln: Vindication of an Autobiographical Legend," *Journal of the Illinois State Historical Society* 93 (Summer 2000): 155–66; *Vicksburg Herald*, June 4, 1905. The company (or parts of it) performed in Springfield several times in this period, complicating a proper chronology of these events. "It is my best story," Jefferson said, "and the best of it is that it is true." *Topeka State Journal*, May 6, 1905. It appears they leased the theater and did not build it.

6 *HI* (Nathaniel Grisby), 111.

7 *HI* (John Hanks), 454.

8 Louis A. Warren, *Lincoln's Parentage and Childhood* (New York: Century Co., 1926), 143.

9 *HI* (Dennis Hanks), 35.

10 *HI* (Dennis Hanks), 39–41; *HI* (A. H. Chapman), 99–102.

11 *HI* (Dennis Hanks), 40; Walter J. Daly, "'The Slows': The Torment of Milk Sickness on the Midwest Frontier," *Indiana Magazine of History* 102 (March 2006): 29–40; Eleanor Atkinson, "Lincoln's Boyhood," *The American Magazine* 65 (Feb. 1908): 362.

12 *HI* (A. H. Chapman), 99; *HI* (Dennis Hanks), 41.

13 *HI* (Sarah B. Lincoln), 597; *HI* (Dennis Hanks), 41; *HI* (Anna R. Gentry), 132.

14 "I don't always intend": MB-AL, vol. 1, 45.

15 *HI* (Joseph Gillespie), 181; *HI* (Matilda J. Moore), 109.

16 *HI* (Nathaniel Grigsby), 113–14; *HI* (Green B. Taylor), 130. "Of the enemies that Lincoln made, none were greater than some members of the Grigsby family. Abraham, it is said, always declared that his sister was not properly treated by the Grigsbys." *Indianapolis Journal*, June 28, 1903.

17 J. G. Holland, *The Life of Abraham Lincoln* (Springfield, MA, 1866), 34.

18 Isaac N. Arnold, *The Life of Abraham Lincoln* (Lincoln: University of Nebraska Press, 1994 [orig. published in 1884]), 31; *HI* (Herndon), 453n.

19 Whitney: *York Gazette*, Feb. 12, 1898; ghosts: *HI* (J. R. Herndon), 70.

20 "cat laugh": Clark E. Carr, *My Day and Generation* (Chicago: A. C. McClurg, 1908), 107.

21 *HI* (John Hanks), 457; Arnold, *Life of Abraham Lincoln*, 31–32.

22 *HI* (Godbey), 449.

23 David Donald, *Lincoln* (New York: Simon & Schuster, 1995), 52–66.

24 *Monmouth* [Freehold, NJ] *Inquirer*, Feb. 17, 1898.

25 *HI* (Anna R. Gentry), 132; Henry C. Whitney, *Lincoln, the Citizen* (New York: Baker and Taylor, 1908), 39–40; Gentry Family Materials, Lincoln Financial Foundation Collection, item 71200908503570. Anna would marry Allen Gentry, with whom Lincoln traveled to New Orleans in 1828.

26 *HI* (Jason Duncan), 539; "buggies": *HI* (Elizabeth Abell), 544; "lacked the attentiveness": *HI* (Johnson G. Greene), 531; "flung him": *HI* (John Lightfoot), 639.

27 Ann Rutledge: *HI* (Mentor Graham), 242–43; *HI* (William G. Greene), 21.

28 John Evangelist Walsh, *The Shadows Rise: Abraham Lincoln and the Ann Rutledge Legend* (Urbana and Chicago: University of Illinois Press, 1993), 6–18, 139.

29 *HI* (Robert Rutledge), 383; gun: *HI* (Henry McHenry), 155; "suicide": *HI* (Mentor Graham), 243.

30 *HI* (Mentor Graham), 243; "from the commencement": *HI* (Leonard Swett), 167; *Tyrone Daily Herald*, Aug. 3, 1893.

31 *HI* (Sarah B. Lincoln), 107; *HI* (Isaac Cogdal), 441; "long face": *HI* (Elizabeth Abell), 557; *HI* (John T. Stuart), 576.

32 *HI* (Isaac Cogdal), 441; *HI* (Mary T. Lincoln), 358–60.

33 Caroline O. Brown, "Springfield Society Before the Civil War," *Journal of the Illinois State Historical Society* 15 (April–July 1922): 478.

34 Catherine Clinton, *Mrs. Lincoln: A Life* (New York: HarperCollins, 2009), 32.

35 *HI* (Elizabeth Edwards), 443.

36 *HI* (John T. Stuart), 63.

37 *HI* (Elizabeth Edwards), 443; *HI* (Joshua F. Speed), 474–77; *HI* (Elizabeth and Ninian Edwards), 592.

38 Jean Baker, *Mary Todd Lincoln: A Biography* (New York and London: W. W. Norton,

1987), 90; Katherine Helm, *The True Story of Mary, Wife of Lincoln* (New York and London: Harper and Brothers, 1928), 89; *The Collected Works of Abraham Lincoln*, ed. Roy P. Basler (New Brunswick, NJ: Rutgers University Press, 1953) [*CWAL*], vol. 1, 233.

39 *HI* (William G. Greene), 21.

40 "the harp": *HI* (Henry C. Whitney), 617; *HI* (Mary T. Lincoln), 566.

41 *HI* (William Herndon), 133.

42 Dorothy M. Kunhardt, "An Old Lady's Lincoln Memories," *Life Magazine* 46 (Feb. 9, 1959): 57.

43 *HI* (Matheny), 251; father's old adage: Lincoln to Speed, Springfield, Feb. 13, 1842, *CWAL*, 269; whispers: MB-*AL*, vol. 1, 195.

44 *HI* (James H. Matheny), 665.

45 William Herndon to Jesse W. Weik, Springfield, Jan. 8, 1886, in Douglas L. Wilson and Rodney O. Davis, eds., *Herndon on Lincoln. Letters* (Urbana, Chicago, and Springfield: Knox College Studies Center, 2016), 189; Jason Emerson, *Giant in the Shadows: The Life of Robert T. Lincoln* (Carbondale and Edwardsville: Southern Illinois University Press, 2012), 7–12.

46 *HI* (Joseph Gillespie), 181; *HI* (Mary T. Lincoln), 357.

47 *HI* (Mary T. Lincoln), 357.

48 Michael Burlingame, ed., *An Oral History of Abraham Lincoln: John B. Nicolay's Interviews and Essays* (Carbondale and Edwardsville: Southern Illinois University Press, 1996), 1; "she devil": *HI* (Turner R. King), 465.

49 Wilson and David, eds., *Herndon on Lincoln. Letters*, 167, 261; *HI* (Elizabeth Edwards), 623.

50 Helm, *The True Story of Mary*, 23–24.

51 MB-*AL*, vol. 1, 359; Eddie Lincoln: Samuel P. Wheeler, "Solving a Lincoln Literary Mystery: 'Little Eddie,'" *Journal of the Abraham Lincoln Association* 33 (Summer 2012): 34–46.

52 *Beaumont Enterprise*, Sept. 15, 1902; *New York Herald Tribune*, July 27, 1926; Wayne C. Temple, "Mariah (Bartlett) Vance, Daytime Servant to the Lincolns," *For the People* 1, no. 6 (Winter 2004): 1, 3; Temple, "Mariah (Bartlett) Vance," *For the People* 2, no. 7 (Spring 2005): 1–2, 4–5, 8; Lloyd Ostendorf and Walter Olesky, eds., *Lincoln's Unknown Private Life: An Oral History by His Black Housekeeper Mariah Vance, 1850–60* (Mamaroneck, NY: Hastings House, 1995), 30, 131, 138, 158–61. The Ostendorf-Olesky book was formed from shorthand notes taken between 1900 and 1904. The latter notes disappeared, leading to one of many doubts about this work.

53 Baker, *Mary Todd Lincoln*, 128. Eddie's stone is preserved at the Abraham Lincoln Presidential Library and Museum in Springfield, Illinois.

54 "had twenty": MB-*AL*, vol. 1, 359; "must eat": Kunhardt, "An Old Lady's Lincoln Memories," 57.

55 "always was": Lincoln to Joshua Speed, Springfield, July 4, 1842, *CWAL*, vol. 1, 290.

56 Arnold, *Life of Lincoln*, 31; Jonathan W. White, *Midnight in America: Darkness, Sleep, and Dreams During the Civil War* (Chapel Hill: University of North Carolina Press, 2017), 149–72.

57 Donald W. Olson and Laurie E. Jasinski, "Abe Lincoln and the Leonids," *Sky & Telescope* (Nov. 1999): 34–35; thirteenth person: Eau Claire *Weekly Telegram*, Feb. 10, 1898; "His mind": Henry Steele Commager, ed., *Herndon's Life of Lincoln* (Cleveland: World Pubs., 1942), 352.

58 bulldog latched: *HI* (J. H. Chapman), 137; off to Terre Haute: *HI* (Frances T. Wallace), 485; Max Ehrmann, "Lincoln's Visit to Terre Haute," Max Ehrmann Papers, DePauw University Archives; madstone: *Evansville Daily Journal*, May 20, 1858; *Crawfordsville Review*, April 27, 1889.

59 *HI* (John T. Stuart), 519.

60 voted nay: *Journal of the House of Representatives*, 38th Congress, 2nd Session (Jan. 31, 1865), 171.

61 election as president: David S. Reynolds, *Abe: Abraham Lincoln in His Times* (New York: Penguin, 2020), 501–3; These views: Donald, *Lincoln*, 222–23; something ordinary: *HI* (Elliott B. Herndon), 459–60; Sidney Blumenthal, *All the Powers of the Earth: The Political Life of Abraham Lincoln, 1856–1860* (New York: Simon & Schuster, 2019), 371, 37.

62 *HI* (George Balch), 595–96; *HI* (A. H. Chapman), 137; *HI* (John J. Hall), 693.

CHAPTER 3: SO OLD WHEN HE WAS YOUNG

1 *FF*, 32.

2 Register, St. Peter's Church (P.E.), volume for 1803–1885, 214, MdHS; Clarke, *The Elder and the Younger Booth*, 107.

3 *Memoir*, 10.

4 *Memoir*, 58.

5 *Memoir*, 46, 69; Clarke, *Booth Memorials*, 79.

6 *Memoir*, 60; Clarke, *Booth Memorials*, 107, 141.

7 *Memoir*, 50.

8 *Harford Gazette and General Advertiser*, April 11, 1851.

9 Mahoney and Milius, "The House That Booth Built," 34.

10 *Memoir*, 43–44.

11 *Memoir*, 54.

12 Donald W. Olson et al., "Walt Whitman's 'Year of Meteors,'" *Sky & Telescope* (July 2010): 28–33; *New York Herald*, July 22, 1860; *Harper's Weekly* 4 (Aug. 4, 1860): 1–2.

13 Thomas L. Clingman, "The Great Meteor of 1860," *Appleton's Journal of Popular Literature, Science, and Art* 5 (Jan. 7, 1871): 10–13.

14 *Richmond Dispatch*, Aug. 15, 1860.

15 Yellow posters: courtesy of James Arsenault; "gypsy witch": *Burlington Daily News*, Jan. 27, 1921; Ronald Decker, Thierry Depaulis, and Michael Dummett, *A Wicked Pack of Cards: The Origins of the Occult Tarot* (New York: St. Martin's Press, 1996), 116–42; "My cards": *Detroit Free Press*, July 16, 1899.

16 *The Highly Important Prophecies of the Celebrated Madame Lenormand of France* (New York: Coster and Guttmann, 1861), 8.

17 Eleanor Atkinson, "Lincoln's Boyhood," *The American Magazine* 55 (Feb. 1908): 363.

18 Herndon to Ward Hill Lamon, Springfield, IL, Feb. 25, 1870, Wilson and Davis, eds., *Herndon on Lincoln. Letters*, 88.

19 Ward Hill Lamon, *The Life of Abraham Lincoln* (Boston: Osgood, 1872), 475.

20 *HI* (Samuel Haycraft), 85.

21 Henry B. Rankin, *Personal Recollections of Abraham Lincoln* (New York: Putnam's, 1916), 122.

22 *HI* (Mary T. Lincoln), 360.

23 Clinton, *Mrs. Lincoln*, 124, 135–37; James B. Conroy, *Lincoln's White House: The People's House in Wartime* (Lanham, Boulder, New York, and London: Rowman and Littlefield, 2017), 16, 35–36.

24 Emerson, *Giant in the Shadows*, 63.

25 Donald, *Lincoln*, 154, 275; Julia Taft Bayne, *Tad Lincoln's Father* (Lincoln: University of Nebraska Press, 2001) 3.

26 Burlingame, *Inside Lincoln's White House*, 16; Lizzie: Elizabeth Todd Grimsley, "Six Months in the White House," *Journal of the Illinois State Historical Society* 19 (Oct. 1926–Jan. 1927): 56.

27 MB-AL, vol. 2, 177.

28 *White Cloud Kansas Chief*, Oct. 10 and 24, 1861.

29 EB to AB, New York, NY, June 15, 1863, HBTL.

30 John Rhodehamel and Louise Taper, eds., *"Right or Wrong, God Judge Me": The Writings of John Wilkes Booth* (Urbana and Chicago: University of Illinois Press, 1997), 55–64, 147.

31 *New Albany Public Press*, Nov. 11, 1885.

32 Asia B. Clarke to Jean Anderson, Phila., n.d., MdHS.

33 *Memoir*, 44, 54, 66.

34 *FF*, 113–16.

35 Excellent recent biographies of Edwin by Daniel J. Watermeier, *American Tragedian: The Life of Edwin Booth* (Columbia: University of Missouri Press, 2015), and by Arthur Bloom, *Joseph Jefferson, Dean of the American Theatre* (Savannah: Frederic C. Beil, 2000).

36 EBG, 149.

37 Gladys Malvern, *Good Troupers All: The Story of Joseph Jefferson* (Philadelphia: Macrae, Smith, 1945), 225; Jefferson, *Autobiography*, 175; Francis Wilson, *Joseph Jefferson. Reminiscences of a Fellow Player* (New York: Charles Scribner's Sons, 1906), 3.

38 Jefferson, *Autobiography*, 229; Bloom, *Joseph Jefferson*, 41, 55; Margaret: Malvern, *Good Troupers All*, 191.

39 Mollie: *Boston Herald*, June 7, 1893; Malvern, *Good Troupers All*, 208.

40 Anne M. Fauntleroy, "The Romance of Mary Devlin Booth," *Ladies' Home Journal*, Sept. 1904, 10.

41 "p—k": EB to June Booth, Oct. 31 and Dec. 12, 1858, HTC.

42 Jervis McEntee, diary, Feb. 7, 1879, Archives of American Art, Smithsonian.

43 L. Terry Oggel, ed., *The Letters and Notebooks of Mary Devlin Booth* (New York, Westport, and London: Greenwood Press, 1987), xii, xiii.

44 Hand in hand: Joseph Jefferson, "In Memory of Edwin Booth," *Modern Eloquence, Vol. 2, After-Dinner Speeches, E–O* (Chicago: John R. Shuman, 1903), 691–93.

45 Mollie to EB, July 17 and Aug. 24 (?), 1859, Oggel, *Letters and Notebooks*, xii, xiii, 11.

46 *Memoir*, 68.

47 "married to please him": Asia B. Clarke to Jean Anderson, Philadelphia, July 11, 1859, MdHS.

48 Asia B. Clarke to Jean Anderson, July 11, 1859, Aug. 1, 1860, and "Thursday" [n.d.], 1860, MdHS.

49 Charles H. Shattuck, *The Hamlet of Edwin Booth* (Urbana, Chicago, and London: University of Illinois Press, 1969), 18–30.

50 Shattuck, *The Hamlet of Edwin Booth*, 29; "Young and happy": Portland *Oregonian*, Jan. 29, 1893.

51 "lady-like": Washington *National Tribune*, April 4, 1895.

52 Adam Badeau, *The Vagabond* (New York: Rudd and Carlton, 1859), 347–54.

53 Adam Badeau, "Edwin Booth. On and Off the Stage," *McClure's Magazine* 1 (Aug. 1893): 255–67.

54 "love-sick schoolgirl": Mollie to Edwin, Dec. 28, 1859, and fruit card: Mollie to Edwin, Dec. [n.d.], 1859, both in Oggel, *Letters and Notebooks*, 23–27.

55 warm, clear: entry for July 7, 1850, RG 27 (Records of the Weather Bureau), Reel 360,
     National Archives and Records Service, Washington, DC; Junius Henri Browne, *The
     Great Metropolis. A Mirror of New York* (Harford: American Publishing Co., 1869),
     654-55.

56 *Troy Daily Budget*, July 10, 1860; Badeau, "Edwin Booth. On and Off the Stage," 263;
     prayer bench: Mabel Osgood Wright to William Winter, Fairfield, CT, June 11 and July
     7, 1893, laid in Folger MS W.a.231, Folger Shakespeare Library, Washington, DC.

CHAPTER 4: GOD'S MOST PRECIOUS TRUTH

1   Wilson and Davis, eds., *Herndon on Lincoln. Letters*, 211-12.

2   *Baltimore Sun*, May 20, 1861; *Daily Nashville Patriot*, May 24, 1861 (her forte); "flub-
     dubs": Donald B. Cole and John J. McDonough, eds., *Witness to the Young Republic*
     (Hanover, NH: University Press of New England, 1989), 382; MB-*AL*, vol. 2, 263, 266,
     272, 280.

3   Julia T. Bayne, "Willie and Tad Lincoln," *St. Nicholas* 24 (Feb. 1897): 277-82; Grimsley,
     "Six Months in the White House," 43-73.

4   Benjamin B. French, "Letter . . . in Relation to the Condition of the Washington
     Canal," Washington, March 11, 1862, *Misc. Doc. No. 57*, U.S. House of Representatives,
     37th Congress, 2nd Session, 1-3; Cornelius W. Heine, "The Washington City Canal,"
     Records of the Columbia Historical Society 53-56 (1953-1956): 1-27.

5   Elizabeth Keckley, *Behind the Scenes, or Thirty Years a Slave, and Four Years in the White
     House* (New York: G. W. Carleton, 1868), 100-103; "a ghost": *Wheeling Daily Intelli-
     gencer*, March 5, 1862.

6   Washington *National Republican*, Feb. 21, 1862; *Wheeling Daily Intelligencer*, March
     5, 1862; Theodore C. Pease and James G. Randall., eds., *The Diary of Orville Hick-
     man Browning*, 2 vols. (Springfield: Illinois State Historical Society, 1925-33), vol.
     1, 530.

7   Michael Burlingame, *The Inner World of Abraham Lincoln* (Urbana and Chicago: Uni-
     versity of Illinois Press, 1994), 103; Keckley, *Behind the Scenes*, 103.

8   Charles E. Lester, *The Light and Dark of the Rebellion* (Philadelphia: George W. Childs,
     1863), 142-44; Embalming: *Weekly Oregon Statesman*, July 24, 1865; *Wheeling Daily
     Intelligencer*, March 5, 1862.

9   *Fremont Weekly Journal*, March 7, 1862.

10 *Philadelphia Inquirer*, Feb. 25, 1862; *Vermont Christian Messenger*, April 3, 1862.

11 Anna L. Boyden, *War Reminiscences, or, Echoes from Hospital and White House* (Bos-
     ton: D. Lothrop, 1887), 52-57; Chris Foard, "Nurse Pomroy, Comforter-in-Chief to the

Lincoln Family," *Military Images* (Autumn 2019): 52–57; Erika Holst, "'One of the Best Women I Ever Knew': Abraham Lincoln and Rebecca Pomeroy," *Journal of the Abraham Lincoln Association* 31 (Summer 2010): 12–20; "I wish I had": Washington *National Tribune*, April 26, 1900.

12 *HI* (Elizabeth T. Edwards), 444; Grimsley, "Six Months in the White House," 67.

13 MB-*AL*, vol. 1, 246–47.

14 Keckley, *Behind the Scenes*, 104–5; Thomas Otto, *St. Elizabeths Hospital: A History* (Washington, DC: U.S. General Services Administration, 2013), 1.

15 *Monmouth Inquirer*, Feb. 17, 1898.

16 Chardon, Ohio *Jeffersonian Democrat*, Sept. 1, 1865; F. B. Carpenter, *Six Months at the White House with Abraham Lincoln* (New York: Hurd and Houghton, 1867), 115–16; Le Grand B. Cannon, *Personal Reminiscences of the Rebellion, 1861–1866* (New York: privately published, 1895), 166–68; *Lincoln Republican*, March 7, 1895.

17 *HI* (Elizabeth T. Edwards), 445; William H. Herndon and Jessie William Weik, *Herndon's Lincoln. The True Story of a Great Life* (Chicago, New York, and San Francisco: Belford, Clarke & Co., c. 1889), vol. 3, 509.

18 London, *Man of the World*, Feb. 20, 1900; "preaches not": Allan Nevins and Milton H. Thomas, eds., *The Diary of George Templeton Strong* (New York: Macmillan, 1952), vol. 4, 265, 292, 439.

19 "Viceregent": Francis Vinton, *The Christian Idea of Civil Government* (New York: G. F. Nesbitt, 1861), 4; "From that day": *Brooklyn Eagle*, Oct. 1, 1872; Stephen Mansfield, *Lincoln's Battle with God: A President's Struggle with Faith and What It Meant for America* (Nashville: Thomas Nelson, 2012), 145–49.

20 Boyden, *War Reminiscences*, 58–62.

21 Boyden, *War Reminiscences*, 67–70; Pierpont: *Obituary Record of Graduates of Yale College Deceased During the Academical Year Ending in July, 1867*, no. 8 of a series, 227; Abe C. Ravitz, "John Pierpont: Portrait of a Nineteenth Century Reformer" (PhD dissertation, New York University, 1955), 301; consoled: C. A. Cummings, "John Pierpont," *The Christian Examiner* 81, n.s. 2 (Nov. 1866): 386.

22 Richard Leisenring Jr., "Requiescat in Pace: Memorial Photographs of the Civil War," https://militaryimages.atavist.com/memorial-photos-spring-2019, accessed April 16, 2019.

23 "No movement": *Biographical and Descriptive Catalogue of "The Ancient Band"* (New York and San Francisco: Pacific Art Union, 1874), 3.

24 Wilson and Davis, eds., *Herndon on Lincoln. Letters*, 173–74; *Daily Illinois State Journal*, Aug. 21, 1874, and Dec. 17, 1878; *Bloomington Weekly Pantograph*, July 29, 1887.

25 William Henry Burr: *Washington Post*, Sept. 16, 1895.

26 Notes provided by Dr. Michael Burlingame from his forthcoming book on the Lincoln marriage; *Massachusetts Ploughman*, March 25, 1865.

27 *Providence Evening Press*, June 14, 1867; *Ottawa Free Trader*, April 27, 1867. Newton was confirmed on June 30, 1862 (*Daily Gate City*, July 2, 1862).

28 "I think": *Olympic Daily Recorder*, June 11, 1910; "I didn't appoint him": *Chicago Inter Ocean*, Dec. 26, 1886.

29 Richmond *Indiana Palladium*, Aug. 24, 1865; wastepaper basket: *Chicago Daily Inter Ocean*, Oct. 5, 1878.

30 *Cleveland Plain Dealer*, Dec. 31, 1893; *Cincinnati Daily Enquirer*, Feb. 1, 1867; *New York World*, Oct. 4, 1872; lettis: *Moore's Rural New-Yorker*, Aug. 30, 1862; foliage: *Macon Telegraph*, Dec. 3, 1887.

31 incident: *Providence Evening Press*, June 14, 1867.

32 chamberlain: Richmond *Indiana Palladium*, Aug. 24, 1865.

33 Nettie Colburn Maynard, *Was Abraham Lincoln a Spiritualist?* (Philadelphia: Rufus C. Hartranft, 1891), 37, 38; *Cincinnati Commercial Tribune*, Dec. 15, 1871; *Jackson Citizen Patriot*, Feb. 22, 1866; William A. Croffut, *An American Procession, 1855–1914* (Boston: Little, Brown, 1931), 57; Harriet M. Shelton, *Abraham Lincoln Returns* (New York: Evans Publishing, 1957), 168.

34 *Philadelphia Evening Telegraph*, Aug. 23, 1866.

35 *Memoirs of Elizabeth Collins, of Upper Evesham, New Jersey* (Philadelphia: Nathan Kite, 1833), 68–69; Upper Evesham Monthly Meeting Men's Minutes (1811–36), 132, Haverford College Quaker Collection.

36 Records of 3226 N St., N.W., Peabody Reading Room Collections, Washington, DC, Public Library; *Philadelphia Evening Telegraph*, Aug. 23, 1866; [Dallas] *Norton's Union Intelligencer*, May 6, 1893; [Boston] *Banner of Light*, Jan. 14, 1865.

37 Maynard, *Was Abraham Lincoln a Spiritualist?*, 36–42; Brian R. Dirck, *The Black Heavens: Abraham Lincoln and Death* (Carbondale: Southern Illinois University Press, 2019), 106, doubts that any séances were held at the White House.

38 Herndon and Weik, *Herndon's Lincoln*, 508–10.

CHAPTER 5: LOVE'S SACRED CIRCLE

1 AB to EB, n.p., April 22, 1860, HBTL; Badeau, "Edwin Booth. On and Off the Stage," 259.

2 *Washington Times*, July 23, 1900.

3 Lillian W. Aldrich, *Crowding Memories* (Boston and New York: Houghton Mifflin, 1920), 1–8.

4   Badeau, "Edwin Booth. On and Off the Stage," 263.

5   "Edwin Booth's Real Self," *Theatre* 24 (Dec. 1916): 360.

6   Badeau, "Edwin Booth. On and Off the Stage," 260–63.

7   Nevins and Thomas, eds., *The Diary of George Templeton Strong*, vol. 3, 14–15; Harry M. Lydenberg, "A History of the New York Public Library, Part 1," *Bulletin of the New York Public Library* 20 (July 1916): 568–74.

8   Bloom, *Edwin Booth*, 85–94.

9   *New York Times*, Jan. 21, 1861.

10 Jefferson, *Autobiography*, 225–27.

11 *Baltimore Sun*, Feb. 20, 1861; burial record of All Saints Church (volume for 1824–1862), 134, Episcopal Diocese of New York Church Records.

12 *Davenport Weekly Democrat and Leader*, May 25, 1905.

13 L. Clarke David, "At and After the Play: Jefferson and Rip Van Winkle," *Lippincott's Magazine* 24 (July 1879): 68.

14 *Davenport Weekly Democrat and Leader*, May 25, 1905.

15 Bloom, *Joseph Jefferson*, 93–98.

16 *New York Star*, Nov. 5, 1886.

17 Bloom, *Edwin Booth*, 50.

18 *Baltimore Sun*, April 4, 1889.

19 William Seymour, ms. draft of letter (1914), Seymour Collection, Department of Special Collections, Princeton University Library.

20 Watermeier, *American Tragedian*, 76.

21 *Frank Leslie's Illustrated Weekly*, Dec. 8, 1860, 35.

22 Emily Cowell, diary, entry of Dec. 28, 1860, in M. Willson Disher, ed., *The Cowells in America. Being the Diary of Mrs. Sam Cowell* (London: Oxford University Press, 1934), 226.

23 EB to Richard Cary, n.p., n.d., 1860, EBG, 132–33.

24 *FF*, 50.

25 Statement of John T. Ford, ms., [Baltimore, 1880s], John T. Ford Papers, MdHS.

26 Edwin M. Alfriend, "Recollections of John Wilkes Booth," *The Era* 8 (Oct. 1901): 604.

27 Alfriend, "Recollections," 603–5.

28 *Richmond Daily Dispatch*, Dec. 1, 1859. The monographs of Angela Smythe at antebellumrichmond.com are must-see studies for John and the Grays at Charles Town.

29 Booth pay claim (April 14, 1860), Box 448, Harpers Ferry Fund, Accounts and Vouchers, Auditor of Public Accounts, Entry 145, RG 48, Library of Virginia, Richmond.

30 flag/execution: *FF*, 26–27, 77–80; "I would like": Philip Whitlock, "Recollections," ms. (1908–1913), Virginia Historical Society, Richmond.

31 *Memoir*, 88.

32 *FF*, 82.

33 *Richmond Daily Times*, Feb. 27, 1887; *Boston Daily Globe*, March 7, 1909; Francis Wilson, *John Wilkes Booth* (Boston and New York: Houghton Mifflin, 1929), 38–39.

34 *New York World*, April 16, 1865.

35 Badeau, *The Vagabond*, 174–75.

36 Badeau, *The Vagabond*, 170; *Topeka State Journal*, April 4, 1888.

37 *The New South*, March 15, 1862; EB to AB, London, Dec. 27, 1861, HBTL.

38 Myra C. Lau, ed., "Emma Forbes Cary's Recollections of Edwin Booth," ms. (1992), author's collection.

39 EB to Emma F. Cary, New York, Oct. 15, 1864, EBG, 165–66.

40 EB to Richard Cary, Boston, Aug. 4, 1861, EBG, 136.

41 Watermeier, *American Tragedian*, 112.

42 R. Todd Felton, *A Journey into the Transcendentalists' New England* (Berkeley, CA: Roaring Forties Press, 2006), 129.

43 EB to Cary, [Boston], [no month] 30, 1861, and Aug. 4, 1861, EBG, 134–35.

44 EB to Cary, Boston, Aug. 4, 1861, EBG, 135.

45 EB to Cary, Boston, Aug. 4, 1861, EBG, 135–36.

46 *FF*, 89–90, 98, 104–7.

47 Henry P. Phelps, *Players of a Century: A Record of the Albany Stage* (New York: Wentworth Press, republished by B. Blom, 1972), 324–26; New York *Sunday Mercury*, Aug. 15, 1886; *Albany Argus*, Feb. 18, 1861.

48 *Providence Daily Post*, Oct. 22, 1861.

49 Bloom, *Edwin Booth*, 51.

50 Bryant: *New York Evening Post*, April 12, 1875; *New York Tribune*, April 12, 1875; antiwar: George A. Townsend Scrapbook, item 131, 162, Townsend Papers, Maryland Hall of Records, Annapolis.

51 *Toledo Daily Blade*, Jan. 2, 1899; testimony of Everton Conger, June 25, 1867, *Trial of John H. Surratt* (Washington, DC: Government Printing Office, 1867), vol. 1, 309; *San Diego Union*, July 15, 1915.

52 *Boston Globe*, Feb. 19, 1893; *New York Sun*, May 13, 1877; *Indianapolis Sentinel*, May 17, 1877.

53 Richard Cary to Helen Cary, Harpers Ferry, Aug. 1, 1861, Richard Cary Letters, Ms. N-1996, Massachusetts Historical Society, Boston.

54 Alonzo H. Quint, *The Record of the Second Massachusetts Infantry, 1861–65* (Boston: James P. Walker, 1867), 63; Richard Cary to Helen Cary, Winchester, VA, March 14, 1862, Richard Cary Letters.

55 Robert K. Krick, *Stonewall Jackson at Cedar Mountain* (Chapel Hill: University of North Carolina Press, 1990), 238, 275; "freak": *New York Herald*, Aug. 13, 1862.

56 *New York Herald*, Aug. 11, 1862; Quint, *The Record of the Second Massachusetts Infantry*, 104–18; George H. Gordon, *Brook Farm to Cedar Mountain in the War of the Great Rebellion, 1861–62* (Boston: Houghton Mifflin, 1885), 332.

57 Helen's appearance is given in her passport application, Oct. 8, 1867, ancestry.com, accessed Oct. 27, 2020.

58 Quint, *The Record of the Second Massachusetts Infantry*, 104–18, 485; *Boston Globe*, June 28, 1918; *Life and Letters of Wilder Dwight, Lieut.-Col., Second Mass. Inf. Vols.* (Boston: Ticknor and Fields, 1868), 278–83; Charles F. Morse, *Letters Written During the Civil War, 1861–1865* (priv. printed, 1898), 80; Gordon, *Brook Farm to Cedar Mountain*, 310–12, 332; "Richard died": Joan Fink, "The Death of a Soldier," [Massachusetts Historical Society], *The Beehive*, Aug. 24, 2012, http://www.masshist.org/beehive-blog/, accessed June 20, 2019; Ronald S. Coddington, "Robert Gould Shaw's Gruesome Task," The Opinionator, *New York Times*, Aug. 12, 2012, https://opinionator.blogs.nytimes.com/2012/08/12/robert-gould-shaws-gruesome-task/; Russell Duncan, ed., *Blue-Eyed Child of Fortune: The Civil War Letters of Colonel Robert Gould Shaw* (Athens: University of Georgia Press, 1992), 223–35.

59 Sarah A. Wallace and Frances E. Gillespie, eds., *The Journal of Benjamin Moran, 1857–1865*, 2 vols. (Chicago: University of Chicago Press, 1948–49), vol. 2, 958.

60 "poorer": EB to Richard Cary, London, March 20, 1862, EBG, 137; Watermeier, *American Tragedian*, 86.

61 Mary D. Booth to Mary L. Felton, New York, NY, Sept. 10, 1862, in Oggel, *Letters*, 81.

62 EB to Mary Felton, New York, NY, Sept. 11, 1862, EBG, 139.

63 "Edwin Booth's Real Self," *Theatre* 24 (Dec. 1916): 360.

64 www.twainquotes.com/Aldrich.html, accessed Oct. 22, 2021.

65 "She had": Lau, "Emma Forbes Cary's Recollections of Edwin Booth"; Aldrich, *Crowding Memories*, 27.

66 Jennifer Putzi and Elizabeth Stockton, eds., *The Selected Letters of Elizabeth Stoddard* (Iowa City: University of Iowa Press, 2012), xxi.

67 Gordon Hendricks, *Albert Bierstadt, Painter of the American West* (New York: H. N. Abrams, 1974), 116; *Buffalo Weekly Express*, Dec. 16, 1862.

68 Ferris Greenslet, *The Life of Thomas Bailey Aldrich* (Boston and New York: Houghton Mifflin, 1908), 21, 67, 77; Florence M. H. Hall, "The Friendship of Edwin Booth and Julia Ward Howe," *New England Magazine* 9 (Nov. 1893): 318.

CHAPTER 6: GHOST KISSES

1   *Leavenworth* [Washington] *Echo*, Oct. 1, 1915.

2   *Detroit Free Press*, June 2, 1867; *Montgomery* [AL] *Advertiser*, Nov. 22, 1889; [Red Wing, MN] *Grange Advance*, Aug. 19, 1874; *Burlington Free Press*, Dec. 13, 1881; *Boston Daily Globe*, March 20 and April 27, 1874.

3   "presentiments": Washington *National Intelligencer*, April 26, 1865; Joe: EB to AB, [Boston], Nov. 1, 1863, HBTL.

4   John C. Brennan, "John Wilkes Booth's Enigmatic Brother Joseph," *Maryland Historical Magazine* 78 (Spring 1983): 25.

5   Life struck Clarke: *Memoir*, 11–12; "He lays": Asia B. Clarke to Jean Anderson, [Phila.], March 3, 1863, MdHS.

6   Asia B. Clarke to Jean Anderson, Philadelphia, July 11, 1859, MdHS; *The Metropolitan Catholic Almanac, and Laity's Directory for . . . 1840* (Baltimore: F. Lucas, n.d.), 67. Thanks to Joseph G. Mannard.

7   Ernest C. Miller, *John Wilkes Booth in the Pennsylvania Oil Region* (Meadville, PA: Crawford County Historical Society, 1987), 69; medal: *New York World*, April 26, 1891; *Washington Post*, June 8, 1903; *Montreal Star*, Dec. 6, 1902.

8   Boston *Daily Evening Voice*, April 15, 1865; *Chicago Post*, April 16, 1865; Howard: "Death of Mrs. J. B. Booth," clipping (1885), HTC.

9   *New York Daily Graphic*, Aug. 1, 1876; left hand: *Newport* [RI] *Mercury*, April 22, 1865.

10 Clara Morris, *Life on the Stage* (New York: McClure Philips, 1901), 101.

11 James H. Wilson, *Under the Old Flag* (New York and London: D. Appleton, 1912), vol. 1, 74, 81–82; tidal information thanks to Dale E. Reddick, research coordinator, Savannah Riverkeeper.

12 nearsighted: *Topeka State Journal*, April 4, 1888; Wilson, *Under the Old Flag*, vol. 1, 89.

13 *New York Commercial Advertiser*, Feb. 21, 1861; *New York World*, Feb. 21, 1861; MB-AL, vol. 2, 29.

14 *Omaha World-Herald*, Feb. 12, 1893; *Newport Mercury*, Sept. 6, 1862; Wilson, *Under the Old Flag*, vol. 1, 191–92.

15 AB to Henry Wilson, New York, May 4, 1862, ABL.

16 "a voice": Wilson, *Under the Old Flag*, vol. 1, 68–69.

17 "Badeau was short": *Louisville Commercial*, March 26, 1889; "'dude'": Washington *National Tribune*, May 24, 1888.

18 Nathan W. Daniels, diary, Mss. Div., LOC, contains valuable material including an undated diary entry in March 1865 about this White House visit; Anderson: *Biographical and Descriptive Catalogue of "The Ancient Band*," 3–4.

19 *Augusta* [GA] *Chronicle*, April 30, 1888.

20 Clinton, *Mrs. Lincoln*, 87.

21 Baker, *Mary Todd Lincoln*, 62.

22 Wayne C. Temple, *Abraham Lincoln: From Skeptic to Prophet* (Mahomet, IL: Mayhaven Publishing, 1995), 59–60.

23 "The only comfort": *MTL*, 271; She told Rebecca Pomroy: Boyden, *War Reminiscences*, 79.

24 Helm, *The True Story of Mary*, 106–7, 111, 227.

25 "the unconscious celebration": Baker, *Mary Todd Lincoln*, 220–21.

26 Gordon Samples, *Lust for Fame: The Stage Career of John Wilkes Booth* (Jefferson, NC, and London: McFarland, 1982), 89.

27 Hall, "The Friendship of Edwin Booth and Julia Ward Howe," 318.

28 *Boston Medical and Surgical Journal* 105 (Oct. 20, 1881): 384; "I have been": Mary D. Booth to Emma Cushman, Boston, Dec. 13, 1862, Oggel, *Letters*, 88; pelvic: MDB to Stoddard, n.p., Dec. 13, 1863, Oggel, *Letters*, 87.

29 Oggel, *Letters*, 103–4.

30 Badeau, "Edwin Booth. On and Off the Stage," 261.

31 Bloom, *Edwin Booth*, 5.

32 "hog Jew": EB to Lawrence Barrett, [New York, NY?], July 1, 1861, HBTL.

33 Nora Titone, *My Thoughts Be Bloody: The Bitter Rivalry Between Edwin and John Wilkes Booth That Led to an American Tragedy* (New York: Free Press, 2010), 281; "Ned": Asia B. Clarke to Jean Anderson, Philadelphia, March 3, 1863, MdHS.

34 Stoddard to J. L. Graham, New York, NY, March 6, 1863, Putzi and Stockton, *The Selected Letters of Elizabeth Stoddard*, 100.

35 Aldrich, *Crowding Memories*, 30; "It startled me": EBG, 143–44.

36 Edwina: Edwina B. Crossman, York Harbor, ME, July 22, 1928, to Edward Valentine, Valentine Museum, Richmond; bowel disease: Mary Devlin Booth, Dorchester, Feb. 21, 1863, vol. 166, page 214, no. 27, Death Records, Archives Division, Commonwealth of Massachusetts, Boston; Louisa Miller: *Boston Globe*, June 7, 1893.

37 EB to AB, Dorchester, March 3, 1863, EBG, 144; Bloom, *Edwin Booth*, 63–64; "Don't tell me": Aldrich, *Crowding Memories*, 37–38.

38 "Look out": David H. Hanaburgh, *History of the One Hundred and Twenty-Eighth Regiment, New York Volunteers (U.S. Infantry), in the Late Civil War* (Pokeepsie, NY, 1894), 35.

39 "We need": James F. Rusling, *Men and Things I Saw in Civil War Days* (New York: Eaton and Mains, 1899), 16.

40 Banks and Sherman, *The War of the Rebellion: A Compilation of the Official Records of the Union and Confederate Armies*, vol. 26, part 1, 6–8, 526–27.

41 Charles McGregor: *History of the Fifteenth New Hampshire Volunteers, 1862–1863* (Concord, NH: The 15th Regt. Assoc., 1900), 296.

42 Wickham Hoffman, *Camp, Court, and Siege* (London: Sampson, Low, 1877), 66–67.

43 council of war: Richard B. Irwin, *History of the Nineteenth Army Corps* (New York: G. P. Putnam's Sons, 1893), 166–69; "blood": Hoffman, *Camp, Court, and Siege*, 70.

44 Badeau, "Edwin Booth. On and Off the Stage," 259.

45 For an overview of the battle, see David E. Edmonds, *The Guns of Port Hudson*, 2 vols. (Lafayette, LA: Acadiana Press, 1983–84), and especially Lawrence L. Hewitt's superb "'They Fought Splendidly': The Struggle for Port Hudson," PhD dissertation, Louisiana State University, 1984 (published in book form by Louisiana State University Press in 1987). Hewitt has continued his masterful study of the battle with *Port Hudson: The Most Significant Battlefield Photographs of the Civil War* (Knoxville: University of Tennessee Press, 2020).

46 *Criminal*: John C. Palfrey, "Port Hudson," *Papers of the Military Historical Society of Massachusetts* (Boston: The Society, 1910), vol. 8, 40; Irwin, *History of the Nineteenth Army Corps*, 168, 177.

47 *The Reminiscences of Neal Dow* (Portland: Evening Express, 1898), 687–94.

48 McGregor, *History of the Fifteenth New Hampshire Volunteers*, 346–48, 396; "Lead them ahead": Otis F. R. Waite, *New Hampshire in the Great Rebellion* (Claremont, NH: Tracy, Chase, 1870), 523–24.

49 "I turned my eyes": McGregor, *History of the Fifteenth New Hampshire Volunteers*, 360, 387; *Milwaukee Semi-Weekly Wisconsin*, June 12, 1863; "like scared sheep": *Topeka State Journal*, April 4, 1888.

50 "brave as a lion": Washington *National Intelligencer*, June 12, 1863.

51 *Detroit Free Press*, June 8, 1863.

52 Surgeon's certificate of Sanger, Bangor, ME, Feb. 20, 1878, Badeau file, National Archives. Thanks to Dr. Lew C. Schon, director, Orthopedic Intervention, The Institute for Foot and Ankle Reconstruction, Mercy Medical Center, Baltimore, for his expert interpretation of Badeau's wound and recovery.

53 "They pulled": Lawrence Van Alstyne, *Diary of an Enlisted Man* (New Haven, CT: Tuttle, Morehouse, Taylor, 1910), 115.

54 the doctors told him: Badeau to Wilson, [New York, NY?], July 29, [1863], ABL.

55 Badeau, "Edwin Booth. On and Off the Stage," 263.

56 EB to AB, New York, June 6, 1863, HBTL.

57 *St. Paul and Minneapolis Pioneer Press*, Feb. 20, 1887.

58 Cary had feared: Cary to Helen Cary, Camp Hicks, MD, Jan. 1, 1862, Cary Papers; "My heart": EB to AB, Dorchester, MA, March 3, 1863, EBG, 141; the key: *St. Louis Republic*, Nov. 1, 1903.

59 EB to AB, Dorchester, March 3, 1863, EBG, 144; Mollie to EB, Aug. 24 [?], 1859, n.p., Oggel, *Letters*, 11.

60 *St. Louis Republic*, Nov. 1, 1903.

61 *Trenton Evening Times*, Sept. 25, 1910; *Washington Post*, Oct. 23, 1879; *Cincinnati Inquirer*, July 24, 1886; *Boston Globe*, Feb. 19, 1893; *Riverside Independent Enterprise*, Dec. 27, 1896; "man of genius": AB to Wilson, n.p., Sept. 12, 1863, ABL.

62 Bret E. Carroll, *Spiritualism in Antebellum America* (Bloomington and Indianapolis: Indiana University Press, 1997), 118.

63 Vivian C. Hopkins, "The Spirits and the Honorable John Worth Edmonds," *Bulletin of the New York Public Library* 10 (Oct. 1958): 479–506.

64 *New York Daily Times*, Nov. 2, 1853; *The Spiritualist Magazine* 2 (July 1861): 292.

65 EBG, 151.

66 AB to Henry Wilson, n.p., Sept. 12, 1863, ABL.

67 *St. Paul and Minneapolis Pioneer Press*, Feb. 20, 1884.

68 MB-*AL*, vol. 2, 528.

69 AB to Henry Wilson, New York, Aug. 2, 1863, ABL; James R. Gilmore, *Personal Recollections of Abraham Lincoln and the Civil War* (London: John Macqueen, 1899), 198–99.

70 Gilmore, *Personal Recollections*, 162–63.

71 Edmund Kirke, *Down in Tennessee, and Back by Way of Richmond* (New York: Carleton, 1864), 243, 281.

72 *Washington Evening Star*, July 2, 1863; "One of the best": Erika Holst, "'One of the Best Women I Ever Knew': Abraham Lincoln and Rebecca Pomeroy," *Journal of the Abraham Lincoln Association* 31 (Summer 2010): 12–20.

73 *Washington Evening Star*, July 15, 1863.

74 Boyden, *War Reminiscences*, 145–46.

CHAPTER 7: WHY WAKE ME?

1 "He has forgotten": William O. Stoddard, *Inside the White House in War Times*, ed. Michael Burlingame (Lincoln: University of Nebraska Press, 2000), 187–88.

2 Lincoln to Hackett, Aug. 17, 1863, *CWAL*, 392–93.

3 Thomas A. Bogar, *American Presidents Attend the Theatre* (Jefferson, NC, and London: McFarland, 2006), 101; called on Lincoln: Michael Burlingame and John R. Turner Ettlinger, eds., *Inside Lincoln's White House: The Complete Diary of John Hay*

(Carbondale and Edwardsville: Southern Illinois University Press, 1997), 127–28; "champagne": [Vail], *The Actor*, 107.

4 Bogar, *American Presidents Attend the Theatre*, 111; Thomas A. Bogar, *Backstage at the Lincoln Assassination: The Untold Story of the Actors and Stagehands at Ford's Theatre* (Washington, DC: Regnery, 2013), 29–30.

5 president had definite ideas: Carpenter, *Six Months at the White House*, 51.

6 Douglas L. Wilson, "His Hour Upon the Stage" (2011), http://theamericanscholar, accessed March 9, 2020; Bloom, *Edwin Booth*, 204; Titone, *My Thoughts Be Bloody*, 311.

7 John M. Taylor, *William Henry Seward* (New York: HarperCollins, 1991), 227; Trudy Krisher, *Fanny Seward: A Life* (Syracuse, NY: Syracuse University Press, 2015), 161–62; Doris Kearns Goodwin, *Team of Rivals: The Political Genius of Abraham Lincoln* (New York: Simon & Schuster, 2005), 155–56, 386; *New York Dramatic News*, June 16, 1878; Grover, "Lincoln's Interest in the Theater," *Century Magazine* 77 (April 1909): 946.

8 "I observed": "Edwin Booth's Real Self," *Theatre* 24 (Dec. 1916): 360.

9 *Inside Lincoln's White House*, 110; *FF*, 140–41.

10 William B. Styple, *The Little Bugler. The True Story of a Twelve-Year-Old Boy in the Civil War* (Kearney, NJ: Belle Grove, 1998), 138; *The Marble Heart; Or, The Sculptor's Dream* [*Spencer's Boston Theatre*, No. LXIII] (Boston: William V. Spencer, n.d.).

11 *New York Herald Tribune*, March 26, 1947; Grover, "Lincoln's Interest in the Theater," 945; *New York Sun*, July 22, 1905; *Boston Herald*, April 9, 1883.

12 "He used to say": William E. Sinn, "A Theatrical Manager's Reminiscences," *Abraham Lincoln. Tributes from His Associates* (New York: Thomas Y. Crowell, 1895), 169; Mordaunt: *Chicago Daily Tribune*, June 22, 1878; *Chicago Inter Ocean*, June 16, 1901; "applause of a negro": *Chicago Times*, April 20, 1865.

13 *HI* (John T. Stuart), 519, and (Ninian Edwards), 446.

14 Noah Brooks, "Personal Reminiscences of Lincoln," *Scribner's Monthly* 15 (March 1878): 675.

15 [Vail], *The Actor*, 83.

16 his request: Washington *Evening Star*, March 2, 1863; Carpenter, *Six Months at the White House*, 49–51.

17 Carpenter, *Six Months at the White House*, 50–51.

18 Bartlett: *Springfield Republican*, Oct. 17, 1863.

19 Bloom, *Joseph Jefferson*, 99–100.

20 Jefferson, *Autobiography*, 245–55.

21 His late wife Maggie: *Mount Airy* [NC] *News*, May 20, 1897; *Davenport Weekly Democrat and Leader*, May 25, 1905; *Indianapolis Journal*, April 26, 1889; Francis Wilson:

Joseph Jefferson: Reminiscences of a Fellow Player (London: Chapman and Hall, 1906), 339.

22 Seed Room: Maynard, *Was Abraham Lincoln a Spiritualist?*, 46; Madison *Wisconsin State Journal*, Aug. 10, 1866; three times: *Harrisburg Telegraph*, Dec. 11, 1867.

23 *Macon Telegraph*, Dec. 3, 1887.

24 Rufus M. Jones, introduction to *The Record of a Quaker Conscience: Cyrus Pringle's Diary* (New York: Macmillan, 1918), 5, 76, 81–92.

25 Jerks: *Phila Evening Telegraph*, Aug. 23, 1866; "Pinkie": *New York Sun*, April 4, 1891; "Dr. Bamford": *Hartford Courant*, May 24, 1831; Carpenter: Maynard, *Was Abraham Lincoln a Spiritualist?*, xi; Elisabeth Lowry, "Pinkie at Play: Postcolonialism, Politics, and Performance in Nettie Colburn Maynard's *Was Abraham Lincoln a Spiritualist?*," in Cathy Gutierrez, ed., *Handbook of Spiritualism and Channeling* (Leiden and Boston: Brill, 2015), 152–70.

26 Joshua F. Speed to AL, Washington, DC, Oct. 26, 1863, Abraham Lincoln Papers, https://www.loc.gov/item/mal2751800/, accessed Feb. 11, 2020; "hardly an honor": Maynard, *Was Abraham Lincoln a Spiritualist?*, 87.

27 Helm, *The True Story of Mary*, 206–27.

28 "nothing is the matter": *Military Images*, Autumn 2019, 52–57; Mary T. Lincoln to Hannah Shearer, Washington, DC, Nov. 20, 1864, *MTL*, 189.

29 Mary T. Lincoln to Hannah Shearer, n.p., Nov. 20, 1864, *MTL*, 188; B. B. French, diary, April 6, 1864, Cole and McDonough, *Witness to the Young Republic*, 448–49; Keckley, *Behind the Scenes*, 117.

30 Mary T. Lincoln to Charles Sumner, "Near Chicago," July 4, 1865, *MTL*, 256; read people better: *HI* (Mary T. Lincoln), 359; for an overview of her visitors, see Joseph George Jr., "Some Lincoln Spiritualist Acquaintances," *Lincoln Herald* 113 (Fall 2001): 162–205.

31 John B. Buescher, *The President's Medium: John Conklin, Abraham Lincoln, and the Emancipation Proclamation* (author: 2015), 81–122; *Hartford Courant*, April 25, 1860; "Lady in Gray": *Washington Post*, Nov. 20, 1895; *New York Sun*, Nov. 30, 1880; for the Lauries, see John B. Buescher, "Unlocking the Mystery of a Lincoln Relic" (Nov. 11, 2008), iapsop.spirithistory.com, accessed Feb. 17, 2020; floral patterns: Emma Hardinge, "Spirit-Art," *The Year-Book of Spiritualism for 1871* (Boston: Wm. White, 1871), 50–55; "far-off look": W. H. Chaney, "Was He a Spiritualist? Reminiscences of President Lincoln," *Religio-Philosophical Journal* 39, no. 21 (Jan. 16, 1886): 5.

32 George C. Bartlett, *The Salem Seer: Reminiscences of Charles H. Foster* (New York: Lovell, Gestefeld, 1891), 86; (Boston) *Banner of Light*, Dec. 7, 1874.

33 *The Spiritual Magazine* 3 (April 1862): 145–53.

34 *London Times*, March 13, 1862; *Banner of Light*, April 23, 1864, and Feb. 14, 1874; no
    trances: Bartlett, *The Salem Seer*, 16; "beyond all bounds": Bartlett, *The Salem Seer*, 84;
    Los Angeles Herald, Oct. 19, 1891; San Francisco *Golden Gate*, Jan. 2, 1886.

35 Bartlett, *The Salem Seer*, 84.

36 *New York World*, March 28, 1864.

37 David Quinn, *Interior Causes of the War* (New York: M. Doolady, 1863), 94–95.

38 "No Faith in Mediums," clipping (1891), "Notes gathered for intended publication
    'Abraham Lincoln's Faith in God,'" Container 11, John G. Nicolay Papers, Mss. Divi-
    sion, LOC.

39 "He was not": Osborn H. Oldroyd, ed., *The Lincoln Memorial* (New York: G. W. Car-
    leton, 1883), 530; William H. Herndon to Mr. Noyes, Chinkapin Hill P. O., Illinois, Jan.
    15, 1874, in Wilson and Davis, eds., *Herndon on Lincoln. Letters*, 115–16; "in order to
    believe": Paul M. Angle, ed., *Herndon's Life of Lincoln* (Cleveland and New York: World
    Publishing, [1949]), 479; lips: *HI* (Mary T. Lincoln), 358.

40 Jackson/Jefferson: *London Times*, June 13, 1863; *Wilkes-Barre Times Leader*, Oct. 21,
    1891; Sickles: *New York Morning Advertiser*, Oct. 20, 1891.

41 *London Times*, June 13, 1863, from the *Providence Post*; wasn't real: Le Grand B. Cannon
    to William H. Herndon, near Burlington, VT, Oct. 7, [1889], *HI*, 679.

42 AB to Henry Wilson, New York, NY, July 28/29, [1863], ABL; AB to Army AG, New
    York, NY, Oct. 14, 1863, fold3.com/image/300498612, accessed March 1, 2020.

43 AB to Henry Wilson, Newport, RI, Sept. 20, 1863, ABL; "Badeau's disgust": AB to
    Henry Wilson, New York, NY, Sept. 13, 1864, ABL; *Windsor* [Ontario] *Star*, Sept. 2,
    1898.

44 AB to Wilson, New York, NY, Oct. 8, 1863; "foolish": AB to Wilson, Newport, RI, Sept.
    10, 1863; "keen pleasure": AB to Wilson, New York, NY, Jan. 26, 1863. All ABL.

45 AB letters to Wilson as follows: n.p., Feb. 13, 1864; Nashville, March 1, 1864; West
    Point, NY, Aug. 28, 1864; and New York, NY, Sept. 13, 1864. All ABL.

46 EB to AB, New York, NY, May 18, 1863, HBTL; Titone, *My Thoughts Be Bloody*, 287.

47 EB to Walter Brackett, New York, NY, n.d., Harry Ransom Center, University of Texas,
    Austin.

48 EB to AB, Boston, July 29, [1863], HBTL.

49 Joe: EB to AB, [Boston], Nov. 1, 1863; Mary: EB to AB, Washington, DC, Feb. 26, 1864,
    both at HBTL.

50 Watermeier, *American Tragedian*, 104.

51 *Mount* [NC] *Airy News*, May 20, 1897.

52 EB to AB, n.p., May 2, 1864, HBTL.

53 Watermeier, *American Tragedian*, 103.

CHAPTER 8: FATAL VISION

1 Washington *National Intelligencer*, Dec. 12, 1861; "sluggards": Michael F. Conlin, "The Smithsonian Abolition Lecture Controversy: The Clash of Antislavery Politics with American Science in Wartime Washington," *Civil War History* 46 (Dec. 2000): 301–23; Henry: *Annual Report of the Board of Regents of the Smithsonian Institution* (Washington, DC: Government Printing Office, 1864), 43.

2 William A. Croffut, *An American Procession, 1855–1914* (Boston: Little, Brown, 1931), 57–61; Brownson: *Daily National Intelligencer*, Dec. 13, 1861; "science of man" and a more accurate variant of Pierpont's disclaimer in Washington *Daily National Republican*, Dec. 16, 1861.

3 "Happy Family": Martin A. Sweeney, *Lincoln's Gift from Homer, New York: A Painter, an Editor and a Detective* (Jefferson, NC, and London: McFarland, 2011), 105; "What puzzles me": Croffut, *An American Procession*, 120.

4 Croffut, *An American Procession*, 109–10.

5 Adam Badeau, *Military History of Ulysses S. Grant, from April, 1861, to April, 1865*, 3 vols. (New York: D. Appleton, 1881), vol. 3, 501–2; "His purity": AB to Wilson, City Point, VA, Oct. 15, 1864, ABL.

6 Badeau/Grant: Washington *National Tribune*, March 28, 1895; "Oh, yes" and "courage of heroes": Wilson, *Under the Old Flag*, vol. 1, 191, 347.

7 "I say": Horace Porter, *Campaigning with Grant* (New York: Century, 1907), 229.

8 stayed up: Badeau, *Personal Recollections*, 21; *New York Daily Tribune*, March 25, 1888.

9 Omaha *World-Herald*, Feb. 12, 1893; time had taught: AB to Wilson, New York, NY, Sept. 30, 1863, ABL.

10 Emerson, *Giant in the Shadows*, 90; AB to Wilson, City Point, VA, Feb. 2, 1865, ABL.

11 "screwed off": Robert's statement, Washington, DC, May 6, 1919, sent to Emily Todd Helm, Robert Todd Lincoln Collection, Chicago Historical Society; "I was probably saved": R. T. Lincoln to E. C. Benedict, Washington, DC, Feb. 17, 1918, in H. C. Brown, ed., *Valentine's Manual of Old New York*, no. 6 (New York: editor, 1922), 182; "narrow escape": "Badeau's Letter," clipping, no ID, Booth Files, HTC.

12 Edwin: Caroline G. C. Curtis, diary, April 18, 1865, Cary Papers, Massachusetts Historical Society; *Springfield Republican*, April 18, 1865.

13 William Bispham: "Memories and Letters of Edwin Booth," *Century Magazine* 47 (Nov. 1893): 132.

14 Watermeier, *American Tragedian*, 107.

15 their father's: Edwin M. Alfriend, "Recollections of John Wilkes Booth," *The Era* 8 (Oct. 1901): 604; Ford: *Kansas City Times*, Feb. 23, 1885; Seymour: William Seymour, "Some Richards I Have Seen," *Theatre Magazine* 32 (June 1920): 502; FF, 157.

16 Raymond: *Boston Herald*, April 9, 1883.

17 Miller, *John Wilkes Booth in the Pennsylvania Oil Region*, 13–19.

18 *Memoir*, 66, 104–5.

19 Edward Steers Jr., *Blood on the Moon: The Assassination of Abraham Lincoln* (Lexington: University Press of Kentucky, 2001), 62–84.

20 William A. Tidwell, James O. Hall, and David W. Gaddy, *Come Retribution: The Confederate Secret Service and the Assassination of Lincoln* (Jackson and London: University Press of Mississippi, 1988), 408.

21 Arnold: Michael W. Kaufman, ed., *Memoirs of a Lincoln Conspirator* (Bowie, MD: Heritage Books, 1995), 44–45; *Memoir*, 85.

22 [Vail], *The Actor*, 179.

23 *New York Herald*, June 19, 1878.

24 *Cincinnati Enquirer*, Feb. 26, 1866; *New York Herald*, Aug. 21, 1865; *Springfield* [Mass.] *Republican*, Dec. 13, 1862; "nothing of": *Buffalo Courier*, Aug. 14, 1865; "jolly appreciation": *Buffalo Courier*, Aug. 17, 1865.

25 Sue Trenchard, "Research on Charles Colchester (Sealby)," June 2020, author's copy; *Leeds Mercury*, March 11, 1843; E. W. Hulburd, *The Life of Little Justin Hulburd, Medium, Actor, and Poet* (Descanso, CA: author, 1909), vol. 2, 234; *Detroit Free Press*, April 15, 1866; John Buescher and Marc Demarest first identified Jackson Sealby as Colchester in a blog post: "Strangers N.Y. City Directory: Charles Colchester and Jackson Sealby" (May 9, 2016). Sealby used his birth name when he registered at Gun and Company's American and General Agency in London in May 1862. This article is important in confirming his identify; *Boston Morning Journal*, June 7, 1862.

26 *Indianapolis Daily Journal*, April 20, 1866; *Cincinnati Daily Enquirer*, Feb. 25, 1866.

27 "playing on": Noah Brooks, *Washington in Lincoln's Time* (New York: Century, 1895), 64.

28 "one of the pleasantest men": L. E. Chittenden, *Recollections of President Lincoln and His Administration* (New York: Harper and Bros., 1891), 238; Warren Chase, *Forty Years on the Spiritual Rostrum* (Boston: Colby and Rich, 1888), 96.

29 Simon Newcomb, *Memoir of Joseph Henry* [1880] (Washington, DC: Judd and Detweiler, 1903), 31–32; Newcomb, *The Reminiscences of an Astronomer* (Boston and New York: Houghton Mifflin, 1903), 409–10.

30 "Why?": William O. Stoddard, *Lincoln's Third Secretary: The Memoirs of William O. Stoddard* (New York: Exposition Press, 1955), 148; Washington *National Tribune*, April 26, 1900.

31 *HI* (Mary T. Lincoln), 360; "long, complicated" and "simple faith": Fehrenbacher and Fehrenbacher, *Recollected Words*, 137, 191.

32 Fehrenbacher and Fehrenbacher, *Recollected Words*, 50; "A sweet comfort": James F. Rusling, *Men and Things I Saw in Civil War Days* (New York: Eaton and Mains, 1899), 15.

33 Even believers in this doctrine prayed. After all, God commanded prayer in the Bible, and that alone was reason to do it. The practice also increased the holy habits of a person as well as allowing him or her to carry out the obligation to praise God, not just ask Him for favors. The insights on this subject by Allen C. Guelzo have been most helpful.

34 Washington *National Tribune*, April 26, 1900.

35 Joshua F. Speed, *Reminiscences of Abraham Lincoln and Notes of a Visit to California* (Louisville, KY: Bradley and Gilbert, 1896), 32–33.

36 Maynard, *Was Abraham Lincoln a Spiritualist?*, 110.

37 Daniels, diary, March n.d., 1864, LOC; a happy sign: Brooks, *Washington in Lincoln's Time*, 74.

38 *Baltimore Clipper*, March 6, 1865; *Morning Cleveland Herald*, March 6, 1865; Washington *National Intelligencer*, March 6, 1865; Donald, *Lincoln*, 566–68; Ronald C. White Jr., *Lincoln's Greatest Speech: The Second Inaugural* (New York: Simon & Schuster, 2006), is a fine study of these events.

39 Carpenter, *Six Months at the White House*, 234.

40 Terry Alford, "Charles J. Colchester's Life Among the Spirits," *Northern Virginia Review* 5 (Spring 1990): 1–6.

41 Louisville *Daily Journal*, May 24, 1866.

42 New York *Herald Progress*, Dec. 27, 1862.

43 Washington *Evening Star*, March 15, 1865; "Men sometimes": James Sheridan Knowles, *The Love Chase* (London: E. Moxon, 1837), 23.

44 New York *Herald Progress*, Dec. 27, 1862; *Louisville Daily Journal*, May 24, 1866; *Cincinnati Daily Enquirer*, Feb. 25, 1866; (Bloomington, IL) *The Pantagraph*, Nov. 1, 1866; *Memoir of Joseph Henry*, 32; Newcomb, *Reminiscences*, 410.

45 "Can you not": Donald C. Pfanz, *Abraham Lincoln at City Point, March 20–April 9, 1865* (Lynchburg, VA: H. E. Howard, 1989), 1–19; David Alan Johnson, *The Last Weeks of Abraham Lincoln* (Amherst, NY: Prometheus Books, 2018), 85–112.

46 Adam Badeau, *Grant in Peace. From Appomattox to Mount McGregor. A Personal Memoir* (Hartford, CT: S. S. Scanton, 1887), 356–60; John S. Barnes, "With Lincoln from Washington to Richmond in 1865," *Appleton's Magazine* 9 (May 1907): 521–24; Porter, *Campaigning with Grant*, 412–14; *Philadelphia Inquirer*, March 29, 1865; Mrs. Ord: John S. Barnes, "The Egotistigraphy of a Rolling Stone," privately printed (New York, 1910), from the internet edition provided by Susan Bainbridge Hay. Julia Grant

presented Mary in a better light in her writings; Julia Dent Grant, memoirs (ms., c. 1887–c. 1891), vol. 4, image 98—vol. 5, image 7, Ulysses S Grant papers, Series 10, Add III, https://www.loc.gov/item/mss233330378/, accessed June 22, 2020; warm, clear: William H. Crook, *Through Five Administrations* (New York and London: Harper and Bros., 1910), 41; "vixen": Strong, *Diary*, vol. 4, 163.

47   *New York World*, April 17, 1887; Nelson Lankford, *Richmond Burning: The Last Days of the Confederate Capital* (New York: Viking, 2002), 218–40.

48   Frederick Maurice, *An Aide-de-Camp of Lee, Being the Papers of Colonel Charles Marshall* (Boston: Little, Brown, 1927), 269; Badeau, *Military History of Grant*, vol. 3, 601–12; AB to Wilson, n.p., n.d. [1865], ABL.

49   "but my own feelings": U. S. Grant, *Personal Memoirs of U. S. Grant*, 2 vols. (New York: C. L. Webster, 1885–1886), vol. 2, 489–90.

50   Arthur C. Parker, *The Life of General Ely S. Parker* (Buffalo: Buffalo Historical Society, 1919), 129; (Ann Arbor) *Michigan Argus*, March 22, 1895; "I am sure": *Cleveland Leader*, June 13, 1886; *Omaha World-Herald*, June 7, 1893.

51   "Lincoln's Last Days," *The Independent* 4 (June 20, 1889).

52   *FF*, 256–57.

53   Exhibit 4 of the conspiracy trial, Memorandum, [1865], Conspiracy Trial, 15/0260-0263, M599, National Archives and Records Services, Washington, DC; "Colchester has been telling": Sylvan J. Muldoon, *Psychic Experiences of Famous People* ([Chicago]: Aries Press, 1947), 153. One needs Muldoon's source, which I have been unable to learn. He was a poor transcriber, giving Colchester's name as Cholcester, an error that I correct in the text.

54   Brooks, *Washington in Lincoln's Time*, 64–66; Daniels, in his diary entry of Sept. 20, 1864 (LOC), wrote that culling information from séance tables was "the slanderer's usual routine."

55   Brooks, *Washington in Lincoln's Time*, 64–66.

56   *Kansas City Star*, Nov. 8, 1897; St. Louis *Sunday Republic*, clipping, n.d., Box 6, F. L. Black Papers, Special Collections, Kresge Library, Oakland University; *Memphis Bulletin*, March 3, 1864.

57   St. Louis *Missouri Republican*, June 18, 1878.

58   Timothy S. Good, *We Saw Lincoln Shot: One Hundred Eyewitness Accounts* (Jackson: University of Mississippi Press, 1995), gathers many key eyewitness statements in handy form. See pages 53, 63, and 67 in particular. Assassination scholars Ed Steers and Michael Kauffman provide reliable accounts of this familiar event, as does James L. Swanson in *Manhunt: The Twelve-Day Chase for Lincoln's Killer* (New York: William Morrow, 2006). For John's weapon, see Sally A. Schehl and Carlo J.

Rosati, "The Booth Deringer—Genuine Artifact or Replica?," *FBI Forensic Science Communications* 3 (Jan. 2001), https://archives.fbi.gov/archives/about-us/lab/forensic-science-communications/fsc/jan2001/schehl.htm.

59 Statement of David Herold, in Edwards and Steers, *The Lincoln Assassination: The Evidence*, 682; *Washington Post*, Dec. 30, 1883, and Nov. 13, 1896.

60 George Alfred Townsend, clipping, "Booths, Father and Sons," [Chicago, June 16, n.y.], Lincoln Financial Foundation Collection, Allen County Public Library, Fort Wayne, IN.

61 Testimonies of James J. Gifford and John T. Ford, in Edward Steers Jr., ed., *The Trial: The Assassination of President Lincoln and the Trial of the Conspirators* (Lexington: University of Kentucky Press, 2003), 77, 102.

62 *New York World*, Feb. 12, 1911; Steers, *The Trial*, 79.

63 Stewart: *New Orleans Times*, April 28, 1865; statement of Joseph B. Stewart, in Steers, *The Lincoln Assassination*, 1197–99.

64 *New York Sun*, May 30, 1897. Stewart's height is given as six feet four inches in his 1858 passport application.

65 "The Route Booth Rode" (ms., c. 1909), 22, James O. Hall Papers, Hall Research Center, Clinton, MD.

CHAPTER 9: ARE WE SO SOON FORGOT?

1 Safford to O. H. Oldroyd, Springfield, MA, June 25, 1903, Ford's Theatre Collection; George Francis to his niece Josephine, Washington, DC, May 5, 1865, Chicago Historical Society.

2 small and drab: *Cincinnati Enquirer*, April 19, 1884; George J. Olszewski, "House Where Lincoln Died: Furnishing Study," published by the Division of History, Office of Archeology and Historic Preservation, National Park Service (1967), 12–14, accessed July 27, 2020, http://npshistory.com/publications/foth/hfr.pdf; napped: *St. Louis Post Dispatch*, May 12, 1881.

3 Charles A. Leale, *Lincoln's Last Hours* (New York: privately printed, 1909), 5–12.

4 John K. Lattimer, *Kennedy and Lincoln: Medical and Ballistic Comparisons of Their Assassinations* (New York and London: Harcourt Brace Jovanovich, 1980), 32–35.

5 Michael W. Kauffman, *American Brutus: John Wilkes Booth and the Lincoln Conspiracies* (New York: Random House, 2004), 37–38.

6 *New York Evening World*, April 16, 1915.

7 W. Emerson Reck, *A. Lincoln: His Last 24 Hours* (Jefferson, NC, and London: McFarland, 1987), 132–55.

8 (Philadelphia) *The Medical and Surgical Reporter*, April 22, 1865, 452–53.

9   *Memoir*, 44, 54, 66; JWB to Moses Kimball, St. Joseph, MO, Jan. 2, 1864, in John Rhodehamel and Louise Taper, *"Right or Wrong, God Judge Me": The Writings of John Wilkes Booth* (Urbana and Chicago: University of Illinois Press, 1997), 93.

10 Aldrich, *Crowding Memories*, 81; Edward Steers Jr., *The Lincoln Assassination Encyclopedia* (New York: Harper Perennial, 2010), 277–79; *FF*, 221.

11 Statement of Thomas A. Hall, April 24, 1865, in Edwards and Steers, *The Evidence*, 630.

12 Thomas A. Jones, *J. Wilkes Booth: An Account of His Sojourn in Southern Maryland* (Chicago: Laird and Lee, 1893), 74–79.

13 *Memoir*, 112.

14 William Hanchett, "Booth's Diary," *Journal of the Illinois State Historical Society* 72 (Feb. 1979): 40–42.

15 *FF*, 306–13, for events at the barn.

16 Testimony of John W. Garrett, June 25, 1867, *Trial of John H. Surratt*, vol. 1, 302–9.

17 *FF*, 309.

18 Conger: Lafayette Baker, *History of the United States Secret Service* (Philadelphia: L. C. Baker, 1867), 537.

19 *Atlanta Constitution*, May 21, 1886.

20 *FF*, 321–22.

21 *Washington Evening Star*, Feb. 16, 1869; *Washington Post*, March 25, 1901.

22 *New York Times*, July 2, 1869; *Baltimore American*, March 2, 1902; *New York Clipper*, July 3, 1869.

23 twenty feet tall: [Oregon, MO] *Holt County Sentinel*, July 15, 1870; "If the richness": *Baltimore American*, June 9, 1870.

24 Sam Tetrault, "Coins on Graves: What They Mean & Why People Leave Them" (July 8, 2021), https://www.joincake.com/blog/coins-on-graves/, accessed July 22, 2021.

25 MB-*AB*, vol. 2, 819.

26 *Chicago Tribune*, Feb. 12, 1900.

27 French, *Witness to the Young Republic*, 498.

28 Crook, *Through Five Administrations*, 69–70; *Washington Post*, Nov. 3, 1895.

29 *Richmond Dispatch*, Dec. 1, 1880; Buescher, "Unlocking the Mystery of a Lincoln Relic."

30 "O, my God": *Boston Globe*, Oct. 17, 1897; *Chicago Tribune*, April 27, 1865; *Bay City* [MI] *Daily Tribune*, Oct. 30, 1910.

31 *New York Clipper*, April 22, 1865.

32 *Boston Daily Advertiser*, Sept. 24, 1896; tall: *Washington Post*, Aug. 21, 1888.

33 *Memoir*, 126.

34 *New York Clipper*, Sept. 2 and 16, 1865.

35 *New York Herald*, Dec. 24, 1865.

36 Watermeier, *American Tragedian*, 126.

37 *New York Tribune*, Jan. 4, 1866.

38 *New York World*, Jan. 4, 1866; *New York Tribune*, Jan. 4, 1866.

39 Clarke, *The Elder and the Younger Booth*, 163–64; *New York Clipper*, Jan. 6, 1866.

40 Melbourne, *The Age*, March 25, 1865; "The war": Bloom, *Edwin Booth*, 106–7.

41 Townsend Walsh, *The Career of Dion Boucicault* (New York: Dunlap Society, 1915), 106–10; "Are we so soon forgot?" and "Live long and prosper": *Rip Van Winkle, As Played by Joseph Jefferson* (New York: Dodd, Mead, and Co., 1899), 47, 171.

42 Wilson, *Joseph Jefferson*, 36.

43 bewildered: Michael Musick, "Thoughts from Beyond," *Surratt Courier* 24 (July 1999): 7; *New York Sun*, April 4, 1891; George, "Some Lincoln Spiritualist Acquaintances," 196–98; Hopkins, "The Spirits and the Honorable John Worth Edmonds," 503–4; Tyler Dennett, ed., *Lincoln and the Civil War in the Diaries and Letters of John Hay* (New York: Dodd, Mead, 1939), 275.

44 Waves of anguish: *Banner of Light*, April 28, 1866; "When I first": *Banner of Light*, Aug. 24, 1872; *Detroit Free Press*, Oct. 9, 1870.

45 *New York Herald*, Aug. 14, 1865; "An Act to provide Internal Revenue" (June 30, 1864), 38th Congress, 1st Session, Ch. 173, 249, 256. "According": *New York Tribune*, Aug. 25, 1865.

46 *New York Mercury*, Sept. 7, 1865; *San Francisco Bulletin*, Sept. 27, 1865.

47 courtroom: *Buffalo Courier*, Aug. 21, 1865; "Old men": *New York Herald*, Sept. 25, 1865.

48 *Buffalo Commercial Advertiser*, Aug. 18–24, 1865; *New York Times*, Sept. 1, 1865.

49 *Indianapolis Daily Journal*, April 11, 1866.

50 *Morning Oregonian*, April 16, 1867; *Lowell* [MA] *Daily Citizen and News*, Oct. 16, 1865; *Charleston* [SC] *Daily News*, Aug. 31, 1865; Bunker Testimony, Conspiracy Trial Exhibits, DNA; "Is it right": Jefferson City *Missouri State Times*, March 1, 1867.

51 *St. Louis Daily Republican*, March 8, 1867; *St. Louis Democrat*, March 7, 1867.

52 *Keokuk Daily Constitution*, April 23, 1867; *Keokuk Daily Gate City*, May 5, 1867; *Banner of Light*, June 1, 1867. "Congestive chill" was a term used in the South and Midwest. James Tyson, *The Practice of Medicine* (Philadelphia: Blakiston, 1907), 77.

53 Alford, "Colchester," 5. Thanks to local historian Douglas Atterberg.

54 Newton: *The Story of U. S. Agricultural Estimates*, USDA Misc. Pub. No. 1088 (Washington, DC: Government Printing Office, 1969), 28; Washington *National Tribune*,

Aug. 17, 1899; "Whatever opinions": Washington *Daily National Intelligencer,* June 20, 1867; Daniels, diary, Aug. 31, 1866, LOC; Cummings, "John Pierpont," 386; *Lowell* [MA] *Daily Citizen and News,* Aug. 29, 1866.

55 *New York Tribune,* June 30, 1892; *New York Sun,* April 4, 1891.

56 Bartlett, *The Salem Seer,* 153; *Chicago Tribune,* Dec. 17, 1885.

57 Henry S. Olcott, *Theosophy, Religion and Occult Science* (London: George Redway, 1885), 243; Laura Edmonds Gilmore to Hamlin Garland, Glen Falls, NY, June 4, 1905, Hamlin Garland Papers, Box 14, Folder 66, University of Southern California, Online Archive of California, https://oac.cdlib.org/findaid/ark:/13030/tf4r29p0q5/.

58 AB to Edward W. Smith, Richmond, April 21, 1865, *Official Records,* Series 1, vol. 46, pt. 3, 882–83.

59 *New York World,* April 17, 1887. Lee's family responded angrily that he never needed or took free food from Badeau. *National Tribune,* April 28, 1887.

60 Henry Wilson to AB, Macon, GA, May 13, 1865, Wilson Papers, AM 15793, Princeton.

61 Joseph Booth to EB, New York, NY, Sept. 27, HBTL.

62 *New York Herald,* March 21, 1896; *New York Sun,* March 21, 1895; younger brother: *Topeka State Journal,* April 4, 1888; rivaled that of the president: (Portland) *Oregonian,* April 18, 1889.

63 *Topeka State Journal,* April 4, 1888; *Bennington* [VT] *Banner and Reformer,* March 29, 1888.

64 *San Francisco Bulletin,* Dec. 4, 1886; *Cincinnati Commercial Tribune,* Jan. 30, 1887.

65 *New York Times,* Nov. 18, 1884.

66 *Louisville Commercial,* April 4, 1889; borrowed money: Grant, *Personal Memoirs,* vii.

67 *Corvallis* [OR] *Gazette,* Aug. 28, 1885.

68 Badeau claimed: *New York Herald,* March 21, 1888; *Muskegon Chronicle,* March 22, 1888; *Trenton Evening Times,* March 21, 1888; "I constructed the work": *Duluth Daily News,* March 21, 1888.

69 *Leavenworth Times,* Feb. 20, 1885; Ron Chernow, *Grant* (New York: Penguin, 2018), 928–59, for Grant's illness and break with Badeau.

70 *Washington Evening Star,* April 3, 1897.

71 *New York Herald,* March 17, 1888.

72 *New York Herald,* March 21, 1888.

73 *Cincinnati Commercial Tribune,* March 25, 1888.

74 *New York Herald,* March 21, 1888.

75 *New York Tribune,* March 21, 1888.

76 Portland *Oregonian,* March 18, 1888.

77 *Corvallis* [OR] *Gazette,* Aug. 28, 1885.

78 *New York Daily Tribune*, March 25, 1888; Chicago *Daily Inter Ocean*, March 26, 1888;
     Salt Lake Herald, April 27, 1890.

79 Mark Perry, *Grant and Twain: The Story of an American Friendship* (New York: Random
     House, 2004), 118, 233.

80 *New York Herald*, March 17, 1888.

81 Washington *National Tribune*, March 22, 1888.

82 *Louisville Commercial*, March 26, 1889; Chicago *Daily Inter Ocean*, March 22, 1888;
     Trenton Times, March 23, 1888; *Fort Worth Gazette*, April 17, 1890.

83 Wilson, *Under the Old Flag*, vol. 1, 192–93.

84 Benjamin F. Butler, *Butler's Book* (Boston: A. M. Thayer, 1892), 860n.

85 *Trenton Evening Times*, March 26, 1888.

86 *Philadelphia Inquirer*, July 16, 1889.

87 *New York Times*, Nov. 6, 1888; *New York Sun*, April 2, 1888, and Oct. 31, 1888.

CHAPTER 10: DEATH CAME AS A FRIEND

1   Keckley, *Behind the Scenes*, 208.

2   *MTL*, 510; *Mineral Point* [WI] *Tribune*, Aug. 6, 1895.

3   *MTL*, 260.

4   Keckley, *Behind the Scenes*, 209.

5   Clinton, *Mrs. Lincoln*, 266.

6   *Chicago Tribune*, Oct. 7, 1867.

7   "Old Clothes Scandal": *MTL*, 432–33; "She has not": *Illinois State Journal*, Oct. 10, 1867.

8   Keckley, *Behind the Scenes*, 335.

9   *MTL*, 572.

10 *MTL*, 502.

11 *MTL*, 501.

12 *Chicago Tribune*, Jan. 1, 1887; *MTL*, 581–82.

13 *Chicago Tribune*, May 14, 1871.

14 *MTL*, 538.

15 *Chicago Tribune*, July 16, 1871; *Rockford* [IL] *Weekly Gazette*, July 27, 1871.

16 *MTL*, 592–96.

17 "Time has at length": *MTL*, 257; renewed her visits to spiritualists: *Waukesha Freeman*,
     Aug. 15, 1872; "She hardly thinks": Robert T. Lincoln to David Davis, Nov. 16, 1875, in
     Mark E. Neely Jr. and R. Gerald McMurtry, *The Insanity File: The Case of Mary Todd
     Lincoln* (Carbondale and Edwardsville: Southern Illinois University Press, 1986), 80.

18 *New York Daily Tribune*, April 22, 1869; Memphis *Commercial Appeal*, March 11, 1872;

Louis Kaplan, *The Strange Case of William Mumler, Spirit Photographer* (Minneapolis and London: University of Minnesota Press, 2008), 92–93, 107, 163. Mumler was featured in the exhibition "The Perfect Medium: Photography and the Occult," held at the Metropolitan Museum in New York in 2005.

19 Eddie Foy and Alvin F. Harlow, "Clowning Through Life," *Collier's Weekly* 78 (Dec. 25, 1926): 30; *Chicago Daily Tribune*, May 20, 1875.

20 Helm, *The True Story of Mary*, 250; Neely and McMurtry, *The Insanity File*, 34; Clinton, *Mrs. Lincoln*, 276, for Robert phrase.

21 Jason Emerson, *The Madness of Mary Lincoln* (Carbondale: Southern Illinois University Press, 2007), is the go-to history of these events.

22 Neely and McMurtry, *The Insanity File*, 21.

23 *Chicago Daily Tribune*, May 20, 1875; Chicago *Daily Inter Ocean*, May 20, 1875; Neely and McMurtry, *The Insanity File*, 137.

24 Rodney A. Ross, "Mary Todd Lincoln, Patient at Bellevue Place, Batavia," *Journal of the Illinois State Historical Society* 63 (Spring 1970): 5–34.

25 *MTL*, 618.

26 *MTL*, 615–16.

27 Kunhardt, "An Old Lady's Lincoln Memories," 59.

28 Sarah Bernhardt, *My Double Life: Memoirs of Sarah Bernhardt* (London: William Heinemann, 1907), 353–54.

29 *MTL*, 618, 716–17.

30 Watermeier, *American Tragedian*, 142; *New York Commercial Advertiser*, Feb. 4, 1869; "she was no": *New York Herald*, Feb. 4, 1869.

31 Putzi and Stockton, *Selected Letters*, 108; Asia B. Clarke to Jean Anderson, London, March 12, 1868, Clarke Letters, MdHS.

32 *New York Clipper*, June 12, 1869.

33 Mary: *Theatrical Sketches Here and There with Prominent Actors* (New York: Merriam, 1884), 16.

34 *Grand Rapids* [MI] *Evening Leader*, Dec. 12, 1881; *Boston Herald*, Dec. 4, 1881.

35 Bloom, *Edwin Booth*, 97.

36 Watermeier, *American Tragedian*, 204–6, 248.

37 Katherine Goodale, *Behind the Scenes with Edwin Booth* (Boston and New York: Houghton Mifflin, 1931), 108.

38 *New York Clipper*, July 16, 1870; Watermeier, *American Tragedian*, 157; Bloom, *Edwin Booth*, 114.

39 *New York Clipper*, Feb. 15 and April 16, 1869, and Feb. 14, 1874; Badeau, "Edwin Booth. On and Off the Stage," 265.

40 Watermeier, *American Tragedian*, 295.

41 *Chicago Tribune*, April 24 and 25, 1879; William Winter, *Life and Art of Edwin Booth* (New York: Macmillan, 1893), 127; *New York Clipper*, May 17, 1879.

42 Watermeier, *American Tragedian*, 239, 247–48; Bloom, *Edwin Booth*, 117; *Chicago Daily Tribune*, Oct. 16, 1881; *Philadelphia Press*, Dec. 3, 1881.

43 EB to Dave Anderson, London, June 6, 1881, in Otis Skinner, *The Last Tragedian* (New York: Dodd, Mead, 1939), 50.

44 *Chicago Daily Tribune*, Oct. 16, 1881.

45 *Boston Herald*, Dec. 4, 1881.

46 *Boston Globe*, June 7, 1893; Mabel Osgood Wright to William Winter, Fairfield, CT, July 7, 1898, Folger MS W.a.231, between pages 24 and 25, Folger Shakespeare Library; Winter, *Life and Art*, 22.

47 *Canton [OH] Repository*, Oct. 20, 1881; *Cleveland Plain Dealer*, Nov. 15, 1881.

48 Bispham, "Memories and Letters of Edwin Booth," 242.

49 *Baltimore Sun*, Aug. 14, 1884, Watermeier, *Between Actor and Critic*, 277.

50 John C. Soliday, "The 'Joint-Star' Tours of Edwin Booth and Lawrence Barrett," 2 vols. (PhD dissertation, University of Minnesota, 1974), vol. 1, 157.

51 *Brooklyn Daily Eagle*, April 5, 1891; *New York Times*, April 4, 1891; *New Haven Register*, April 4, 1891.

52 Description and ages of Niles in her passport applications of Nov. 4, 1874, and March 3, 1893, and census returns: ancestry.com, accessed Nov. 6, 2020.

53 *New York Times*, April 30, 1875; *Philadelphia Times*, April 30, 1875; *New York Herald*, April 28, 1875.

54 *New York Commercial Advertiser*, June 26, 1875, *New York Tribune*, Nov. 7, 1874.

55 *New York World*, Dec. 15, 1899; *San Francisco Bulletin*, Jan. 30, 1877.

56 Chicago *Daily Inter Ocean*, Jan. 27, 1877; *American Law Review* 31 (Nov.–Dec. 1897): 917–19.

57 John Y. Simon, ed., *The Papers of Ulysses S. Grant*, vol. 26 (Carbondale and Edwardsville: Southern Illinois University Press, 2003), 184–85.

58 *New York Times*, Nov. 18, 1884; Washington *Daily Critic*, March 18, 1886; Shattuck, *The Hamlet of Edwin Booth*, 30; Chicago *Daily Inter Ocean*, March 27, 1888; *Sioux City Journal*, March 9, 1889.

59 Henry Adams, *The Education of Henry Adams* (New York: Modern Library, c. 1931), 263–64; William B. Moore to Fred Grant, March 27, 1888, Silmon, *Papers of Grant*, vol. 31, 280.

60 U. S. Grant to AB, Mt. McGregor, New York, July 12, 1885, Simon, *Papers of Ulysses S. Grant*, vol. 31.

61 *Pulaski [TN] Citizen*, Dec. 16, 1886.

62 *Topeka State Journal*, April 4, 1888; Badeau Family Tree, ancestry.com, accessed October 5, 2020.

63 Badeau, "Edwin Booth. On and Off the Stage," 265–66.

64 John W. Trebbel, *A Certain Club: One Hundred Years of The Players, New York, 1888–1988* (New York: Wieser and Wieser, 1989), and George W. Stewart, *The Players After 75 Years* (New York: The Players, 1968), are the standard club histories.

65 *Baton Rouge Daily Advocate*, April 4, 1890; *Springfield* [MA] *Republican*, Feb. 17, 1889; *Pulaski* [TN] *Citizen*, Oct. 21, 1886.

66 Badeau, "Edwin Booth. On and Off the Stage," 266–67.

67 *St. Louis Republic*, June 7, 1893.

68 "Unfortunate": William T. Sabine, *"The Land Mourneth" the Death of Abraham Lincoln, President of the United States* (Philadelphia: W. P. Atkinson, 1865), 11; marginal people: *Washington Daily Critic*, Jan. 21, 1871; New Orleans *Times-Picayune*, Feb. 12, 1871; *New York Tribune*, July 22, 1894; "Then, I say": Jefferson, *Autobiography*, 339–40.

69 *New York Tribune*, June 9, 1893.

70 New Orleans *Times-Picayune*, June 10, 1893.

71 *Sun and New York Press*, June 10, 1893.

72 *Boston Daily Advertiser*, June 10, 1893.

73 "Disaster in D.C.: The Curse of Ford's Theatre" (2019), https://www.historynet.com/d-c-disaster-the-curse-of-fords-theatre.htm, accessed October 20, 2020; *New York Tribune*, June 10, 1893; *Washington Sunday Star*, June 8, 1930.

74 George J. Olszewski, *Historic Structures Report. Restoration of Ford's Theatre, Washington, D.C.* (Washington, DC: Government Printing Office, 1963), 7; *Washington Post*, Dec. 16, 1883.

75 Skillful research by Diane T. Putney on the history of the building indicates that Congress ultimately paid thirty-one official death claims from the disaster.

76 "Saturn's Men," *The Illustrated American*, July 1, 1893, 773.

EPILOGUE

1 Thomas J. Craughwell, *Stealing Lincoln's Body* (Cambridge, MA, and London: Belknap Press, 2007), is the standard history; see also John C. Power, *History of an Attempt to Steal the Body of Abraham Lincoln (Late President of the United States of America) Including a History of the Lincoln Guard of Honor, with Eight Years Lincoln Memorial Services* (Springfield, IL: Rokker, 1890), 27–67; trial: *Springfield Daily Illinois State Register*, May 31, 1877; Fleetwood Lindley: *Life* 54 (Feb. 15, 1963): 88; Arthur L. Meriam, "Final Interment," *Journal of the Illinois State Historical Society* (April 1930–Jan. 1931): 171–74; Emerson, *Giant in the Shadows*, 189–203.

2   *Chicago Tribune*, Jan. 17, 1887.

3   *St. Paul and Minneapolis Pioneer Press*, Feb. 20, 1887.

4   *Washington Post*, March 21, 1895.

5   *New York Tribune*, March 23, 1895.

6   *Boston Globe*, March 23, 1895.

7   *Catalogue of the Literary Possessions of Gen. Adam Badeau* (New York: John Anderson, 1901). The Adam Badeau Collection at the Bolger Heritage Center, Ridgewood, NJ, Public Library, consists of material that escaped the sale. The artifacts are well cared for by Sarah Kiefer, Local History Librarian.

8   *New York Times*, Dec. 1, 1908; *Catalogue of Mr. Edwin Booth's Valuable Collection* (New York: Alexander Press, 1908), copy courtesy of Amherst Library Special Collections; *New York Times*, Dec. 6, 1908.

9   Bloom, *Jefferson*, 278, 283.

10 Bloom, *Jefferson*, 284.

11 Wilson, *Joseph Jefferson*, 339–40.

12 Eugenie Paul Jefferson, *Intimate Recollections of Joseph Jefferson* (New York: Dodd, Mead, 1909), 12, 19.

13 *Palm Beach Daily News*, April 1, 2012.

14 *New York Times*, April 2, 2012; Angela Smythe, unpublished manuscript (2021) titled *Saving Grace: John Wilkes Booth in the Richmond Grays*, courtesy of the author.

15 Buescher, *The Other Side of Salvation*, x–xi.

16 Ann Braude, *Radical Spirits: Spiritualism and Women's Rights in Nineteenth-Century America* (Boston: Beacon Press, 1989), 162–91.

17 *Memoir*, 97.

ILLUSTRATION CREDITS

Page 4: Folger Shakespeare Library, Creative Commons Attribution-ShareAlike 4.0 International License

Page 8: Don Olson, Texas State University

Page 19: Folger Shakespeare Library under a Creative Commons Attribution-ShareAlike 4.0 International License

Page 23: Library of Congress, Prints and Photographs Division, LC-USZ6-2095 (b&w film copy neg. post-1992)

Page 29: Courtesy of Rick A. Harris

Page 38: Daguerreotype collection (Library of Congress), Library of Congress, Prints and Photographs Division

Page 49: From the Lincoln Financial Foundation Collection

Page 52: Library of Congress, Prints and Photographs Division, LC-USZ62-5409 (b&w film copy neg.)

Page 57: TCS 18 (Jefferson, Joseph). Houghton Library, Harvard University

Page 61: Brady-Handy photograph collection, Library of Congress, Prints and Photographs Division, LC-DIG-cwpbh-00094 (digital file from original neg.)

Page 66: Abraham Lincoln Library and Museum

Page 78: War Department. Office of the Chief Signal Officer (8/1/1866–9/18/1947)

Page 83: Lincoln Financial Foundation Collection

Page 97: Massachusetts MOLLUS Collection (Vol. 94, p. 4757L) at USAHEC

Page 113: From Richard J. S. Gutman and Kellie O. Gutman

Page 117: Library of Congress, Music Division

Page 128: Courtesy, American Antiquarian Society

Page 138: National Portrait Gallery, Smithsonian Institution

Page 147: Lincoln Financial Foundation Collection

Page 151: The J. Paul Getty Museum, Los Angeles

Page 163: Private Collection Photo © Christie's Images / Bridgeman Images

Page 181: © Victoria and Albert Museum, London

Page 187: Florida Center for Instructional Technology

Page 197: Library of Congress Prints and Photographs Division

Page 222: Lincoln Financial Foundation Collection

Page 228: The Rare Book & Manuscript Library, University of Illinois at Urbana-Champaign

Page 239: Library of Congress Prints and Photographs Division Washington, DC

INDEX

Page numbers in *italics* refer to illustrations